DRAMA AND IDEOLOGY IN MODERN ISRAEL

A large number of political plays have been written in Israel over the past fifty years, and they are perceived, by audiences and critics alike, as major interventions in the country's ongoing political debates; the result is that Israeli drama is at the centre of many public controversies. In this first full-length study of Israeli political drama Glenda Abramson shows that during the early years of the State of Israel most of its intellectuals were identified with the 'official' interpretation of Zionism. After the Six-Day War in 1967 an influential group of playwrights, concerned with the evolution of Zionist ideology in the modern nation state, began to question the ethical basis of Zionism. Hanokh Levin, Yehoshua Sobol, Yosef Mundi, Miriam Kainy, Amos Kenan and others have gone on to examine Zionism as it affects contemporary Israeli society.

Glenda Abramson is Cowley Lecturer in Post-Biblical Hebrew at the University of Oxford, and Schreiber Fellow in Modern Jewish Studies at the Oxford Centre for Hebrew and Jewish Studies. Among her publications are *Modern Hebrew Drama* (1979), *The Great Transition* (with Tudor Parfitt, 1985), *The Writing of Yehuda Amichai* (1989) and *Hebrew in Three Months* (1993). She edited *The Blackwell Companion to Jewish Culture* (1989), *Jewish Education and Learning* (with Tudor Parfitt, 1995), *Tradition and Trauma* (with David Patterson, 1995), *The Oxford Book of Hebrew Short Stories* (1996) and *The Experienced Soul: Studies in Amichai* (1997). She edits the *Newsletter* of the European Association for Jewish Studies.

DRAMA AND IDEOLOGY IN MODERN ISRAEL

GLENDA ABRAMSON

CAMBRIDGE
UNIVERSITY PRESS

PUBLISHED BY THE PRESS SYNDICATE OF THE UNIVERSITY OF CAMBRIDGE
The Pitt Building, Trumpington Street, Cambridge CB2 1RP, United Kingdom

CAMBRIDGE UNIVERSITY PRESS
The Edinburgh Building, Cambridge CB2 2RU, United Kingdom
40 West 20th Street, New York, NY10011–4211, USA
10 Stamford Road, Oakleigh, Melbourne 3166, Australia

First published 1998

Printed in the United Kingdom at the University Press, Cambridge

Typeset in Baskerville 11/12.5pt [CE]

A catalogue record for this book is available from the British Library

ISBN 0 521 44159 5 hardback

To Joel Burton Abramson, with love

Contents

vii

Illustrations

Acknowledgements

The generosity of theatre people is well known. In Israel the magnanimity of playwrights, directors and theatre and drama scholars, all willing to help an outsider understand their world, is unparalleled. My grateful thanks, therefore, to Aliza Israeli, Tom Levi, Yitzhak Laor, Motti Lerner, Miriam Kainy, Rivka Maoz, Avraham Oz, Ben-Zion Tomer, Yedidya Yitzhaki, and many other playwrights, scholars and critics in Israel and elsewhere whose suggestions, advice and material moved this book along. An exhilarating afternoon spent with the late Professor Hayyim Shoham will not be forgotten. The untiring efforts and kindness of Naava Carmel and her team at the Israel Goor Theatre Museum and Archive well exceeded the call of duty. This marvellous resource is invaluable for any form of research into theatre in Israel. Ruth Blumert's hours of conversation, somehow found within a harrowingly busy schedule, were exceedingly helpful. To Moshe Zimmerman, who made his pathbreaking thesis available to me, I owe a great debt, and to Dafna Cohen-Mintz, who acted as go-between, my grateful thanks. So too to the Cameri Theatre for a gift of material from its archives, to Melanie Christoudia at the Theatre Museum in London, Ian Herbert of the *London Theatre Record*, Charles Ward for researching a crucial item, Tal Ben Zwi, for her incisive insights and information and Noah Lucas for his careful reading of a portion of the manuscript. To all, my most sincere appreciation.

To Linda Bree, my editor at Cambridge, my eternal thanks for her calm encouragement, even in the most despairing days.

To Dan Urian, above all, for his unstinting gifts of time, advice, encouragement and material, my most profound gratitude.

To David, thanks, as always, for his patience, understanding and support.

The author is grateful to the following for permission to reprint extracts from published papers: Dr Efraim Karsh, editor of *Israel Affairs*; Dr Ulf Haxen, editor of *Copenhagen Proceedings*.

NOTES ON THE TEXT

When a play has been read as a photocopied typescript or an unpublished playtext, no publishing details are available. In some cases, there have been no page numbers. All such texts are indicated in the notes.

Introduction

In 1896 Dr Theodore Herzl, a 36-year-old Viennese journalist and playwright, published *The Jewish State, an Attempt at a Modern Solution of the Jewish Question* which advocated the recreation of a sovereign Jewish state. As an assimilated Jew, with little nationalist feeling, he did not share the territorial ideals of the Jewish people, but Herzl realised that the only solution to the problem of Jewish homelessness and anti-Semitism would be the re-establishment of a Jewish homeland in Palestine (the Land of Israel, *Eretz Yisrael*), that was openly recognised and legally secured. It was logical in the wake of European nationalism that Jewish nationalist aspirations should be focused on the ancestral land which had been the subject of literature and prayer for almost 2000 years.

In August 1897 the first Zionist Congress (the first international Jewish parliament) took place in Basel. Two hundred and eight delegates from sixteen countries including the United States attended, even though Zionism did not represent all Jewry. The congress did, however, propose the interconnectedness of all Jews, the creation of 'a new type of Jew', the settlement of farmers and labourers in Palestine and the strengthening of a Jewish national consciousness. The World Zionist Organisation was established, with Herzl as its president; it adopted a national flag and an anthem, *Hatikva*. From that time 'Zionism' denoted the movement whose aspiration was the legal return of the Jewish people to the territory promised to them by God. It promoted the idea of 'normalisation', transforming the Jews into 'a nation alike all other nations', 'a secular nation, settled on its own territory, bearing responsibility for its own defence, economically self-supporting, developing basic social institutions and fostering a unique culture of its own'.[1]

In Tel Aviv, in May 1948, fifty-two years after the publication of *The Jewish State*, David Ben-Gurion proclaimed the establishment of the State of Israel, of which he was soon to become the first Prime Minister. The foundation of the state resulted from a combination of Jewish settlement in Palestine and international Zionist diplomacy, initiated by Herzl. The state was born three years after the end of the Second World War and the attempted Nazi genocide of the Jews.

Palestine had never been empty of Jews although their numbers were small. Under Turkish rule (from the 16th century) the community grew and by 1880, before the launch of the Zionist movement, the total Jewish population had reached 25,000. Generally the Jews who lived there devoted themselves to a life of Orthodox religious observance, supported by the charity of international Jewish communities. They constituted what is known as the 'Old *Yishuv*', *yishuv* being the word for 'settlement', later indicating the Jewish population of Palestine. By the 1880s, in the spirit of Jewish renewal and for the purpose of personal emancipation, Jewish immigrants, predominantly non-religious Zionists, had begun arriving in Palestine from Eastern and Central Europe, establishing the 'New *Yishuv*'. By 1907 there were perhaps 70,000 Jews in Palestine, a small proportion of them working on the land. The Zionist pioneers (*halutzim*) founded collective settlements (*kibbutzim*), drained the swamps, irrigated deserts, sank wells and planted forests. Some were independent farmers who employed Arab labour. By the Second World War there were almost a half a million Jews settled in Palestine.

According to one of the tenets of Zionism, the settlers were determined to create a Hebraic culture for Palestine. Its language was to be Hebrew, the language of the Bible, rather than Yiddish, a language associated with exile and life in the diaspora. Eliezer Ben-Yehuda (1858–1922), himself an immigrant, founded the movement for the revival of Hebrew as a viable *spoken* tongue. Yiddish (contemptuously termed 'the jargon' by its critics), the *lingua franca* of the East European Jewish masses, was not to be identified with the demand to remove Jewish culture from the political and cultural margins of non-Jewish societies to centrality in a politically self-determined Jewish state. Hebrew, not Yiddish, had been one of the languages of political autonomy in ancient history. It was recognised in 1913 as the official language of the Zionist movement. The Palestinian settlers placed their children in Hebrew-language schools and tried to use Hebrew as their daily idiom.

From the early years of the twentieth century Zionism and socialism discovered a compatible partnership, despite their contradictions. A number of young Jews had been actively involved in the Russian Revolution and many pioneers and intellectuals of the period before the First World War were influenced to some extent by socialism. This was reflected in the belief that the Jewish state could be created only on socialist principles, with a return to the soil a tangible fulfilment of socialist ideology. Reconciliation of the contradictions – the Labour Zionist movement embodied the ideals of national redemption, as well as 'the redemption of men in society' – led to the creation of a new nationalist philosophy. The Israeli labour parties grew out of this messianic blend of Zionism and socialism, the Labour Zionists setting the ideological tone for the State of Israel, which they governed when the state was proclaimed in 1948.

By the First World War Zionism had been transformed into a major political force. While most early Zionists saw the possibility of creating a socialist, egalitarian, secular Jewish society in Palestine, it was inevitable that several profound ideological differences should have developed among the early settlers. By the 1920s, the conflicting ideologies of the Jewish community in Palestine had crystallized into the political parties which still exist in Israel today. From the start, for example, Zionism encountered opposition amongst some Jewish religious factions who objected to its secularity, claiming that only God could restore the Jews to their land. Other religious elements were part of the World Zionist Organisation. In 1902 one of these groups formed its own party, the *Mizrahi*. In 1956 The National Religious Party (NRP) was created in Israel by a merger of *Mizrahi* and a group called *Agudat Yisrael* which was more extreme in its opposition to certain aspects of Zionist ideology. The right-wing revisionist faction in the Zionist movement did not share the same values as the labour factions who promoted physical labour and agricultural and industrial growth. By contrast, the right wing espoused ideals of toughness and militarism, and did not stop short of terrorism. The revisionist movement, from which the contemporary *Likud* party has evolved, believed that the Jewish state should encompass the entire territory of Palestine, on both sides of the Jordan. Yet both labour and revisionist factions postulated the same myths and symbols which had become accepted as part of an authentic Jewish self-perception. This included Herzl's ideal of the

'New Jew' who would be proud and independent, strong and dignified, implying everything that diaspora Jewry was not.

In 1917 the British government, which was later to hold the mandate over Palestine, signed the Balfour Declaration which approved the establishment of a Jewish national home in Palestine. This was endorsed by certain European powers and the USA but it signalled the start of relentless and ferocious Arab opposition, particularly to increased Jewish immigration. Until shortly after the Balfour Declaration, the Zionist movement as a whole had given little serious thought to the question of the Arab population of Palestine, although certain individuals in the movement had sounded notes of warning. Jewish immigration continued to be the issue during the inter-war years, with Arab riots causing Britain to curb it even more. Freedom of immigration for Jews became crucial with the rise of Nazism in Germany in the 1930s. The Arabs, however, continued to oppose it with open violence.

Eventually the British government referred the problem to the United Nations which, in 1947, recommended the division of Palestine into independent Arab and Jewish states. Following the armistice agreement after the Second World War, the Old City of Jerusalem was placed under Jordanian control, as was the west bank of the Jordan. One day after the British withdrawal from Palestine – at the termination of the mandate on May 15, 1948 – five Arab armies, supported by the Arab states, simultaneously invaded Israel, leading to the War of Independence (1948) which ultimately secured the Jewish state for the Jews. This was at an enormous cost to the *yishuv*: the Jewish losses in the war were proportionately the same as British losses in the First World War. Many Arabs fled or were driven from their homes to settle as best they could on Jordanian territory. A small proportion remained in Israel.

Securing the state did not secure peace. Arab attacks continued and the Israelis continued to retaliate. On May 14, 1967, Egypt's threatened attack was pre-empted by Israel; the Egyptian army (supported by Jordan and Syria) was overcome by the Israeli forces in six days. The so-called Six-Day War resulted in Israeli hegemony over areas on the West Bank and the Gaza Strip that had been under Jordanian rule since 1948, the Sinai Peninsula up to the Suez Canal (later ceded to Egypt), and the Golan Heights in the north. These were subsequently referred to as the Occupied Territories. The war also brought about the reunification of Jerusalem under

Israeli control. Israel not only gained these territories (the area now designated as Palestine) but also their angry and resentful populations. About a million Palestinian Arabs came under Israeli military administration, creating a further stimulus to Palestinian Arab nationalism which remained unmitigatedly hostile to Israel. The Arabs as a whole refused to accept Israel's existence or recognise the right of Jews to a state of their own.

Victory in the Six-Day War brought self-assurance to the Israelis, and prosperity to their country. At the same time it shattered the myths of moral self-righteousness that had been gained with the War of Independence and the establishment of the state so soon after the Holocaust. The so-called 'festival of victory' was shortlived. The aim of Zionism had always been to establish a *Jewish* state in Palestine;[2] yet after 1967 the Jewish state became the conqueror and ruler of a large non-Jewish population. Acquiring the territories led to another potentially divisive development: the rise of *Gush Emunim* (Bloc of the Faithful), a group of militant religious nationalists. Its members declared all the areas gained by Israel in the 1967 war to be the inalienable possession of the Jewish people, not to be ceded. Consequently they advocated settlement, legal and illegal, in those areas in order to reclaim the entire Land of Israel (*Eretz Yisrael*, 'Greater Israel') for the nation, according to the biblical promise.

In October 1973, on the Jewish Day of Atonement (*Yom Kippur*), Egyptian and Syrian forces attacked Israel which, for the first time, was relatively unprepared. The Yom Kippur War was a crisis for Israel in many respects, but primarily because it brought the political domination of the Labour Zionist 'old guard' to an end. In 1977 the right-wing *Likud* party, led by the revisionist Menahem Begin, came to power. The war had also crystallised changes within Israeli society. Far from rejecting the image of conqueror, the majority of Israelis appeared to relish it. A formerly united nation, concerned above all with its survival, 'turned into a divided, irresolute, complacent rabble chasing after money and pleasure'.[3] Serious divisiveness about the shape of Israel's future followed the disintegration of the consensus about the manner of national survival. The realisation of its vulnerability led Israel to a national trauma and a re-examination of its collective self. This intensified in 1982 when Israel invaded Lebanon, primarily to expel the Palestine Liberation Organisation and to halt missile attacks on Jewish settlements and towns in northern Galilee. The operation provoked widespread dissent among the Israeli public, and sometimes violent protests by artists and writers.

The tensions between the ideals of the Zionist founders and the realities of state-building and statehood were enormous from the start, and have increased with continuing problems across the Green Line, Israel's pre-1967 borders. Once the state had been founded, the question of the purpose and validity of classical Zionism began to be aired. Issues of return, nation-building and national aspiration were deemed to be irrelevant in the face of the established state. Zionism became the centre of a debate which focused on crucial changes of definition in the light of conquest and control of the Palestinian population, growing Arab nationalism, Israeli self-preservation and survival. At the heart of the argument was the transformation of Zionism, a liberal, nationalist movement, into the militant 'revisionist' vision of the entire Land of Israel, a vision reinforced by a comparatively small group of religious extremists dedicated to the same purpose: the securing of 'Greater Israel'.

II

Drama in Hebrew was almost unknown until the foundation of the State of Israel. It was limited to sporadic allegorical works in dramatic form scattered over four centuries, and a few realistic plays set on the *yishuv*. Isolated examples of drama are not sufficient to establish a dramatic tradition, nor can a tradition develop without a spoken language. Within the dispersed, diglossic Jewish communities throughout the ages, Hebrew, the language of the sacred texts, had been reserved for more elevated discourse than play-acting. Yiddish theatre, on the other hand, flourished even without its own land because it had the great advantage of a spoken language. Nowhere in the diaspora was there a Hebrew-speaking audience, and there was no folklife in Hebrew as in Yiddish. With Hebrew adopted as the vernacular in the *yishuv*, Hebrew literature became the 'normal' literature of a nation living in one territory and speaking one language. Only then could a Hebrew-speaking theatre audience be cultivated.

It was on the *yishuv* from the 1880s onwards that the embryonic Hebrew theatre began to play a fundamental role in acculturating the new immigrants and teaching them Hebrew, first in the rural settlements and then in the cities of Jaffa and Tel Aviv. Many of the earliest plays written in Palestine dealt with biblical and historical subjects, and as the Jewish settlement grew, playwrights began to describe life there. Some idealised it to the point of propaganda while others portrayed the hardship of the pioneering effort, providing support and reinforcement for the pioneers. It was not great drama but it was written in Hebrew, and it offered its audiences slices of their own lives, as well as education.

During the *yishuv* period and the early years of the state, the majority of the young nation's intellectuals, including the writers, were identified with the 'official' state interpretation of Zionism through its institutions, the *Histadrut* (labour union) and the youth movements, and they concentrated on issues of national concern. Members of the so-called *Palmah* or *dor ba'aretz* generation of writers born during the first quarter of the twentieth century adopted the conformist collective ideals of the founding fathers, including 'love of country, passionate idealism and readiness to sacrifice the fruit of their Zionist education tendered at home, in the youth movement and in school'.[4] Playwrights of this generation continued to fulfil their creative obligations from a social and didactic, rather than an aesthetic, point of view. Their plays were predominantly social dramas in which the new, developing society was evaluated according to the principles of the labour movement. The plays were credited with 'serving purposes, describing an environment and setting intellectual values ... The environment in Israel is the holiest entity and the play's primary obligation is to picture it and to display ourselves'.[5] The *yishuv* playwrights had already established a drama that was temporal and localised, relevant for an audience that was both auditorium and stage, participant and spectator. After 1948 the drama perpetuated the representational, realistic mode, most of the plays reporting factually on events that were at once familiar to audiences.

In its early years Israeli drama predominantly – although not exclusively – reflected the modern, secular world of the influential Ashkenazi cultural minority, Jews of European origin, many of whom were native-born, or had immigrated at an early age.

It is not surprising, therefore, that the writers wrote about soldiers and not civilians, about *sabras* [native-born Israelis] and [those who were] almost *sabras* and not new immigrants and members of the *gahal* [foreign conscripts]; about people on the *kibbutzim*; about intellectuals like themselves and therefore about the élite upon whom all the attention rested ...[6]

This élite – who perceived almost uniformly the historical events responsible for the nature of their existence – represented a shared political ideology which they featured in their drama. Even after 1967, with many cultural and demographic changes, theatrical representations by and large continued to ignore the altered social constructions of ethnicity and religious and political orientation.

After the Six-Day War, control of the territories and their populations plunged Israel into a crisis which involved not only issues of *realpolitik* but of identity and culture. The ideological gap between left and right widened into a gulf. The drama stepped into the arena of debate. A group of playwrights, whose influence was disproportionate to their number, took Israeli politics as their central topic. This is not to say that they wrote about party politics or, until much later, about members of parliament, or that they campaigned from the stage. Their focus was the ideological substructure of Israeli political life: Zionism and its evolution in the modern nation state. It was the ethical basis of Zionism that concerned them as much as its territorial mandate. Playwrights including Hanokh Levin, Yehoshua Sobol, Yosef Mundi, Amos Kenan, Hillel Mittelpunkt and Danny Horowitz – examined Zionism as it affected contemporary Israeli society. They discussed the nature and quality of the state, and the lines of cause and effect underlying the theories of Zionism, as they underlie all moral thinking. The Occupied Territories, with their Jewish and Arab populations, were central to the playwrights' political investigation.

A number of women playwrights, notably Miriam Kainy and Shulamit Lapid, began to make their mark from the 1970s, also through political or social comment. So far there has not been a movement in the theatre to correspond with the sudden and brilliant growth of young women novelists; no such phenomenon has graced the Israeli drama due to the traditionally masculine orientation of the theatre's various hierarchies. The mainstream women writers' themes largely mimic those of their male counterparts but they have tended in the 1980s and 1990s towards the creation of new voices which speak less stridently about current events. Female playwrights, such as Hagit Ya'ari and Edna Mazya, for example, tend also to view social realities from a personal perspective, offering individual responses to the same national phenomena, war and the *Intifada*, for example, and attaining a pathos which has eluded the male writers.

Although political drama was not the only form of drama being written, it seemed to be the most representative until the mid-1990s. In 1993, for example, forty-two per cent of the total theatre takings were for ten plays, nine of which were original works which dealt in one way or another with the social and political problems of Israeli society. This was also the case the following year: nine of the ten most successful plays of 1994 were local works dealing with socio-political issues. Each of these plays ran on an average of five times more than all other plays, imported and local, during the season.[7] This confirms that a large part of the Israeli audience of the time chose to attend performances of particular plays in order 'to strengthen the link with Israeli society'.[8]

If the playwrights required a symbol for their investigation of Zionism, they found it in the character of the New Jew, who had originally been supposed to represent the positive self-image of modern Jewry. In his Israeli incarnation he was the *sabra*, male hero of the War of Independence, and cultural, political and military arbiter of the new state. It was this part-mythical, part-historical formulation that attracted the opprobrium of the post-1967 writers, their rebellion against heroes who were, despite their virtues, 'mono-lithic in their political existence.'[9] The *sabra*-hero was perceived as the symbol of militarism and the glorification of might. In the post-1967 decades, together with increasingly savage outbursts against political hierarchies (demarcated by the playwright Yehoshua Sobol as 'politicians, demagogues and various interests' and by others as the 'consensus'), this heroic stereotype was rejected. Not only he, but the entire mythology generated by the processes of national rebirth, was probed and disparaged.

Open politicisation, the obsession with the crisis of definition engulfing Zionism, and the theme of Jewish and Israeli identities, are particularly apparent in the drama of this period. Its central tension was forged by the gap between the utopian dreams that nourished Israel's founders and the difficult reality experienced by their heirs. The drama has moved from an almost wholehearted support of Zionism in the 1950s to an antithetical, critical position that saw the Jews in Israel as the victims turned victimisers of the Palestinians. The character at the heart of this perception, the Arab and Palestinian 'other', is represented in the post-1967 drama variously as victim, collaborator, alter-ego, lover and bitter political antagonist.

The rise of *Likud* in 1977, and the Lebanon War in 1982 – which severely unsettled the national consensus – led to an eruption of plays attended by controversy, public debates, sometimes even demonstrations. A growing concern of the political drama was the growth and influence of religious groups. Playwrights began to air anti-Orthodox grievances from the stage, in polemical plays which fed the Orthodox-non-Orthodox *kulturkampf.* Theatre censorship (which existed from 1927 to 1991) became even more intrusive. It was, at this time 'possibly particularly instrumental in causing the theatre to raise fierce objections to the religious groups, thus reinforcing their negative image'.[10]

From the start, then, Hebrew drama perpetuated its original function as a unit within the social debate, both as a reflection of and an 'active intervention'[11] in Israeli social and political life. Ben Ami Feingold, the veteran critic and drama scholar, confirms the drama's political character. 'Israeli theatre,' he writes,

is a political theatre. I'm not referring to political theatre in the sense that it deals with political topics, a dominant and perhaps the most important element, but to the politicisation, the commitment the 'savouring' as an artistic confinement and a cultural and intellectual barrier, not to be found in any other contemporary western theatre. It's a theatre that can't deal with questions of religion and faith, Jews and Arabs, settlement and Zionism, history and actuality, except from within a defined and dogmatic ideological standpoint.[12]

From the 1950s this was the direction taken by Israel's drama, despite many plays which dealt with individual and family issues. Attempts by playwrights to leave the political arena were sometimes characterised as 'escapism', particularly after the outbreak of the *Intifada*, the Palestinian revolt against Israel's occupation of the Territories, which began in December 1987. Oded Kotler, former artistic director of the Haifa Municipal Theatre, commented that while a play should contain aesthetic value it should also have a 'non-cultural use', it should not just be art for art's sake but a means of examining other social processes. Other writers similarly stress the drama's 'relevance'. Even the Holocaust is politicised, and granted a central position within the debate.

III

Israel's large cities are home to subsidised theatres, each of which possesses a culture of its own. In Haifa, the Haifa Municipal Theatre has dedicated itself to discovering original plays, many of them politically provocative, and encouraging native talent, Jewish Israeli, Arab Israeli and Palestinian. Consequently the percentage of original plays in its repertoire has been higher than that of the other municipal theatres and it has developed what has become known as 'the Haifa style'. In Tel Aviv the Cameri Theatre has maintained a standard repertoire throughout its existence, but it has taken many risks both at the box office and by frequently attracting the attention of the Censorship Board. While the Cameri's repertoire is more conservative than that of the Haifa Municipal Theatre, in the early 1990s it took up the cudgels against religious extremism with a series of plays that fed into the *kulturkampf*. The Habimah National Theatre embodies the middle way, presenting a classical repertoire in addition to a number of original Hebrew plays. Other subsidised theatres exist in Beersheva and Jerusalem. In 1993 thirteen public theatres in Israel performed to general audiences in over a hundred locations. Forty-eight per cent of the plays produced were original, a trend that continues. Every original play runs on average almost twice as long as a translated foreign play.

Israeli audiences conform to Susan Bennett's definition of core theatre audiences as belonging to middle aged, high income, highly educated, professional, managerial and white collar groups.[13] The most active self-motivated theatre visitors are well educated (13 or more years of education) native Israelis or Ashkenazi immigrants. The majority of them are secular Jews.[14]

In addition to the regular theatre-going population, Israeli audiences are supplied by institutions, cultural organisations and trade unions which are allocated tickets. There is also the *Art for the People* project which was established at the beginning of the 1950s to bring Israeli culture and Hebrew to outlying areas. From among 132 communities in which *Art for the People* functioned in 1989–90, thirteen were on the West Bank and Gaza and seven were Arab settlements. *Art for the People's* repertoire, carefully selected from the available theatrical productions, is therefore frequently understood in ways unintended by those responsible for the selection.

The Israeli Fringe has provided the framework for many political plays, especially those directly concerned with the Arab-Israeli conflict. Most noteworthy of the peripheral theatrical activities is the annual theatre festival held in Acre. Arabs and Palestinians have participated in it for some years as both audience and actors. Because most of the participants are young, the festival's topics reflect those that most concern them. It is therefore revealing that nine plays on the subject of the Holocaust were staged in Acre in the first half of the 1990s. A threat to the festival (apart from constant lack of funding) is the establishment from 1985 of small stages in the main urban theatres which present dramatic themes and styles similar to those favoured by Acre, for example Habimartef (the small stage at Habimah) and Bamah 3 at the Cameri. Many plays have moved from the festival to the main stages of established theatres, two notable examples being Ilan Hazor's *The Masked Men* (*Re'ulim*), and Shmuel Hasfari's *Tashmad*.

Far from the male-dominated mainstream another phenomenon is growing: women who have established their own theatre groups, the first of which was the Jerusalem Theatre Company. This and similar groups still find their most effective place on the fringe or even further afield, on the West Bank. Whereas mainstream theatre tends towards more-or-less structured narrative styles, the dedicated women's theatre groups present their material in unstructured, abstract, fragmentary form, often with audience participation. Music and movement are essential components of their theatre. Their plays are not limited to expressing responses to political events and often indicate their deviation from the canonic norm by reinterpreting classical Jewish texts, including biblical stories and rabbinic writings.

The Israeli press and professional journals are the principal sources of information about Israeli theatre and drama. A few full-length studies have been published, in Hebrew and English. With the development of departments of theatre in Israeli universities, more scholarly studies are being undertaken which will result in a greater volume of publication on the subject. It has to be said that media comment on the original drama is often conditioned by the critic's political views.

IV

The approach throughout this book has been one of textual analysis, drama rather than theatre. It is concerned more with what the playwrights are saying than their manner of saying it. A playtext represents only part of a complex procedure placed before the audience in live performance. A printed text has its own semiotic which is different from that of the performed play, and it is changed when enacted on the stage. Any text 'postulates its own receiver as an indispensable condition of its potential for meaning'.[15] In the theatre the 'receiver' is not alone in his or her interpretive generation of the text but is guided by the director who manipulates it, and the actors who are also permitted a certain flexibility. Presumably every performance of the same text can vary.

Textual analysis on its own omits all these exciting, dynamic processes. It can provide a valuable insight into the drama as literature and, through careful examination of stage directions, offer an *idea* of the literature as drama. Obviously this can only represent a small part of the interactive relations between text, stage and audience although the playwright Yehoshua Sobol demands that the critics read the texts. Still, the analysis of dramatic texts that follows in this book does allow an idea of their staging, but more crucially, of the relationship between Israeli drama and its society.

In Israel there is an added dimension to the texts: their value as *documents* that reflect extra-theatrical social reality and which therefore possess autonomous importance. This is Israeli drama's most important characteristic, the one most responsible for its authoritative status within the contemporary culture. The Israeli theatre repertoire is not 'just a "list of plays" but a compilation of works that reveals the high frequency of discussion of social and political problems'.[16] Political texts, with which this book is primarily concerned, serve in Israel less as examples of theatrical art than as statements that converge on current political discourse. They are *perceived* as documents by audience and critics alike, the result being many public controversies and arguments, post-production public discussions with playwrights and directors, polemics in the press, and censorship (which is, after all, almost always performed on the text, not the enacted play). It is therefore the play as text rather than as theatre with which this present study is primarily concerned.

CHAPTER I

The 'Enterprise' and its reinforcement in the drama of the 1950s

The literature of the 1950s is an element in our understanding of Israeli society at that time, for while it may not advance our real knowledge of events it does, to a certain extent, map the society's emotional landscape. According to Kafka, literature represents 'the keeping of a diary by a nation, which is something entirely different from historiography'.[1] This presupposes that the diary charts the inner life of the nation – the inner lining, so to speak, of the fabric of sociopolitical life – and attempts an honest analysis. In the 1950s, Israeli literature saw itself as something between the diary and historiography, creating a new document which contained components of both. More importantly, it articulated many social and ideological convictions that were extensively challenged after 1967.

Jewish labour idealists considered writers to be 'the principal creators of national symbols – banner-bearers of the spirit'.[2] Hayyin Hazaz put it more succinctly: 'One upon whom the responsibility for society lies, this is Hebrew literature today'.[3] Since many writers themselves saw the cultural and educational systems as a means of strengthening the new national order, they consequently reinforced the institutional uses of creative literature. Hebrew fiction and drama of the *yishuv* and the early years of the state were therefore distinguished by their engagé quality and documentary fidelity to daily events. Writers continued to function as political commentators and mentors presumably because of the tendency to contextualise them within the Jewish prophetic tradition. In fact, Israel's early political leaders occasionally called upon writers for advice which, according to Amos Oz, they rarely took.

In the late 1950s the Labour establishment and the left-wing youth movements already controlled most of the canonic literary activity in the country. Official bodies assumed the power to decide the politics of publication and translation and also to determine literary norms.[4]

Israel's first Prime Minister, David Ben-Gurion, felt strongly that the entire intellectual community must participate 'in heart, soul and deed'[5] in the statebuilding effort.

Most Hebrew drama complied. It was enlisted, at the time, in the mission of mass education of which Zionist ideology was a significant part. This was nothing new: the Hebrew theatre had already established itself as an educational forum, particularly for the acquisition of Hebrew on the *yishuv* in the 1920s. Over three decades later, in 1957, a critic asked: 'When will those responsible for our [theatre] stages finally understand that the theatre is a vast school for the nation?'[6] Like the fiction of the time, the drama saw itself as a functional social instrument rather than predominantly as an art form. Playwrights tended to abide by the Marxist injunction that all artists should assume the responsibility for reflecting public concerns in their work since theirs is a public voice. Perhaps the drama did not directly influence social processes; at best it offered the consolidation of complicated polemics, simplified and personified for a non-specialist and somewhat interactive public.

Israeli plays were judged only partly on their style and structure and primarily according to their sociopolitical content. Soviet criteria of literary creation and production influenced both content and intent of *yishuv* writing to a large extent. Later, a standard Israeli value judgment decreed that Hebrew literature concerned with the society's collective needs and interests was acceptable; literature that centralised the individual, that 'forgot about Zionism and the enterprise of the war' was 'existentialist' and therefore suspect.[7] These judgments ideologically juxtapose two systems of authority: Zionist collectivism and Soviet functionalism.

In order to fulfil its sociological function, to interpret the substance of documentary reality created primarily by the media, and to attract audiences, the drama adopted the genre of realism. Playwrights' preoccupation with the present was no doubt fuelled by a conviction that those participating in the nation-building efforts were determining the pattern of Jewish history. The choice of realism was made in spite of the critics of the time who were intemperate and repetitive in their condemnation of the drama's 'reportage'. They were, however, somewhat self-contradictory: they applauded the ideologically sound precepts which framed the playwrights' social realism while lamenting the banality of the plays. Critical definitions of 'realism' and 'reportage' were in any case inaccurate. The 'reportage' was selective, at times no more than a nominal reference to events. In fact most of the plays written in the 1950s saw 'reality' as part of a rigid ideological system that influenced social and individual life. This *ideological* formulation impeded a non-doctrinaire representation of reality. By offering what *appeared* to be the documentary reality of everyday life the theatre could constitute a unifying mechanism for a culturally and linguistically diverse audience, enacting for them their shared, communal experience.

The dramatic 'social realism' both admired and censured by the critics was a structure based on the broadest essentials of post-1948 Israeli urban living, together with certain romantic and usually unachieved expectations. In fact, in common with other literary genres, the early drama was inspired by a series of founding myths rather than social reality. Certain of these myths had been held in common by the entire *yishuv* in Palestine and were augmented by the 1948 war and the establishment of the state. While many of them rested on strong factual foundations, others offered no more than wish-fulfilment. There was often a strong divergence between factual truth and the constituents of the collective memory.

One of the methods by which the mythology was disseminated was through the creative literature which played its part in manipulating the collective memory. The ideological complicity of the drama in particular led to the transformation of the founding myths into something more, the kind of material that closely resembles propaganda. Fiction and poetry answered a pressing need in the wider public: the young nation urgently required texts to serve a national ritual of atonement and celebration, texts which would bring a transcendental dimension to the achievement of the war, its sacrifices and its aftermath.[8] The focus of the 'mythology' was its leading character, the *sabra* hero, a new phenomenon in Jewish history, who was closest to the writers in age, origin and education. Through this character they perpetuated their own predetermined self-image, a reification of the image of the pioneer. In a play by Yoram Matmor a character asks:

Do you remember that same liberated, proud and simple character our ancestors aspired to cultivate on the land of the new homeland? The young leader, the one who knew how to be the inspiration during the time of the war and before it, who consolidated all that the youth was doing?[9]

While the literary *sabra* was also a throwback to the nineteenth-century romantic hero, he was an appropriate spokesman for his milieu and its ideology, representing a generation that belonged explicitly to one chapter of Israeli history. Included in his uncompromising personality was a taxonomy of historical, ethical and pragmatic virtues; he was the repository of good.

If there is a vocation for the Hebrew literature, for the Hebrew culture in the forthcoming periods, it is the function to eternalize the figure of the fighting Hebrew youth, the whole figure in all its glory, in its faults and angles, in its laughter and anger. A nation whose descendants will be educated in the light of this eternal figure, who would look up to it as a model for living – cannot be destroyed by any instrument of death. In the same line with the conquerors of Canaan, the Judges, prophets, the resettlers of Zion, the returners to Zion, the Hasmoneans, the Zealots of Jerusalem, the martyrs . . .[10]

This persona of whom Shamir said, 'He was a hundred young men, if not more', was a *kibbutznik*, the kibbutz being represented as the vanguard of the Zionist movement and the hero's ideological locus. As an ideal creation for the collective memory he could not fail as an archetype of the Zionist enterprise.

Many of the writers composed their works as memorialisation for members of their families or comrades-in-arms who had fallen in the war, further reinforcing the idea of the hero's perfection. One of the most representative of many memorial volumes of the 1950s was a collection entitled *Haverim Medabrim al Jimmy* (Comrades Tell Stories About Jimmy), memorial writings by and about 'Jimmy' (Aharon Shemi) a *Palmah*[11] commanding officer killed in 1948. This volume and others like it served to confirm and entrench the popular literary stereotype, that of the strong, sensitive hero. Yet it was acknowledged that his image was largely symbolic and incorporated the outstanding qualities common to many *sabras* of that generation.[12] According to a young French immigrant, a member of Jimmy's platoon, Jimmy was a true *sabra*, but significantly different from the 'Jewish boy who grew up in France', that is, the *golah* Jew. Jimmy was considered to have been the archetype of the *Palmah* commanding officer who always led his men into battle, adjured bravado, bluster and compromise. 'This book was the most representative of the War of Independence in general and the *Palmah* in particular. It was like a key to the profundity and heroism, beauty and fear, legends created during the war.'[13]

Three playwrights of the 1950s exemplified in the broadest terms the general literary discourse of the time; Yigal Mossinzon because of his adherence to the founding ideology and popular mythology, Natan Shaham because of his evaluation of them, and Yoram Matmor because of his attempt to deconstruct them. Mossinzon's *Be'arvot Hanegev* (In the Wastes of the Negev), (1949),[14] is the most topical and perhaps the most representative of the three, incorporating the attitudes attributed to the groups involved in the 1948 war. It sets out popular perceptions almost systematically. The play takes place in a bunker on a kibbutz in 1948. Like most of the plays on the subject of war, pre- and post-1967, the war is represented by an enclosed, besieged space, a location of the *few*, with the *many* encroaching outside. The kibbutz is surrounded by the enemy, food and arms are dwindling and the number of casualties growing while a father and a son, both of whom occupy positions of responsibility, attempt to work out their own relationship. Avraham, the father, is in conflict with others as well, a senior kibbutz functionary and a military officer who advocate retreat in the face of the advancing enemy rather than a diehard stand. Avraham, the kibbutz leader and area commander, a member of the pioneer generation, argues strongly for remaining. According to contemporary reports, the arguments aroused strong responses in the audiences of the day. Danny, Avraham's son, is the only one with the necessary qualifications to cross enemy lines. Against much opposition, Avraham decides to send his son to certain death. This decision reflects the playwright's perception of a collective ideology that proposes personal sacrifice for the sake of national salvation.

The play comes close to being a taxonomy of stereotypes, chief among them the *sabra* to whom the older pioneers relate as if confronted by a strange but wondrous beast: 'As if they are a nation but not a nation. A barbaric race is growing here. They don't even look Jewish ... You *sabras*, it seems sometimes that flowers grow on you instead of thorns ... Our *sabras* are ashamed to show their feelings to the outside world ...' They are complex people 'whose parents, people of the third and fifth *aliyot*,[15] worry too much about education ...'[16] The young men and women self-consciously speak a patois of slang which mystifies and irritates their elders. Language is used as a means of distinguishing the soldiers from their parents and from new immigrants who are uninitiated into the army jargon. The soldiers admit that trivialising their language prevents their having to face the horror of killing 'before they've had a chance to stroke a girl's hair'; a belief, as in our time, that language on its own is able to alter reality.

An important component of the play's ideological subtext is the story of the binding of Isaac (Genesis 22), the *Akedah*: 'We are a cruel generation that kills its young sons! The old ones continue living – but send their young to die!' The reference is to the biblical Abraham's willingness to sacrifice his son, on God's command. Mossinzon's Avraham, father of the archetypal hero, is deemed no less heroic for having willingly sent his son to his death. Danny's death represents a form of fulfilment of Avraham's ego and that of the nation, embodied in the long tradition of martyrdom and salvation.

AVRAHAM Bik'at Yoav won't fall. But we have to take Dan from Bik'at Yoav for burial. Shosh, tell Givoni: 'Bik'at Yoav rejoices today.' Yes, Shosh, tell him. 'Bik'at Yoav is rejoicing in the knowledge [that they are about to be relieved].' We'll go and bury Danny who gave his life on this hill. Yes, we've all paid a high price. All of us.'[17]

The play comprises a collection of romantic clichés and rhetoric, offering stereotypical material to a putatively stereotypical audience, and it achieved great success. According to the playwright Danny Horowitz (later one of the chief organisers of the artists' protest against Israeli activities on the occupied West Bank), *In the Wastes of the Negev* possessed a truly ritualistic power at the height of the War of Independence in spite of its weakness. People, claims Horowitz, 'simply came to see themselves'.[18] The audience identified with the events portrayed on the stage to the extent that during the performance, 'the sounds of bitter weeping were heard'.[19] Despite his admission of the play's lack of artistic value, Yisrael Goor writes,

I remember well the excitement in the audience. Many wept quietly for a long while. After the play had ended many members of the audience crowded into the corridors of the theatre and heaped praise and gratitude upon the actors. So you see, an atmosphere of sacredness and transcendence caressed you that evening.[20]

The play's value apparently lay in its fidelity to the national mood, rather than to aesthetic principles:

This play is little but dramatised reportage written with great tension and emotion and it was staged during the battles. The playwright knew how to take advantage of the audience's feelings and in his story of heroism on

Bik'at Yoav he drained the qualities of melodrama to their limits. Let us recall that in great profusion there are ideas of fidelity to and love of place to the point of sacrifice, love of the land, dreams about fulfilling social ideals on the one hand, and dramatic effects on the other, such as the lighting of [Sabbath] candles in the bunker, and Sabbath songs ... and the heartrending ending when the bereaved mother sings a lullaby to her dead son.[21]

Authenticity, however, was questioned:

Explain this to me: for what reason has the playwright created such a caricature of the native-born Israelis and why did he bother to explain their 'complex soul'? For it is clear: no native-born Israeli has seen himself in the *sabras* on the stage. He hasn't loved their loves and enjoyed their wit. If so, what? It seems to me that Yigal Mossinzon has done something interesting for tourists, for new immigrants, for any kind of people who are distanced from life. He lets us talk nonsense, utter words that even I don't understand ... so that someone will 'split his sides' laughing at the differences between a prattling new immigrant and a prattling *sabra* ... He has to lay it on with a spade. ... And I ask: where is the artistic restraint, the sense of proportion? ... Believe me, I wouldn't have written these things if I didn't feel that the audience is streaming to receive these caresses and longs for them.[22]

In the Wastes of the Negev is constructed upon a variety of cultural and historical sources which assume the dimension of myth: the biblical story of David and Goliath, the *Akedah* and the history of Massada. Massada was a fortress on the western shore of the Dead Sea where the last Jewish fighters held out after the Roman conquest of Jerusalem (70 CE). They eventually committed suicide in 73 CE. The most potent idea in the play is that of Danny's death bringing salvation, or at least of salvation following his death (which did not, in fact, have any consequential effect). Mossinzon both perpetuated a mythology by means of his play as a mythopoeic text on its own, and reinforced to his audience the existing historical myths. Danny's self-sacrifice is akin to an act of appeasement, a ritual offering thrown to the gods. There follows a happy ending, all are saved and Avraham's lonely conviction about holding ground is finally justified. It is no wonder that many critics disdained the play as it distorts historical events into banal formulas, something which would not have been permitted, for example, if this were a story about the Holocaust. Generally, the War of Independence was swamped in the drama by a deluge of rhetoric, clichés, fake heroism and false internal conflicts. Bereavement in Israel was perhaps too recent and acute for undiluted realism and it is possible that a certain amount of counterfeit, together with positive and reinforcing propaganda, provided the consoling formula by which audiences could confront the war and their own losses.

Some of the plays, however, were not entirely predictable. An example of a much more ambiguous mien in the drama of the 1950s is Shaham's *Hem Yagi'u Mahar* (They Will Arrive Tomorrow)[23] which, like many other plays of the period, was adapted from a short story. The play has been revived twice since its first performance in 1950, in 1966 and 1973. In accordance with the dramatic custom of the time it blends an ideological argument into a dramatic plot. The play is about the moral decline of a platoon of Israeli soldiers during the war in 1948. The platoon has captured a landmined hill from the Arabs. Having lost the map indicating the location of the seven mines, each soldier, in his fear of detonating one of them, invents excuses for remaining inside the barracks and finds pretexts for sending his comrades and two Arab prisoners outside to step on the mines. One of the two COs, Jonah, manufactures tactical excuses for refusing to set foot outside and is accused of cowardice by his counterpart, Avi, a man of sensitivity and integrity. Despite a dramatic external story it is the conflict between the two commanding officers, Jonah and Avi, which provides the primary dramatic and ideological tension of the play.

They Will Arrive Tomorrow reads like a canon of prevailing popular truths or myths. It entrenches national stereotypes, amplifies ideology and seamlessly mingles fact and fiction. Jonah and Avi may be antithetical sides of the same hero: Jonah, the hard, practical soldier whose real concern for his men is concealed beneath a brusque, even cruel exterior; Avi, the sensitive, compassionate man, the positive stereotype. Yet both these commanding officers (the duality in itself a satirical comment) appear to embody *and* to reject the stereotypical qualities of the *Palmah* hero: courage, physical attractiveness, brusqueness, sensitivity and uncompromising moral integrity. Jonah's view of the tasks of the commanding officer could be a cover for cowardice; Avi's moral propriety is compromised in his agreement to keep the mines a secret; Jonah's concern for his men is tainted by his callous attitude to his Arab prisoners, and so on. Shaham is already questioning the myth of the hero of the War of Independence, the Israeli *sabra*.

This play provides an early dramatic foretaste of the dialectical and moralistic fiction of the later 1950s, particularly S. Yizhar's gigantic novel, *Yemei Ziklag* (The Days of Ziklag), (1958), which dissolved many of the popular myths. Unlike *In the Wastes of the Negev*, *They Will Arrive Tomorrow* did not have an upbeat, positive ending, one which would reinforce popular beliefs, but ended on a note of warning, the last unexploded mine, the only transparent political statement in the play. One by one the ideas of the day – premises derived from Zionist philosophy that were largely taken for granted by audiences who settled down to an evening of self-reinforcement in the theatre – are examined in the play. Courage, patriotism, the youth movements, the individual and the collective; idealism, the pioneering spirit, the relationship between the pioneers and the *sabras* and the conduct of the war are all dissected by the playwright with a certain candour, but still not the candour that would exceed the ideological parameters of the society and the period. The debate between the two men remains within the overriding propositions of new statehood, a kind of political correctness of the time. For example, Shaham perpetuates the intellectual stereotype of the Arab as the unfortunate, innocent and often naive victim, but he also indicates, with unusual frankness, that as an army the Arabs were a force to be reckoned with.[24]

Like many authors Shaham places controversial ideas in the mouths of his less popular characters. For example, in fiction of a later period Palestinian characters articulated certain nationalist sentiments, principles of the author and his milieu that were unacceptable to the contemporary Israeli liberal conscience. In Shaham's play the alien, the disaffected, the unpopular persona is permitted to express debatable opinions, such as Jonah's 'Even in the army there is only one moral obligation – to win. And if we destroy certain principles along the way – we'll get our punishment in the end.'[25] This sentiment might have found an echo in audiences of the time, but Shaham's own ambivalence is revealed in his choice of its proponent.

For all its apparent radicalisation of current topics the play belongs firmly to its time because of its relationship to reality. A state of siege was a familiar element of the war. There was nothing unusual about men being forced to remain in dangerous, inhospitable terrain, or even about their heightened responses to the trauma of confinement. Yet because the space of the play is not geographically defined it also becomes an obvious embodied trope, reinforcing one of the national myths, the *few* against the *many*. The metaphor of a small, almost defenceless group besieged in a dangerous arena, surrounded by foes but fighting on to the end by fair means or foul, is irresistible (despite the controversial issues raised by the playwright), manifesting, as it does, one of the most trenchant truths of the war and of postwar propaganda.

Because of its ideological anomalies at least one scholar described the play as being in the mould of Sartre;[26] another situated it within the tradition of the Absurd.[27] These are means of shifting the play's focus from a debate that did not always conform to prevailing attitudes and which was often perceived as provocative. Yet one factor remained constant, itself a constant reflection of the ideology of the day: the implicit identification of the purpose of the war with the teleological purposes of Zionism. This was not part of the argument, which consequently remained a matter of form rather than substance. The reason for the success of Shaham's play, despite its dialectical, even controversial, quality, was his firm conviction of the validity of the national enterprise. Yizhar similarly remained within acceptable confines in *The Days of Ziklag* which *appeared* to stretch them to the limit and at times to cross them.[28]

With all the rebellion of Yizhar's heroes against the boredom, the demands, the obligations, pettiness, uselessness, real or imagined, they never doubt the principle. This is beyond argument or hesitation, an axiom that needs no proof, the enterprise that sets the most exalted boundaries against rebellion.[29]

Yitzhak Laor confirms this view but with less approval:

Yizhar is an important literary creator within the sphere of the dominant ideology in Israel but his limitations as a spiritual man and as a narrator rest first of all in his obedient relationship to this ideology, this dominant ideology. It may be that there are entire sections of this ideology that he doesn't like ... but in this entire wonderful story [*The Days of Ziklag*] there is not one attempt to rebel against the 'enterprise' [*mif'al*], to use David Canaani's term.[30]

As far as the drama was concerned, 'Even when the [original] play began to reflect a little on quality, to sharpen its gaze and to reveal blemishes and even to scold and rebuke, it still did not free itself of one-sidedness, of serving a specific idea, of being the bearer of a world view.'[31] Despite its apparent ideological anomalies, Shaham's play was a paradigm of the drama of the time, presenting its thesis in a dialectical, even didactic format. Yet its truthfulness was curtailed in accordance with the society's beliefs and sensibilities. Throughout the early drama – unlike that of the following generation – the question of the validity of the nation's founding values rarely arises; the belief in all of them was total.[32]

According to Lucien Goldmann, good artistic works reveal the intellectual structure of the dominant social class or level of the society in which they are written.[33] This is true of Israeli drama which reflects the major preoccupations of the dominant group in its society. In the 1950s, the drama's firmly Ashkenazi focus ignored the entity which at the time was termed, with some contrition, 'the other Israel', the oriental and North African immigrants. They were not relevant to the war plays and even in the plays of 'social realism' they are depicted by Ashkenazi playwrights as little more than victims of the new state's ineffectual bureaucracy.

What, then, of the drama's attitude to the European immigrants? Clearly, this was largely ambivalent despite the immigrants' contribution to the Zionist 'enterprise'. Popular creeds and 'mythologies' were most apparent within the relationship between the Israelis and the European survivors of the Nazi concentration camps who came as refugees to Israel from 1948. Some twenty-five per cent of the fighting forces in the War of Independence and fifteen per cent of the casualties were Holocaust survivors.[34] War casualties were almost equal among the Israel-born, the veteran immigrants and the refugees who arrived in the 1940s, one third of whom had been in concentration camps.[35] According to Emanuel Sivan, the contribution of these immigrants to the War of Independence has not been appropriately evaluated, partly because of the ethos of the early literature, and partly because early Israeli historiography ignored them. If the literature saw them at all it was, initially, as traumatised refugees or deficient soldiers who 'don't know where they're fighting, they don't know the terrain; they've been sitting in concentration camps in Germany and Cyprus ... They don't know how to hold a gun, to dig in, to take advantage of the terrain. In the end too many of them are hit.'[36]

Mossinzon's immigrants speak nothing but Yiddish. They have alighted from the ships a metaphorical 'two days' previously. Baruch, the Commanding Officer, complains that these members of the *gahal* (foreign conscripts) have been forced upon him. To him, as to his men, there is no other dimension to the unilateral stereotype 'immigrant': they remain for him one single entity. Even in death the separation between 'ours' and 'theirs' is presumed:

SOLDIER A (*enters*) I've brought a few certificates for Moishe Gross. He was a good lad. He was with us in Cyprus, he was in the concentration camps in Germany. Yes, he's been in the country once before, in the Haifa port for one day until the British sent him away. He's on a stretcher, up above. (*He gives the death certificate to Baruch*) Rivka, let's go up to him. One of our people must mourn him at his funeral. Yes, it's a bitter cooperation.[37]

The perception of the newcomers as nothing but untrained cannon fodder (a view shared by many Israelis at the time), is part of the drama's ideological tapestry. Because of the self-reflexivity of the literature as a whole, they were marginalised or ignored, perhaps also as a consequence of their position in the war: the so-called 'ownership' of military casualties provided a group's most dramatic claim to centrality in Israeli society.[38] In Yizhar's novel, as late as 1958, the 'others' were subtly classified, recognised by their 'diasporaness' (*galutiyut*), always boastful, hungry, parsimonious, and obliquely accused of cowardice.

The early drama exemplified the myth that the war was fought and won, and the new society established, by native Hebrew-speaking youth. Generally the plays were bound to the *sabracentric* view, to use Laor's term,[39] characteristic of the dominant Israeli ideology. Yisrael Goor quotes as 'very touching' the evidence of the French immigrant whose resolution to abandon the kibbutz as a result of his sense of segregation and alienation was changed after a discussion with Jimmy led to his joining the *Palmah* instead.[40]

Women had little part to play in the literature of the 1950s, which was mostly a paean to machismo. Throughout the decade woman's roles in fiction and drama were secondary, despite the functional part that women had played on the *yishuv* and in the war, and their comparatively heavy civilian losses.[41] According to the literature, the War of Independence was a male war, fought by brave, resourceful, tough but sensitive and morally elevated men. Women had no place in this exclusive club. They appeared almost exclusively as adjuncts to the men, girlfriends, fiancées, wives and mothers. In *They Will Arrive Tomorrow* the appearance of Avi's sister, Noga, as a radio-operator was questioned by the critics who saw no useful role for her in the play. While she is a part of the platoon, her story is still the stereotypical one of frustrated love, and her death is wilful, melodra-

matic and linked to love and nothing else. In the heat of battle and
the threat of mines killing her brother, her lover and their comrades,
Noga does nothing but confess her love for Jonah, plead his case to
Avi and weep over her betrayal of a previous lover. Her purpose in
the play is perhaps a means of highlighting Jonah's lack of sensitivity
or her own helpless feminine submission to male power, but most
likely it is to provide the 'love interest' which authors of the time
deemed necessary. Later 'social realism' frequently singled out the
women as the principal victims of the new postwar urban life, bored,
passive and displaced, or complaining and demanding malcontents.
This facile creed represented the creation of a new mythology of
women, without an authentic history as an antecedent.

Both Mossinzon's and Shaham's plays exemplified other myths,
many of them to be interrogated by later dramatists:

> We were and always will be pure and a minority, we never wanted war, of
> course, and we are much weaker and of course besieged and we always rise
> again from the flame in order to win only because we are forced to,
> because we're commanded to . . .[42]

While Laor somewhat mischievously exaggerates the national
beliefs, his calibration of them is reinforced by their dominance in
the writing of the first decade, leading him to comment on 'the
limited function of the literature'.

The *limitations* of the drama were often revealed when the war was
its central topic. The young Israeli generation were the heirs of a
tradition which, perhaps because of its history, tended to sublimate
suffering and death, transforming it into the vital determinant of
salvation. Playwrights of the 1950s displayed some difficulty in
confronting the war, perhaps because traditional responses to catastrophe were no longer appropriate as paradigms, or perhaps because
of the technical problems of conveying war on the stage. The war in
their plays is hazy and romanticised, heroic and, above all, a *wordy*
war, earnestly concerned with the ideological positions of the day. A
few years later when the country was able to take stock of the
tragedy of its casualties for the first time, Yizhar expressed – through
fiction rather than drama – the terror, sadness and heroism of the
time, but even he tempered his inquiry with an affirmation of the
salvatory aspect of the war and the national enterprise.

Yoram Matmor's *Mahazeh Ragil* (An Ordinary Play), (1956),[43]
provided an almost unique challenge to the claim that the War of

Independence gave rise to a unified genre of heroic literature whose values were an uncritical reflection of the Zionist ethos. The play aroused heated criticism quite out of proportion to its quality. This was primarily because Matmor's dissension encompassed the early myths, questioning the ideological consensus and validity of the war itself. It provided forthright answers to the questions raised, for example, by Shaham's work. Matmor's play describes a generation that trod the difficult path from a unique historical achievement directly into a society which was rapidly normalising. The main burden of the play is the self-sacrifice of the young ex-fighters to a society increasingly embourgeoised, in which they have no place. According to the poet Avraham Shlonski, there was a need 'to turn the war generation into a peace generation'.[44] The play creates a portrait of Israel's first 'lost generation', those 'who refuse to live an illusion and yet are incapable of living in reality'.[45]

An Ordinary Play takes place in a theatre where a writer and producer are rehearsing a new play about Israeli youth after the War of Independence. The play-within-the-play's players themselves are Israeli youth immediately after the War of Independence, as are their stage characters. In an ironic coup Matmor's actors imitate the fictional cast *and* their characters, like multiple mirror images. The living actors were, in fact, playing themselves. The audience in the auditorium and the 'audience' of the play-within-a-play were able to unite as one audience, creating a single ideological entity. Joseph Millo, the director of *An Ordinary Play* for the Cameri theatre, reports that fierce arguments broke out among members of the cast about various topics raised by the play, causing the postponement of rehearsals for a while. After a long break it was decided to incorporate many of the ideas that had arisen from the arguments in *An Ordinary Play*. The play therefore contains a painful authenticity which contributed to the heated critical response. When Matmor offered his play to the committee of the Habimah theatre, a spokesman commented, 'If this is the truth it's better to present a lie'.[46]

In 1948 Matmor had created a character named *Danny Keresh*, Danny the Board (or Plank), the hero of a one-act play produced by the Carmel company. The plank, representing Danny, is central to *An Ordinary Play*, positioned on the stage in place of the main character who never appears. From 1948 to its final staging at the Cameri in 1956, Matmor rewrote the play about fourteen times. His few admirers praised him extravagantly for his honesty. He rejected 'the hollow drama of the 1948 generation' with its 'empty pasteboard characters with blond *bloriyot* [fringes of hair, cowlicks], blue eyes ... a mixture of Fenimore Cooper and Gary Cooper, singing Russian songs in Hebrew transposition or dancing Druze dances in Israeli guise'.[47] All the critics, admirers and detractors alike, ignored the currently popular hero, or anti-hero, of English, American and European literature of the 1950s, the disillusioned postwar urban dweller, rootless, angry, nauseated, a *talush* (rootless person). Matmor's Danny Keresh owed a good deal to Camus' urban *déraciné* and Osborne's 'angry young man'. This anti-hero recurred later in Israeli fiction as a rootless urban intellectual, who like Danny, was unable to order his life, keep a job or complete his work. In the post-1948 Israeli context such a character, the anti-type, was unacceptable and unexpected, particularly given the generally self-reinforcing drama and fiction of the time.

Matmor's critics and supporters alike accentuated his characters' view of Israel, its post-war corruption and deterioration. Certain fiction of the time similarly dwells on the sense of futility, the desperation of characters when faced with the so-called 'new reality'. Yet few authors effectively dissected this new reality, so that it remains hazy and undefined. Many writers, including Shaham, reinforced the new negative responses by writing about the bureaucracy and the evil of urbanisation, but their attempts to explain their characters' discontentment in terms of actual social, political or economic truths were lame and unspecific. The writers submitted the clinical picture of malaise without investigating its cause; even the presentation was fragmentary, always featuring the same symptoms.

The post-war literary angst was engendered by a number of factors: first, the inevitable disappointment inherent in the romantic vision of the new generation. The brief period of Israeli pastoralism was a clear reflection of the pioneering enterprise, Labour Zionism and its promise of physical and metaphysical redemption. However, a combination of the Jewish urban ethos and unresolved conflicts in post-1948 Israeli society overwhelmed this faith in the land and romantic utopianism. Second, there was a far greater adoption of contemporary European literary trends than was recognised by the majority of Israeli critics. Third, the post-war 'normalisation' was bewildering. The author of Matmor's interior play, the play-within-the-play, reads from his own notes:

With slow tread they step off the stages of history, tired, dirtied with blood and dust, hungry for peace, stinking, burnt, bearing scars in their bodies and in their souls. The groaning of a wounded comrade still rings in their ears, and the black fear is still fused to their bones.[48]

The 'author' declares that they have been brought from the battle-field to a world that has become alien to them. Those who have been 'on the stages of history', involved in the making of history, find the aftermath empty and purposeless with little to do of importance. According to Ehud Ben Ezer,

The War of Independence, the encounter with killing and cruelty on both sides, the disappearance of the Israeli childhood world and the inability to 'come to terms' with the new Israel, with the new daily life ... and the 'dissolution of values' resulted in a trauma in the soul of this generation. There was a sense of alienation in the Israeli child confronting the landscape that had changed utterly with the conquests, the departure of the Arabs, the waves of mass immigration and the rapid building that had no hint of romanticism about it ... there was a confusion of landscapes and a confusion of values.[49]

Young men whose adulthood had so far been defined only by heroism and death, who had to grow up abruptly after losing their youth on the battlefield, were bewildered by the sudden need to settle down in a society whose criteria were becoming western and middle-class. One of Matmor's characters describes the dislocation that this caused:

YITZHAK I was on the kibbutz for a few years but I left, it didn't suit me. I tried to study but I wasn't interested in studying. I simply couldn't concentrate. Recently I've been wandering around without doing anything. You understand ... before the war, in the underground, it wasn't important what the job was. It was very satisfying, maybe because I had responsibility. I'd like work like that ...[50]

The fourth factor, the contradiction between the ideological premises of Zionism – that the State of Israel would be established by appeasement, and its actual establishment through bloodshed and eviction – generated a profound dismay, as did the rapid transition from *halutziut* (pioneering) to *mamlakhtiyut* (political state-hood).[51] Most significantly, the actual scale of losses in the War of Independence, the destruction of a promising élite not unlike that of the First World War, together with the growing awareness of the enormity of the Holocaust, led to a period of national depression and guilt. This sense of worthlessness and low self-esteem was not greatly ameliorated by the Sinai Campaign of 1956. It is this that Matmor's protagonists represent, the unacknowledged depression precipitated by events rather than by the country's 'corruption'. The post-war society's dreadful abnormality is signalled by a teacher in *An Ordinary Play* who, on casually meeting Danny's mother, asks her if Danny is still alive.

It is unlikely that Matmor set out on a deliberate myth-shattering initiative but he astutely challenged the myth of the *sabra*-hero's perfection, a severe blow to a society whose national soul was implicated in one archetype. The point is not lost on Matmor:

DIRECTOR What I'm missing, apart from a more dramatic story, is that in this whole business there isn't one positive character. To put on an original play which has not even one positive character? This isn't acceptable to us.[52]

In accordance with his need to infiltrate his society's unconscious Matmor, the diarist, made few concessions to prevailing ideological requirements. His most nonconformist stroke is the character of Danny Keresh and his circle of ex-army companions. Matmor's *Palmah* heroes are negative stereotypes, inversions of the Avi-Jonah-Jimmy composite whose moral imperative was dictated by the collective. To strengthen his ironic point, Matmor has Danny Keresh conform to the profile of the ideal *sabra* to the extent that he is a proven prewar hero and a distinguished commanding officer, but he is also a flawed young man, lazy, drunken and devoid of the values attributed to the hero archetype by two literary generations.[53] The *keresh* (plank) on the stage is, of course, symbolic of *absence*: it is passive and lifeless, unrelated to its environment, an image of non-existence. The actor who is to play Danny in the biographical interior play is also killed at the end: both Danny and his *alter ego* are therefore worthy only of death.

The play's cultural implications were profound: the *Palmah* writers – representing the dominant intellectual class – had tendered the War of Independence in romantic packaging to a community that was either unwilling or powerless to scrutinise it with detachment. Those responsible for the packaging also governed the cultural systems of the 1950s. Matmor attempted to redress the ideological balance and to tell a different story which was largely rejected by mainstream critics and audiences, although scholars of a later period, including Gidon Ophrat and Hayyim Shoham, devoted considerable attention to it. Significantly, there is a wealth of contemporary critical and analytical material, memoirs and anecdotes concerning *They Will Arrive Tomorrow* and *In the Wastes of the Negev* but little other than biographical sketches of Matmor.

Characteristically for its time *An Ordinary Play* was not evaluated entirely according to dramatic criteria but within its historical and ideological contexts. To the critics, both positive and negative, Matmor's attack on national beliefs was paramount and they responded as representatives of an anxious, defensive, newly-formed nation. Moshe Shamir, popular novelist and playwright, thundered in a review: 'The thesis of the play claims that the *Palmah* generation suffered a decline and spiritual disintegration after the war ... is it so bad today? Aren't there creativity and *halutziut* [pioneering] and self-sacrifice and truthful values today?'[54]

[T]he veterans of other armies ... pour out their nonsense in the cafés of the new left or in Greenwich Village, but not our army. Their disappointment, if it exists at all, is not indifferent, it is not nihilistic ... it is painful, calling out and striving for restoration ... we know today why we fought yesterday. Everyone, without exception, is ready to fight that same war with the same fire even tomorrow.[55]

A political furore grew around Matmor's play; he was censured on the one hand for failing to justify his attack on Israel's treatment of the Arabs and, on the other for allowing the leading character, Rafi, to be killed by Arab infiltrators, thereby exacerbating the atmosphere of fear in the country. Temperate words of praise for the play, such as those of the feared and influential drama critic Hayyim Gamzu, were subsumed by a torrent of indignation. Life and art were so closely intertwined in Israel that a national event as monumental as a war could be taken to be a reproach to a renegade artist: the 1956 Sinai campaign appears to have come as a reprieve for the 'lost' generation which was once again able to prove its mettle. Shamir commented about *An Ordinary Play*:

And so, and without asking the Cameri or any one of us, suddenly in the middle of a nice autumn day the Sinai war broke out and suddenly the newspapers were again filled with 'our wonderful youth' and suddenly I know that the presenters of *An Ordinary Play* felt uncomfortable. For ten days or two weeks the play stopped being truthful, the complaint about the rottenness of the generation stopped sounding justified.[56]

Despite his irony, there is a probably unconscious admission in Shamir's words that the complaint had some justification.

In addition to his acrid social commentary, Matmor attacks the so-called realism of the day and recapitulates the failure of his generation of dramatists to confront reality and present more than an idealised gloss on the events of the early years of statehood. By its iconoclasm *An Ordinary Play* underscored the rhetoric of the other plays of the 1950s, notably *In the Wastes of the Negev* and Shamir's *He Walked in the Fields*. These had achieved success by strengthening the public self-image and serving as an encouraging boost to the Zionist consensus.[57] Matmor's 'playwright' complains about his inability to write a drama:

> I've come to the conclusion that it's impossible for anyone to write a true play; there's no connection at all between what is done on the stage and the reality taking place outside the walls of the theatre. Because reality... isn't well-rounded, it isn't squeezed into two and a half hours and there aren't two intervals in between. Your theatre is very far from being a mirror of life.[58]

Gamzu offered a surprising confirmation of Matmor's brand of realism by placing the play within 'the documentary library of the eight years of the state between its establishment and the Sinai Campaign, [as] a stenographic document concerning the mood of the generation which fought to establish the state but could find no place in it'.[59]

While Matmor was primarily concerned with the aftermath of the war, he did not flinch from the battle itself. His greatest deviation from custom is his presentation of the war in a style which mingled the Absurd with almost documentary realism. He differs greatly from Shaham and others in this respect. In certain instances of battle description, his writing becomes exceedingly strong and effective, conveying the unsanitised experience of war to his audience and rejecting the customary denial or ennoblement of suffering. He mocks the glorification of the war:

THEATRE MANAGER One must point with pride to the positive achieve-
    ments. Satisfying scenes about the positive achievements. Satisfying
    pictures, the youth's volunteering, bloody battles, horrors, comrades'
    suffering – and at the end – the victory.
AUTHOR Yes and no, when one looks from close up the ideas change as
    well. The spirit of the battles and the spirit of volunteering change to
    crawling in a field of thorns, to ambush. To lobbing grenades. To a
    machine gun that's stuck, to running under crossfire to be bandaged;
    and the horrors are armed mines, flies and the ordinariness of death.

> This is the way the soldiers see the war; the glory, the splendour and the adulation are attached to it when peace comes.[60]

This passage is closer in spirit to the poetry of the First World War than most other Israeli writing on the War of Independence.

With all this, many of the accepted doctrines of the day and the myths were still to be found in Matmor's play. The mélange of documentary and myth was so commonplace in early Israeli drama that it created a new truth, a new 'stenographic document' which Matmor did not discard in its entirety. For example, among the *dramatis personae* there is not one immigrant character able to put his or her point of view as another or an 'other' category within Israeli society. Danny and his friends are representatives of the customary literary milieu, the Ashkenazi Hebrew-speaking Israelis, who supply the officer classes during the war.

Women are not affirmatively portrayed by Matmor. Danny's mother is a weeping, cringing figure, constantly complaining about her son, using the refuge of ill health to wheedle him into better behaviour, a *yiddishe momme* stereotype. The young women in Matmor's play are no more than sexual partners without substantial function: one, Zipporah, will ultimately confine her husband to a life of middle-class boredom, being incapable of understanding his nostalgia for his vigorous wartime past.[61] The image of bourgeois living, at the centre of which is the tedious wife, is a commonplace in early Israeli literature:

CHICHO [one of the ex-soldiers]: Zipporah wants to get married, to live in a two-roomed flat, she wants a child, to buy a refrigerator ... she wants to waste life. And every day on the way to the office and in the high rise I'll die a little, and for what? So that I'll have a comfortable life? That's not what I want.[62]

This attitude generated its own mythology, for in fact the women were as emotionally involved in the war and the post-war 'enterprise' as the men.

An Ordinary Play set the tone for what was to become, in the 1960s and after, an increasingly brutal examination of Zionism and its realisation in Israeli society. Matmor's unusual moodiness indicates that even in the 1950s the 'enterprise', represented by a large portrait of Theodor Herzl onstage throughout his play, was not immune to the society's, perhaps unstated, misgivings.

Stating these misgivings is one reason for the play's unpopularity;

it is not difficult to find others. Matmor spared no one in his savage dissection of his society. Even bereaved parents are mocked in the play by the trivialisation of their grief and by sullying the memory of the fighting men. Yet Yizhar, whose book was in the making at the time Matmor's play was staged, later reiterated some of Matmor's concerns.

With all this, Matmor could still be subsumed under Yitzhak Laor's categorisation of those whose rebellion was performed within the parameters of the dominant ideology. Matmor strayed further beyond the borders of the ideologically acceptable than the others, but not sufficiently far to appropriate the distinction of a truly revisionist, dissident examination of his society for his drama. Nevertheless, Matmor was vilified and then ignored for his pains. He died alone in Portugal in 1975, having written a second play and a novel in English which remains untranslated into Hebrew and unpublished in Israel.

In the 1950s, unlike in later decades, the drama did not accurately reflect, satirise or parody its society. It followed its own imaginative agenda, comprising half-truths, myths, some historical facts, ideologically-founded ideas and characters drawn primarily from the stuff of Israeli everyday life. It lacked critical thrust. With other genres of the time, the drama marginalised the issues that were troubling the society. For example, there were few Arabs on the Israeli stage and those that did appear were stereotypes, reflecting Israeli society's inability to deal with them socially or politically. There was no serious theatrical engagement with religious issues, although oriental Jewish traditionalism surfaced as a topic in often paternalistic plays about the oriental communities.[63] There was minimal estimation of the experiences of the war, the aftereffects of the traumas of the war and the Holocaust, and the actual problems of European refugees. These were considerations which in later decades shifted from the margins of the drama to become central. The drama of the 1950s stringently avoided political confrontation. Neither the significant social debates of the 1950s, occurrences of the next decade, such as the scandal known as the Lavon Affair in 1960, or the decline of the *Mapai* (Labour) party and Ben-Gurion, found a place in the drama of the time.

The playwrights were, in fact, self-censoring and diluting the issues so that the drama retained a mere hint or outline, a watered-down summary of the concerns of the day. They did this for cogent reasons, one of which was fear of official disapproval, another their reluctance to challenge the national ideology. When they did depict contemporary social conditions, they rarely placed them within an *authentic* social context or exhibited a sense of the underlying social and economic movements of the period. Playwrights appeared to debate the implications of the growth of a new urban culture, speaking about materialism, urbanism and loss of direction[64] but we are not sure that their plays, despite this 'social realism', progressed or clarified the audience's knowledge of the broader sociopolitical situation of the time. More importantly, the playwrights offered little indication of the public mood.

If Israeli drama of the 1950s was a chapter of Kafka's 'diary', it was a selective record. Audiences saw themselves portrayed on the stage in a positive, self-reinforcing light, as a group possessing a refined moral conscience, dismayed by events in the country but not impelled to probe them too deeply. In this way the drama certainly fulfilled its ordained role of ideological reinforcement: it enhanced the dominant Zionist consensus, disseminated positive nation-building propaganda and entrenched positive archetypes and stereo-types, and largely avoided subjects which were likely to impair national morale.

Dissent was yet to come.

CHAPTER 2

Zionism on the stage: years of protest

The literature of the first decade of statehood provided later writers with the means for cultural rebellion by presenting patterns of ideology that had to be dismantled. From 1967, as the nature of the collective changed and political thinking became more divisive, the substance of the drama changed as well. It moved from almost unequivocal support of Zionism to criticism, from mythic models to fallen heroes. The War of Independence had infused the nation with a sense of glorious achievement, akin to David overcoming the giant Goliath, the few prevailing over the many. The Six-Day War was different: after the initial triumphalism it provoked a moral crisis in an influential minority of the population who recognised their responsibility to the Palestinians under the country's control. The altered Israeli self-image, from victim-hero to conqueror and occupier, led to an ideological crisis, an attenuation of the consensus concerning Zionist ideology, which divided the nation. Zionism itself became the target of a debate that juxtaposed the ancient dream of national renewal in the Land and contemporary *realpolitik*. Ancient aspirations embodied in modern Zionism were considered by certain groups to be irrelevant to the twentieth-century nation state with its increased affluence and powerful army. What mattered now was the conflict between Zionist ideology and its extension through conquest. Questions of militarism and power and the growth of religious extremism were debated within the new problematisation of Zionism.

The drama continued to be a sensitive antenna of any political disquiet. In their intense social and political scrutiny, playwrights had to 'cut out a piece of their society' for analysis and inspection.[1] In Israeli cultural history, Zionism constituted such a 'piece' and the analysis, the re-evaluation of national mythology, was to become the underlying preoccupation of Israel's serious political drama for three decades.

Attention to social and political reality dominated not only drama but fiction from the 1960s to the 1980s. Due to the prominence given to political writing at the time it is easy to believe that no other genre was being produced. Most of this writing was generated by the Israeli Left. The fury of right-wing spokespeople at the tone, for example, of the protest poetry produced in Israel after the war in Lebanon in 1982 was aroused to a large extent by their belief that a national medium was being used for the political interests of a vocal minority. They were incensed by the fact that the recipients of major Israeli prizes for fiction and drama were, almost without exception, representatives of the left-wing intellectual stratum of Israeli society. Outraged conservatives were convinced that the 'other side' did not raise its voice

because in the small world of the political theatre all the places are taken, all the talented directors are committed and most of the actors are also identified. So talent will not help and money won't help. There is not a stage for the ideas of the right and in fact there isn't even a stage for the ideas of the centre, only the extreme left rules, only it has a stage and a subsidy.[2]

After Hanokh Levin, the *enfant terrible* of the Israeli stage, had won the Leah Porat Prize in 1983, Rabbi Haim Drukman, a right-wing member of the Knesset (Israeli Parliament), expressed his anger:

Hanokh Levin, the author of plays like *The Patriot*, and *The Great Whore of Babylon*, was chosen by the Institute of Culture and the Arts to receive the most important and prestigious prize among the arts prizes in Israel . . . The State of Israel encourages a blow to the basic values of Judaism, the nation and the state.[3]

With withering irony the Right mocked the literary establishment which, it claimed, consists of people who 'apologise for their existence', the 'auto-anti-Semites', preoccupied not by forty years of Hebrew independence but forty years of Palestinian oppression.[4]

Much Israeli drama of this period was certainly radical in the sense that it struck at the most powerful weapon of social control, Zionism, the national ideology. The political plays took this as the springboard for protest in the name of the Israeli liberal establishment. Because of their internal prominence and their accessibility in translation to foreign readers and audiences, left-leaning to radical playwrights and fiction writers were widely regarded as national mouthpieces. Members of conservative to right-wing political groups had not yet found a convincing literary voice. Amos Oz asks, in a speech to members of Gush Emunim:

Why are most of the creative people in the country, heaven help us, 'leftists'? Is it a conspiracy? Has Damascus bought out Hebrew literature lock, stock and barrel? How do you explain the fact the artistic, ideological and philosophical creativity in Israel is these days taking place – not all of it but most and perhaps even the best of it – in a defeated, wounded, crumbling camp? No, don't try to say that this is the fashion all over the world. There are fascinating creators and thinkers everywhere who are completely removed from the left ... Why is your world a barren desert of creativity?[5]

The answer is probably that a conservative government has no need for what is, in effect, protest literature. Also, conservative leaders tending to anti-intellectualism do not often seek expression through creative art. There is certainly little creative literature in Israel which reflects the Right.[6] In fact, nowhere is there a political *theatre* of the Right. A London *Times* review of Howard Brenton's *Greenland* at London's Royal Court theatre included the following comment:

Political theatre is in trouble: it hasn't really acquired a language to deal with the Thatcher age. We have, of course, no right-wing political theatre, and I dread to think what it would be like if we had. Anyway, the right doesn't need it: the right, at the moment, is where the action is, while the left is busy licking its wounds.

In Israel the 'wounds' (according to the Left) derive from the founding philosophy of Zionism which has for them become the new conservatism.

The problem has been attacked in Israel with arsenals of rhetoric, both in and outside the Knesset, and in 1984 Yossi Sarid, a Member of the Knesset declared, in response to the angry claims of a right-wing opponent:

The difference between us is a very simple one, and therefore your symbols, too, are not ours. You and I do not belong – I don't know why – to the same nation, to the same culture, to the same tradition, to the same values, to the same norms.[7]

This idea is, perhaps unwittingly, emphasised by a theatre group established on the West Bank. Its members have provided one of the few responses from the Right through creative drama. Fifteen religious West Bank Jewish women, under the leadership of Zippora

Luria, created a play, *Mirkam* (Weave), (1994), which they presented
to all-women audiences. It consisted of monologues, poetry and
movement. Their narratives are drawn from their own lives, from
the domestic to the political (for example, descriptions of clashes
with Israeli soldiers during demonstrations). Their discourse is
aimed directly at the audience, in the first experiment by a community theatre created beyond the Green Line to give expression to life
in the highly politicised settlements on the West Bank. Masks with
which the performance begins are soon cast aside, a symbolic act of
withdrawing the barrier between normative Israel and the 'other'.
The purpose of this group is to counteract what they perceive as
Israeli audiences' prejudice against West Bank settlers, and the
negative perceptions of those writing from outside the culture of
religious settlement in the territories. Dan Urian comments that the
majority of the scenes

feed on pathos: a pathos of the pioneering land myth that returns the texts
to the original period of settlement, the Zionist play and the framework of
the 30s and 40s; a pathos supported by the use of rhetorical Hebrew –
unique to this group, spiced with religious expressions.[8]

The pathos extends to stories about their collective experience and
their realtionship to the state. The popular – and fashionable –
notion of a women-only theatre, combined with curiosity about their
lives and the emotional power of their performances, have ensured
success for the group although by its nature it is unable to penetrate
into the established theatre.

Political dialectic in Israeli literature is not simply a matter of
protest against an unpopular government, since it spans the entire
history of the State of Israel. It cannot be compared, for example,
with the upsurge of artistic protest from the Left in the UK during
the Thatcher period. In Israel, protest has been a constant feature of
literature as much during the Labour years as under *Likud*. The
mainstream group of Israeli writers have exhibited radical tendencies even when nominally supporting and traditionally identified
with the government. There is, therefore, an added quality to the
political literature of Israel, one which more specifically defines its
radicalism and places it on an ideological plane above that of simple
protest. It takes the form of a *moral* argument derived from the
various developments associated with Zionism. As early as 1948,

Yizhar raised the moral question in a short story entitled 'The Prisoner' in which he described the treatment by a group of young Israeli soldiers of an Arab shepherd they had captured. Almost forty years later the preoccupation with morality remains constant. While the *aspiration* of return to the Land was rarely questioned, the *method* of achieving security and peace for Israel lay at the heart of the moral argument. Most of the drama which achieved the greatest prominence was focused upon this, whether clarified through the problems of war, post-war repercussions or a direct confrontation with the philosophy of Zionism itself.

In the drama, the experience of the Six-Day War was extended to incorporate its most contentious consequences: *hitnahlut* (settlement in the Occupied Territories), the rise of religious nationalism and the growth of ultra-Orthodoxy. In addition, there were the questions of the Jewishness of the State of Israel, the consequences of extended *mamlakhtiyut* (statehood), the evolution of Palestinian nationalism, the conflict – which became the central theme of at least one prominent dramatist – between Judaism and Zionism, and the subsequent redefinition of 'normalisation'. Generally the literature revealed the weakening of the founding mythology and its dominant symbol, the *sabra*, the icon of Israeli self-determination. Theatre scholar Avraham Oz has gone so far as to suggest that the ideological conflict aroused by the growing confrontation with Zionism should be the basis for tragedy, given that tragedy describes the challenging by mortals of moral or metaphysical determinism.[9] The contradictions inherent in Israel's founding ideology seem to make this kind of dramatic exercise feasible, yet so far the tragic mode has not been employed for the purpose of exploring Israel's complex political problems.

The drama became the primary opposition to the heroic norm of the 1950s, rejecting the presentation of reality through epic or mythic models and challenging the national consensus. The collective had lost its potency, the artistic propaganda machinery was winding down. Even before the Six-Day War, the deconstruction of the memory of 'those days' in fiction and drama had begun. A. B. Yehoshua's allegorical novella, *Mul Haye'arot* (Facing the forests), (1962), pointed to the flaws in early Zionist ideology, and a collection of soldiers' writings published after the 1967 war expressed doubts about aspects of the war itself.

Yehoshua's family drama, *Laylah Bemai* (A night in May), (1969)[10] was among the first of the new-wave plays to examine Zionism in relation to the Six-Day War. The play set the tone for the ensuing destruction of the clichés so dear to the *Palmah* writers; everything which had characterised the early war plays was laid to rest by Yehoshua through a series of ironic scenes: the old fighters, now facing another war, are seen as derelicts, madmen and failures. The play combines many themes with which the drama was concerned at the time: mockery of a fantasised past, symbolised by a film made of the 1948 war which is now blurred and fuzzy; nostalgia for lost idealism symbolised by romantic *Palmah* poetry now locked away in a suitcase. This idealism is destroyed when an ex-*Palmahnik* publicly expresses doubt about Israel's ability to win the war in 1967. In Yehoshua's play there is no longer a hero, individual or group, there are no battles or sieges, no weary soldiers trudging down from the hills, no glory. The battleground has shifted to the internal landscape of fear and madness. The war belongs to a different generation, one whose ideology has evolved beyond that of the heroes' in Shamir's *He Walked in the Fields*, the first original play to be performed in Israel.

Novelists such as S. Yizhar, Benjamin Tammuz and Yehoshua himself had been posing moral questions that predated *A Night in May* by some years. Now, for the drama too, all caution disappeared as it took up political and sociological cudgels in a clear break with the idea of artists constituting the representative voice of the ideological establishment. Playwrights, no longer seeing themselves as acquiescent commentators, did not hesitate to speak their mind.

Three major changes took place in the political drama: the submergence of the positive hero, the establishment of a clear divergence from the united communal face that the playwrights had initially shown to the world, and a weakening of their moral responsibilities engendered by patriotism and national unity; and the fact that the plays were no longer adaptations of novels or stories, rendered for the stage by theatrically inexperienced authors. After 1967, political drama was composed from the auditorium for the stage by playwrights who were trained in theatrecraft and who frequently directed their own work. The medium and the message therefore achieved equal importance.

From 1972 the *enfants terribles* of the Israeli stage came into their own. Almost exclusively to the political left, they were subsequently able to lay the blame for what had in fact been happening all along at the feet of the right-wing government which came to power in 1977. War, occupation, social inequity, materialism, loss of idealism – these were merely the inheritance of Menahem Begin's *Likud* government, to which it proceeded to add what the playwrights saw as a new and ambitious imperialism. Events such as the American-brokered Camp David peace accord between Israel and Egypt in 1979, the Lebanon War in 1982, and the emergence of right-wing militancy led to a wave of documentary and realistic plays. Much of the argument in these plays centred on the political catchphrase *ein brerah* ('no choice'), a notion attacked by the radical writers. Some of them characterised this philosophy as a lie through which the government was able to justify its policies. Above all, the plays were concerned with examining the national myths, among which *ein brerah* was considered to number, and exploring the gap between the vision of Zionist redemption and its realisation in modern Israel. Plays on this topic constituted about ten per cent of all original plays from 1967.

One of this theatre's most popular genres was political satire in the form of cabaret or revue. Cabaret is an easily accessible presentation of matters of serious and immediate importance, in accordance with Eric Bentley's opinion that when political theatre is good it is often very simple.[11] The Israeli cabarets revealed the influence of the European thesis plays of the interwar years and more directly that of the political theatre of Ernst Toller and Erwin Piscator, perfected in Berthold Brecht's Epic Theatre – all of which had their roots in political cabaret. In interwar Germany the cabaret had grown out of opposition to official pomposity and conformity, an exaggerated national pride and a sense of shame about the past. Satirical cabaret allied itself with anti-chauvinist ideology which perceived the danger to the individual of artificial nationalist values.

Israeli satire rested upon three strongly based pillars, all implicated in the edifice of Zionism: the army, the social good, and Jewish ultra-Orthodoxy to which religious Zionism was later added. Even so, regardless of its topicality, early Israeli satire attempted to avoid offending the public, for in Israel the satirists, even those adopting a dissident stand, never saw themselves as being outside 'the camp'.[12] They did not at that time lose the sense of the tension between their opposition to certain political policies on the one hand, and their dedication to the national entity on the other.

The conflict between [the satirist's] faith for which he is prepared to give his life and the faith that he is forced to support and defend (to the point of giving his life) is the most characteristic and central element of the world of the new Israeli political satire.[13]

This changed with the advent of Hanokh Levin and Yehoshua Sobol, both icons of the Israeli theatre since the 1970s. Apparently free of ethical conflict in their satires, they initiated a more pointed, sophisticated, often brutal version of the cabaret.

Levin's *Malkat Ha'ambatya* (The Queen of the Bathtub), (1970)[14], was the most notorious of the satires that followed the Six-Day War. It was a representative example of a number of post-war literary works, poetry, fiction and drama, which denigrated the post-1967 'festival of victory'. Immediately after its end, the Six-Day War was universally perceived as having been the heroic action of a nation fighting for its survival, and a declaration of Israeli military prowess to the world. Many Israeli plays bolstered this view but there were others which criticised the psychological effects of the victory on Israeli society. Interestingly, the plays which took a traditionally heroic view of the war achieved less popular success than the iconoclastic satires, perhaps because of the public scandals the latter aroused. Levin went entirely over the top in his nihilistic view of his country, his anal and excretory imagery becoming a metaphor for its rot and wastage.

The primary target of *The Queen of the Bathtub* was Israeli self-congratulation after the war. It attacked the nation's glorification of its own power through a satire on the *sabra*-hero, and it mocked the Israelis' sense of moral superiority, their apparent veneration of sacrifice, their chauvinism and national paranoia.[15] Levin set out to taunt the so-called consensus whose supporters, according to him, were smug and self-assured. These are represented in the play by young, middle-class professionals who would elsewhere be charac-terised as 'yuppies'. Their key phrase, repeated many times, is *hakol beseder* (everything's okay), leading Levin contemptuously to define them as '*anshei beseder*' (the people of 'Everything's okay'). Unlike Yoram Matmor, writing in the mid-1950s, Levin is sufficiently distant psychologically and politically from the *Palmah* generation to be able to dispel the myths of 1948 without sentiment.

His soldier-hero, Boaz (a wartime call-sign), characterises himself as a simple soldier who is doing his duty. He is, however, an urban stereotype rather than a *kibbutznik*. He refers to one of the most compelling semiotic features of the *Palmahnik*, his untidy lock or quiff of hair (*blorit*), and to his mischievous eyes. Boaz's biography parodies the idealised biography of the hero of the *Palmah*, down to his parents' occupations, both of them bourgeois professionals. His girlfriend, Hulda, is the prototype of an entire series of narcissistic female characters glorying in egocentrism, an enduring component of Levin's writing.

Levin's revisionism is derived from what appears to be a dialogue with the 1950s texts through which he derides the blatant rhetoric of the earlier plays. His destruction of the *sabra* character is so drastic that *The Queen of the Bathtub* seems to constitute a direct response to Mossinzon's *In the Wastes of the Negev*. For example, Hulda declares, 'I'm actually an autumnal girl who carries great existential sadness within her'.[16] Mossinzon's Shosh analyses the *sabra*'s internal misgivings when confronting the necessity of war:

Include them, those who aren't here, who don't exist any more, and tell them that you don't want to kill, you don't want war ... we don't want to dig too deeply in case we see an open abyss – because Uzi and Uri are killers of people at an age when they haven't even stroked a girl's hair ... I've been visiting the hospital ... and there were young men there without hands and a without legs ... I wanted to cry – and I knew it wasn't allowed![17]

In *The Queen of the Bathtub* Boaz mocks the *sabra* metaphor,[18] thorny outside, soft and sweet inside: 'I cover myself with a hard skin in order to conceal the softness of my heart and my natural gentleness'.[19] 'You *sabras*, sometimes it seems that flowers grow on you instead of thorns,' says Abraham in *In the Wastes of the Negev*.[20] Boaz characterises himself as 'not at all a simple fellow'.[21] 'These young men,' says Zvi in *In the Wastes of the Negev*, 'are very complex ... they are very complex people who become confused by complexity'.[22] Their emotional reticence ('Our *sabras* are ashamed to show their feelings to the outside world ... '),[23] their courage, lightheartedness and, above all, complexity, are demolished in Levin's characterisation of Boaz, the antitype. It is likely that Levin is attacking the *sabra*'s fabricated image, his *literary* incarnation, an emotional distillation of the qualities of many young soldiers further glorified by the texts. This archetype epitomises the ideological buttress against which Levin and his contemporaries deploy their dramatic arsenal.

No one is spared in Levin's satire. He highlights the Israeli's defensiveness and sensitivity to any form of criticism, particularly of national institutions. More significantly, he attacks the attitude of the wealthy, secure and materialistic Ashkenazi towards the impoverished Sephardi. A particularly biting sketch presents two well-heeled Israeli matrons tormenting an Arab waiter at a café in terms which are uncomfortably reminiscent of South African satires portraying the treatment of blacks by whites during apartheid. The women in Levin's sketch justify their racism by the one being the mother of a soldier and the other the daughter of Holocaust survivors. In a satirical monologue the Arab is represented metaphorically as a fly, revealing his bourgeois master's stereotypical racism in addition to his contempt for the *untermensch*.

In *The Queen of the Bathtub* Levin is even able to take issue with the Ten Commandments which, he says, are not appropriate for a nation constantly at war, and he devotes an entire scene to the *Akedah*. The sacrificial power is interpreted in the play as the most brutal force of all, the state, which victimises its citizens. Zionism invokes a new *Akedah* through which obedient fathers send their sons to die in battle. In the sketch Abraham, unwilling but dutiful, prepares Isaac for the sacrifice while Isaac goads him on: 'When God says to you, kill your son like a dog, you must run and kill him'.[24] After a heated quarrel Abraham is halted by Isaac who hears the angel's voice. Abraham muses: 'I think to myself, what would it be like if other fathers had to kill their sons. What would save them?' In one version of the play Isaac replies: 'Well, there could always be a voice from heaven'[25] and Abraham responds: 'Okay, if you say so';[26] in a second version he adds: 'But between you and me, you know there's no God'.

A central theme of *The Queen of the Bathtub* was to become a constant preoccupation of Levin's, the destructiveness of war and the loss of young lives. One of his more serious lyrics tells of a small child who must learn about war too soon. Another expresses the soldiers' longing to die a natural death between battles. The climax of the satire occurs with the dead son imploring the father not to be brave about his death: 'Don't stand up so proudly . . . father. Weep for me, don't be silent in my honour. Don't speak of me as a sacrifice because I was the one who died. Don't say exalted words, for I've been brought very low'.[27] The lyric ends with the son demanding that the father beg forgiveness, which particularly enraged the critics and aroused a furious debate in the press.

A son who has been killed accuses the father of having sent him to his death. This is malicious brutality aimed at thousands of bereaved parents whose hearts are bleeding and whose world has been destroyed ... Have you ever seen how people train a puppy who has made a mess in the living room? They take his head and shove it in the mess. Any intelligent dog will understand the meaning. Blessed is he who takes the playwright by the hair of his head and shoves it into that same pile so that he understands that there are sanitary places in which one casts excrement, not on a public stage.[28]

Levin's lyrics attack the memorial rhetoric and the post-war rituals, all of which involved some religious discourse. He vilifies attitudes like Avraham's in *In the Wastes of the Negev* – the father who, despite his grief, is proud of his son's noble death. Levin's message is that dead soldiers should not comprise a part of the national ritualisation of grief. One of the most poignant lines is the son's rebuke: 'Something more important than honour is resting at your feet, my father'.

Levin condemns the entire political system together with its approving followers. His primary target is the ideology which legitimises the politics represented by the hero of 1948 to whom he attributes all the country's later ills. This revisionism, which is an accepted part of contemporary Israeli left-wing rhetoric, was at the time seen as subversion:

In the name of 'freedom of speech' and the 'sacredness of the citizen' it seems to be permitted to do any kind of wicked deed even if it explicitly means undermining the state. The wounding of the spirit of a nation engaged in a war for its survival is much worse than concealing a bomb in the supermarket ...[29]

There remains something unresolved about the *Palmah* period, with continuing disputes about whether the founding 'mythology', is to be preserved or obliterated. It is obvious that this wrangle possesses political overtones. Much contemporary Israeli writing, in addition to Levin's, implies that retaining the early heroic stereotypes implies the glorification of the origins of the present Israeli crisis. The *sabra* hero embodied militarism, nationalism, machismo – traits less acceptable today; increasingly, therefore, the icon is being rendered void like Matmor's Danny Keresh.

Following the sections about war and loss, the *The Queen of the Bathtub* degenerates into a cruder satire on the political establishment and the national consensus, and outlines a vulgar portrait of Golda

Meir enthroned on a toilet as the Queen of the bathtub. Some of
Levin's supporters viewed the play as a sign of a healthy society in its
perception of the dangers of *hubris* after an historic victory,[30] while
those opposed damned it as a 'lavatorial requiem', 'rubbish whose
only appropriate place is the toilet', 'a bath of counterfeit and
mendacious anger'.[31] In April 1970 the play was removed by the
management of the Cameri theatre after fewer than twenty performances. The Board of Criticism of Films and Plays (the Censorship
Board), a branch of the Ministry of the Interior, had demanded the
excision of certain scenes from the text. Once this was done, it
passed the play for performance but the decision to remove it from
the stage was taken by the theatre management itself, using public
pressure as its justification following riots and demonstrations, and
death threats against members of the cast. The controversy about
the play's thesis then shifted to a discussion about the principle of
freedom of speech.

The *Queen of the Bathtub* and Amos Kenan's *Haverim Mesapperim 'al
Yeshu* (Comrades Tell Stories About Jesus) (1972),[32] (set the tone both
thematically and structurally – as well as in their myth-destroying
tendencies – for much of the radical drama that followed. Kenan's
title itself was provocative on two counts: the name of Jesus which
contributed to the play's banning by the Censorship Board, and the
satirical reference to the 'Jimmy' book. In the play a sacrificed
figure, representing the hero of 1948, hangs from a cross throughout
the action: the active hero, the once adored *sabra*, has become
impotent and motionless, like Danny the Plank.

Kenan supplies a savage caricature of Israeli society during the
1960s with its worship of materialism on the one hand, and its
recourse to slogans on the other, 'synthetic values, false memories –
the primary stuff of satire'.[33] The play strikes at the established belief
in the cycle of catastrophe and redemption realised through the
Holocaust on the one hand, and the establishment of the state on the
other. Accordingly, the play mocks the historical icons (pioneering,
greening the desert, draining the marshes), turning the accepted
rhetorical terminology back on itself so that it becomes a reprimand
for complacency and the reliance on mythology and slogans.
Kenan's most derided target is the army and the war, heralding two
decades of anti-war and anti-army protest plays in a new mythology
of war.

The play is a lament for dead youth. In a series of vignettes Kenan condemns the sacrifice of young men and the public, ritualised response of bereaved parents who are seen, through Kenan's distorted lens, as smug keepers of the children's memories. Two dead soldiers speak:

YOUNG MAN He was a youngster, almost a boy. When he killed me he burst out crying.
MAN Afterwards he began writing poetry.
YOUNG MAN Yes, yes, we were marvellous. We'll never forget ourselves!
MAN We'll never forget how much we wanted peace.[34]

Kenan relies on this kind of *galgenhumor* (gallows humour) throughout the play. With the insouciance of the mythic hero, the two soldiers discuss their many deaths in previous wars, and in those still to come, as if it were an adventure or a business deal:

YOUNG MAN What's new? I haven't seen you in years!
MAN Me too. D'you remember the last time we were killed?
YOUNG MAN Old pal, do I remember! As if it were yesterday.[35]

Later they agree: 'Yes – those were the days!'[36] Mingled with the literary clichés of battle ('I dragged you on my back') is the acceptance of the eternality of war by the mention of a date, 1974, still in the real future for the playwright but the distant past for the characters of the play.

Referring to canonic texts ('He walked in the fields, he walked and walked and in the end he was killed in the fields')[37] two mothers outdo each other in the matter of their dead sons' heroism (in a mockery of the tone represented by Mossinzon's Avraham) and in their own suffering as pioneers clearing the swamps and enduring the fever. Their absurd quarrel over ownership of an egg reduces the Middle East conflict to farce. Kenan is not mocking the bereaved, but the ideology of sacrifice and the systems of collective grief in which national ideology was paramount. The play contains many anti-military passages, which helped to ensure its unpopularity with the Censorship Board and also indicated the distance that drama had travelled since Matmor's *An Ordinary Play*.

Despite its serious, even powerful moments, *Comrades Tell Stories About Jesus*, like Levin's, *The Queen of the Bathtub*, created a furore in Israel. This was not only due to its content. Unlike Levin's play, which had been removed by the theatre itself, *Comrades Tell Stories About Jesus* was officially banned in its entirety after seven performances, the official reason being 'offence to the Christian religion'.[38]

Despite the widespread belief that the banning had a political motive, the Censorship Board insisted that Christian leaders in the Occupied Territories had protested to the Prime Minister, Golda Meir, requesting the proscription of the play. Even after Kenan had changed the name of the play, replaced the crucified man with a scaffold, and the play was passed by the Board without further alteration, he could not find a theatre prepared to stage it. While *Comrades Tell Stories About Jesus* was often in bad taste, it was symptomatic of a need to re-examine an the established ideology. It released a torrent of similar anti-social treatises, the very volume of which, if nothing else, had to be taken seriously.

The politicised Israeli drama, the result of 'a thirst for political satire',[39] was, in the 1970s and 1980s increasingly devoted to cabaret, documentary or revue. However, one reviewer commented at the time that in a country where 'News Review' (*Mabat Lahadashot*) was the 'funniest programme on television', political satire would not bring Begin's followers to a rational examination of their actions.[40]

Another genre – the semi-documentary, episodic play – also gained popularity in Israel from the early 1970s. The American-born director Nola Chilton mounted a series of plays which uncompromisingly described and often condemned the Israeli Ashkenazi middle class. This was somewhat paradoxical considering that these exercises, like Levin's satires, were staged by a subsidised mainstream theatre, something akin to an American protest theatre burning real money onstage whilst demanding subsidies. Chilton obtained her material through interviews and court proceedings which playwrights adapted for the stage. Her productions covered a multitude of social problems, from the care of the aged to poverty-stricken Oriental communities and the growing violence among the alienated Sephardi[41] youth. Chilton's distinctive theatre grew out of her belief that the stage had lost its opportunity to change people's lives. Her production of Yehoshua Sobol's *Kriza* (1976)[42] – a collection of monologues concerning the second generation of Sephardi immigrant families – was aimed at the 'white' Ashkenazi establishment, but it was developed by members of that establishment rather than by the oppressed subjects of the exercise themselves. This is the anomalous face of protest theatre: the protest is perhaps no less valid when made on behalf of others, but it is less authentic.

Present in *Kriza* was the element that underscored many of the protest plays of the 1970s and 1980s: the underlying presence of the 'dream' and its potential realisation in the Declaration of Independence. Just as Yehoshua Sobol began the play *Repentance* (1972) with Ben-Gurion's voice intoning the text of the Declaration, Chilton strung a banner across the stage bearing enlarged quotations from the works of the Zionist founders in *Kriza*. Beneath this banner, contradicting those old ideals, events from life in Israel took place. *Kriza* raised the question of the practical value of this kind of dramatic presentation which bordered on publicism since it contained a direct appeal to the government to change discriminatory laws. Some reviewers accused Chilton of exploiting the theatre for propaganda, and also revealed Israel's discomfort at seeing itself portrayed with ugly racist overtones that hurt the public as much as Hanokh Levin's attacks had done. Many critics detested the play, seeing themselves – the Ashkenazi intellectuals – as among the accused.

In basement cafés and cabaret clubs and on the stages of subsidised theatres, satirical and documentary material, whether by seasoned playwrights such as Sobol or Hillel Mittelpunkt, or in workshop productions, increasingly viewed the army and its hierarchy as a major antagonist in Israeli society. The proliferation of quasi-Brechtian plays, quantity often at the expense of quality, led one critic to comment:

We are rich in problems in this country but not as rich in dramatic creativity. Therefore, when three plays are staged at the same time, all denouncing the Defence Force and making it culpable – there is cause for a moment of concern.'[43]

The army and military government are at the heart of Yosef Mundi's *Moshel Yericho* (The Ruler of Jericho), (1975),[44] which constituted an effort to encapsulate the problems of Israel, the Arabs, and diaspora Jewish identity in the surprising form of a comedy. Its plot concerns the absurd pretensions of the Israeli military establishment which are observed by a number of Palestinians. Mundi drew upon the gallery of stereotypes which dominated Israeli Hebrew agitprop of the 1970s and 1980s, for his *dramatis personae*: the military Ruler, his deputy, his female Israeli secretary who is possibly an Arab spy, a Palestinian terrorist called Muhammed, a Russian Jewish itinerant vendor and a 'schizoid' Israeli – all of whom symbolise players in the real political game. One departure is the Arab girl, Lila, who differs from other Israeli theatrical Arabs, a character, according to Zimmerman, who combines the Arab's romantic aspect popular in *yishuv* literature with the destructive, and threatening aspect prominent in the literature of the 1960s.[45] Lila – who may or may not also be Naava, the Ruler's clerk – is a modern Rahab[46] who becomes the Ruler's lover and represents an earthy, exotic middle-eastern ambience. The 'schizoid' and Muhammed provide both sides of the Israeli-Palestinian conflict with some additional Israeli angst:

SCHIZOID Why don't I want your blood, why do you frighten me with death all the time, why aren't you afraid of me, I don't want your death but you want mine, I don't hate you and you hate me, I don't want to kill you and you want to kill me. [*Takes him by the throat*] Why don't I kill you, what's stopping me, why don't I finish you once and for all. [*Shouting*] Why?[47]

At the same time Mundi satirises the stock Israeli perception of the inferior group by their betters:

SCHIZOID I'll never understand them. Never. I hate them! I'm built differently. There'll never be peace between me and them. Their ways are strange to me. I'm a child of Europe.[48]

In accordance with Israeli symbolism in other works,[49] both the 'schizoid' and the Palestinian are equally imprisoned by the conflict, and in the play they actually share a jail cell. The play's arguments reiterate various political positions within Israeli society: love of the land, entitlement to and possession of it, hatred of the enemy, guilt.

NAAVA We're sitting on their land and claiming that historically it's ours!
RULER So what, there's a wilderness here, the land belongs to the one who works it, makes it fruitful; the one who looks after it and does what's necessary is its legal owner.
NAAVA They're Muslims and we're Jews, they once ruled us and now we're ruling them, they're a majority and we're a minority. They only want a little and we want it all. They have time and we don't.
RULER So what if they're right, so what ... who put these ideas into your head?[50]

Later Muhammed cries: 'You think [the land] is yours alone. Get out of here! Get out! You're strangers here'. Yet Muhammed's militancy and readiness to kill Jews is contradicted by his cowardice: he would rather be caught and do time in an Israeli prison than be punished by his own leaders. Audiences were therefore presented with a

craven Arab man and an erotic Arab woman. Stereotyping conge-
nial to the implied viewer remained intact.

Mendel, the Jewish peddler, is the true child of Europe, a
burlesque of a diaspora Jew: a vagrant concerned only with his profit
but dreaming of his intellectual prime in St Petersburg. He disdains
the Levant, always recapitulating the encounter between the intellectual superiority of the European Jew and the boorish Israeli, but
he is cringingly obsequious to his Israeli military masters. Mundi's
dislike of him is indicated not so much in the characterisation itself
but in a stage direction: 'Mendel nods his head and doesn't forget to
take his suitcase containing his wares with him before he goes out'.
This image of the black-clad diaspora Jew clutching his merchandise
to his chest is akin to an anti-Semitic caricature. However, when a
loaded gun is placed in Mendel's hands he enjoys shooting and calls
for more ammunition. The Jew, when armed, becomes dangerous.

The Ruler of Jericho dreams of being a supermarket manager; his
aide imagines buying a stereo set, Mendel fires rounds of machine-
gun fire at random, the Palestinian terrorist opts to remain in jail.
All of them seek a non-existent wall believed to surround Jericho, an
imaginary wall which nevertheless prevents their escape, a symbol of
both a political and an existential dead end. They are trapped
together by history, geography and politics. Mundi portrays the
conflict between the Zionism which promotes acquisition of the
land, and present day political ineptitude, through the technique
previously untried in political drama: the Absurd which rendered
the conflict as irrational as the characters themselves.

Yehoshua Sobol's *Joker* produced by the Haifa Municipal Theatre
(1975) aroused the customary controversy. It is the tale of five
reservists in a bunker during the Yom Kippur War. It incorporates a
discussion between various representatives of Israeli society, notably
an Ashkenazi clerk who by default becomes the commanding officer,
and a religious Sephardi (played by Makram Khoury, an Arab
actor). The bunker is an allegory of Israel at war and, according to
Israel Goor, it reveals only the negative, unheroic, passive side of the
soldiers.[51] Writing from a traditional ideological standpoint, and
shortly after the shock of the Yom Kippur War, Goor contrasts the
people of *Joker* with Jimmy (of *Comrades Tell Stories About Jimmy*) and
Shaham's Avi in *They Will Arrive Tomorrow*. Sobol's revisionist insight
is certainly contrary to the reinforcing vision of these earlier works,
although it is equally selective. He attempts to expose the weariness

of people at war, their ordinariness, banality and ultimately their compromised morality when they send out a young, inexperienced soldier to set up a dangerous ambush.

Because many critics of the old school see Israel's wars only in terms of the endeavour of the War of Independence, a portrait of war without the superimposition of mythology becomes offensive. Due to the sensitivities of the society, war must be romanticised, an effect against which Matmor, in his earnest drama, attempted to protest. With *Joker* Sobol offended not by having composed a poor play but because, according to Goor, he denigrated 'a justifiable war for the survival of a nation confronting those who wish to destroy it'.[52] Many plays of the 1970s possessed elements of consciousness-raising, similar to Sobol's, counteracting the ideological bluster of the 1950s and 1967 which the Yom Kippur War terminated once and for all. While *Joker* was itself rough in structure and characterisation, and accorded with the prevailing fashion of alienation and dissent, Sobol was able to convey a sense of the nastiness and futility of war and its effect upon its fighters.

A streak of masochism affects much of the Hebrew political drama of the 1970s and 1980s. In Hillel Mittelpunkt's satirical cabarets, Israeli society is represented by its outcasts, the criminals and madmen. Regarding a cabaret he wrote with Sobol entitled *Hastriptiz Ha'aharon* (The Last Striptease), (1980), he declared,

When we saw what is happening in the state, we felt the need to shout out our anger ... we looked for a framework which would suit reality and we settled on the cabaret. By means of strong visual scenes like a striptease or the appearance of a transvestite we attempted to transmit our political message ... we don't see many positive phenomena in this country and we are therefore not ashamed to show the negative.[53]

Consequently his satire is peopled by the grotesque, perverted and deformed, not least of all a crippled Begin. Towards the end of the satire this character becomes so weakened that the others are obliged to move his limbs for him. Each character represents an element of modern Israel: the faltering economy, a fragmented society, political crises, war and *yerida* (emigration). *The Last Striptease* and other satirical cabarets successfully achieved the ideal charge of theatre, to 'probe a community's weaknesses, call its leaders to account, desacralize its most cherished values and beliefs, portray its characteristic conflicts and suggest remedies for them, and generally take stock of its current situation in the known world'.[54]

Israeli playwrights themselves appear to find the definition of 'political' difficult and anomalous, for drama which takes political actuality as its topic does not necessarily need to address directly the world of 'politics' or mimetically reproduce social or cultural processes. It appears, according to playwrights' own critical categorisation of drama, that 'naturalistic' – which to them means relating to current affairs – directly equates with the word 'political' in its original sense of pertaining to the *polis* as a whole. Their protagonists regard their personal fate as intimately involved with social and political events. The comment by an unnamed reviewer concerning a right-wing nationalist character in Sobol's *The Palestinian Girl* provides the proposition upon which not only the political drama but its criticism rests: 'He learned to love his nation before learning to love himself'.[55] In any case, our 'anticipated sense of the whole'[56] derived from our awareness of certain playwrights' most consistent preoccupations, prevents our taking their plays as anything but political. One of the disabilities of political writing is that even when politically identified writers attempt to avoid political bias, reviewers and scholars will inevitably impute it to them one way or another.

Political literature generally requires the reader to step beyond the usual boundaries of analysis since the extra-literary knowledge of the author's political stand is essential for the interpretation of his or her work. This applies equally to criticism which, in Israel, is frequently as politicised as the literature. If there is any doubt about the political nature of Israeli plays one has only to look to the critics. The veterans, for example – many of whom developed their critical skills with the drama's development – were offended by what they saw as attacks against the state and Zionism, and rushed to their defence. Their successors' judgements have also become a part of political rather than aesthetic discourse. All these critics either reinforce or reject *content* before evaluating style.

Israeli literature's political nature is not, however, entirely the responsibility of the writers, critics, readers or audiences, for Israel itself is automatically a politicised setting, like the South Africa of Nadine Gordimer or the Peru of Mario Vargas Llosa, among many others. The politics of place tends to override other concerns in a work of art in times of upheaval or unrest, whether or not its creator attempts to assume a neutral stance.

The aim of the popular semi-professional experimental Israeli group, *Hateatron Hapashut* (The Simple Theatre Company) encapsulated the precepts of political theatre in Israel: '[O]ur plays should always be realistic, not in the sense of a newspaper article, but in the sense of reflecting, of an artistic elevation of the reality in which we live ... Theatre is obliged to be actual and relevant'.[57] 'Relevant' and 'political' are almost interchangeable adjectives. A. B. Yehoshua confirmed in an interview that merely by being interested in Israeli social reality one is politically conscious.[58] Within these definitions it is possible to establish at least a politics of *content*. Israeli playwrights tend on the whole to avoid issues which fall beyond the peculiarly Israeli definition of 'political' – that is, which pertain to Zionism. Problematised issues that continue to exercise the political imagination of writers abroad – issues of class, gender, conservation, racism (outside the context of armed conflict) and sexual orientation – have been less prominent in Israeli dramaturgy.

The number of plays with political content presented in the annual theatre festival in Acre increased significantly during the 1980s, and since the best of these plays have reached the 'legitimate' theatre this is seen as a significant trend. Regarding one of these festivals Giora Manor, a seasoned dramatic critic, pointed out that there was hardly a presentation which did not deal seriously with important topical problems.[59] Some years ago an amateur playwright accused a drama competition selection committee of rejecting his play due to its radical content. The critic Michael Handelsaltz pointed out that no member of the selection committee was identifiably right-wing and expressed astonishment that any non-political plays had been accepted at all.[60]

Despite the particular character of the Acre Festival, drama (all that is written, produced and performed) and theatre (a hegemonic space of institutional and official control),[61] are not generally oppositional in Israel. The radicalisation of the dramatic subject remains unmatched by a radicalisation of either its form or its context. From the start, for example, the Haifa Municipal Theatre proclaimed an overtly political agenda which encouraged outspokenness and included the work of Arab and Palestinian playwrights and actors. It is widely regarded as the theatre of opposition, an idea which originated in 1969 with the theatre's founder, Joseph Millo. Yet both the

Haifa Theatre and its offshoot, Neve Tzedek, remain subsidised. There is, therefore, not a great disparity in Israel between the drama and the theatre, and until the mid-1990s there were few attempts at new theatrical forms. Playwrights, including those identified with the Left, use the subsidised institutional theatre as their forum, with the result that the most radical of Israel's drama functions within orthodox structures of theatre. Nola Chilton and Motti Baharav were two of the few playwrights and directors who attempted to synthesize the oppositions 'theatre' and 'drama' by working through special social theatre projects and youth workshops. Generally, however, political drama is not reserved for fringe or community theatre although in many notable cases that is its point of origin.

Although the political drama, whether it be staged by the Haifa Municipal Theatre, the Cameri or other subsidised theatres, is concerned with political procedures and beliefs that require change, with all the elements of oppositional politics, the creators of this drama still function within the same ideological framework as that of the national consensus. 'Even when the radical writers explore the distortions of the ideas of Zionism they don't doubt the ideas themselves'.[62] Because of ideological unity between the playwright, the director, the actors and the theatrical establishment – and even a significant section of the audience – the playwrights are for the most part functioning within a consensual framework. Their work assumes the posture of a political manifesto. Other than during the Begin years, they demonstrated little disaffection along party lines. It is perhaps for this reason that 'theatre' and 'drama' remain closely united in Israel.

The fact that the playwrights are by and large speaking predominantly to like-minded audiences and critics, that they are not in the true sense dissidents, does not detract from the political, social and historical value of their work. In his letter of 15 January, 1889 to the literary editor A. N. Plescheyev, Checkhov noted the difference between prose and drama: 'Writing prose is a quiet and sacred activity, like being with a lawful spouse. But drama is an impressive yet insolent, loud and tiring mistress'. Israeli political theatre, loud and insolent as it may be, is one of Israel's most impressive – and effective – cultural creations.[63]

CHAPTER 3

'The Israeli-Palestinian War'

The political and psychological watershed of the Six-Day War induced an awareness among the Israelis of the Palestinians as a potential nation. Their problem became central to the Israeli intellectuals' altered perception created by the war. Up to that point the Palestinians as a people, rather than the Arab as victim stereo-type or over-romanticised oriental, had scarcely been mentioned in the literature. In 1970 the Haifa Municipal Theatre took a bold step in producing a documentary play compiled by Mohammed Watad and directed by Nola Chilton, entitled *Dukiyum* (Coexistence). This was a collection of monologues based on newspaper reports concerned with the lives of the Israeli Arabs. While it portrayed their difficulties it was not entirely negative. After that, many plays problematised Arab/Palestinian-Israeli relationships, some proposing cautious optimism, others reaching the conclusion that no solution was possible. The playwrights' concern about the status of the Palestinians increased, especially after the rise of the right-wing *Likud* in 1977.

The period between the Yom Kippur War in 1973 and the Lebanon War in 1982 brought about a critical political change in Israel. The Yom Kippur War, which profoundly shocked the nation, altered Israel's perception of war, stripping it of the last vestiges of romanticism and destroying Israel's belief in its own invicibility. Some sense of optimism was restored by the Camp David peace accord between Israel and Egypt in 1977 which also reinforced certain liberal views of the Arabs. With the new desire for reconciliation came anxiety about Israeli treatment of the Palestinians on the West Bank, anxiety which was fully exploited by the drama. As a consequence of the unpopular incursion into Lebanon in 1982, six plays about the Lebanon War were staged in 1983 alone. This war, the *Intifada* and the growing power of right-wing militancy and

57

religious Zionism solidified the artistic opposition to the official Right and ultra-nationalist factions, and strengthened the playwrights' need to become involved in political action.[1]

Dominating the repertoire from 1982 to 1993 was the so-called 'Palestinian question'. Almost a hundred plays, not all of them staged in mainstream theatres, dealt directly or indirectly with the subject. Some were produced within an oppositional framework on fringe stages and at the the Acre Festival but, out of keeping with these venues, many adopted the genre of realism since playwrights aimed to portray actual events and issues to engage the audience.

The general sense of all this literature – whose topic was increasingly designated in the early 1990s by writers, including Amos Oz, as the Israel-Palestine War – is that of reality represented as nightmare. In works about the Occupied Territories, for example, normality – usually constituted by moral judgement, interpersonal relationships and normative language – is distorted, producing a world turning upon its own unique behavioural, moral and cultural axis. Anger, hatred and death become the new norms, language is metamorphosed into a system of repeated codes incorporating overworked rhetoric and telegraphic communication in mixed Arabic-Hebrew nourished by Israeli army proclamations and Palestinian public manifestos. The stage became a favoured forum for a discussion of this world, and the intimation of dialogue between stage and audience made it a particularly appropriate medium for debate. Once again warfare and theatre were juxtaposed in ideological confrontation. No longer did audiences sit in the auditorium for self-reinforcement as they had done in the 1950s; they came to listen to the arguments and to behave in a properly Brechtian manner.

In 1956 the Sinai Campaign had apparently disproved Yoram Matmor's negative claims about young Israelis; in 1987 the Intifada fuelled Yehoshua Sobol's charges against Zionism. The Intifada began on December 9, 1987, a few days after the first performances of Sobol's *Sindrom Yerushalayim* (Jerusalem Syndrome). This was an indictment through allegory of Israeli politics and the army, staged in the context of the fortieth anniversary celebrations for the state. Like many of Sobol's plays, this work compares phenomena in the Jewish past and the Israeli present. Paradoxically the play is set in the near future and draws its historical analogy from the period of the Roman destruction of the Second Temple (70 CE). Soldiers of a modern Israeli army, wandering tired and hungry, meet a group of strolling players, all mentally or physically disabled, who put on a play about the rebellion against the Romans that resulted in the Temple's destruction. Sobol's message rests in the correspondence between the potential destruction of Israel in a Third Temple age and the events in the Occupied Territories.

The play enraged certain elements within the public, including many who were not theatregoers. Those who took offence saw, as in Matmor's time, a denigration of Jewish heroism, the historical acme of which was the last stand against the Romans at Massada. Sobol was by that time the *bête noir* of the Right, who had begun their campaign even before the play opened.

[The right-wingers] demonstrated at the theatre entrance and then carried out a noisy, violent demonstration in the hall itself, in the middle of the performance [by throwing stinkbombs onto the stage]. The media roundly condemned the violent attempt to interfere with freedom of expression. Unfortunately, however, the critics condemned the play itself on the grounds of artistic merit.[2]

A member of the Knesset accused Sobol of self-hatred (a common canard of the religious Right), 'a superficial destruction of national and religious morals and a moral weakening of the power of Israeli opposition to Arab terror'. The matter reached a plenary session of the Knesset during which another MK voiced his views of a 'corrupt play ... [which] dishonoured the army and its casualties'. One of the most vociferous of the right-wing spokespeople, Geula Cohen, suggested that Sobol commit suicide.[3] This entire fracas lead to his resignation – and that of his colleague and director of the play, Gedalia Besser – as artistic directors of the Haifa Municipal Theatre.

Not all the plays on the topic of Israeli-Arab relations were as provocative. Some were constructed around a love story between an Arab and a Jew, such as Nola Chilton's *Na'im* based on A. B. Yehoshua's novel, *Hame'aheav* (The Lover). The central element in a play by Miriam Kainy, *Hashiv'ah* (The Return) (1973, 1981)[4] is an empty Arab house occupied by an ex-kibbutz Israeli family. Their son Ruben develops a friendship with a young Israeli Arab, Riyyad, whose family had previously owned the house. Their accord becomes a triangle when Riyyad's Jewish girlfriend, Alona, becomes interested in Ruben and their relationship subsequently destroys the friendship. Riyyad completes his law studies and marries a girl from his village while Ruben studies medicine in the United States. On the eve of the Six-Day War he returns and the three meet again. Ruben is killed in battle and his parents collect material for a memorial book. His father had once remonstrated with him over his friendship with an Arab, declaring such a thing an impossibility. At the end of the play the spotlight cuts through the darkened stage to light Riyyad and a photograph of the dead Ruben. Riyyad concludes, 'I lost not only a friend – I lost a dream'.

Kainy's was the first authentic Arab hero in Israeli drama. While *The Return* is not strictly a political play its ideological – or idealistic – value was sharpened by the fact that in 1973 an Israeli Arab actor, Makram Khoury, played the Arab character. Kainy commented that for many Israelis who were aware of Arabs only as people who work in restaurants, this might have represented their first encounter with an Arab who possesses human qualities.

Other works were adapted from foreign plays which had been moulded to fit the topic. For example, Joseph Heller's *Catch 22* was produced by the Khan in 1975, soon enough after the 1973 war; Beckett's *Waiting for Godot* (1984) explores the problem of the Israeli Arab by characterising both protagonists as Arab labourers; a production of *The Merchant of Venice* (1994) reincarnated Shylock as a militant West Bank settler; in Aeschylus' *The Trojan Women* (1983) the Trojan women are Palestinian refugees, an interpretation which caused so great a controversy that it was deemed by its critics to be PLO propaganda. In *Romeo and Juliet* (1994) Romeo is played by a West Bank Palestinian actor and Juliet by an Israeli.

The political culture of the Haifa Municipal Theatre particularly lent itself to controversial political issues and it continued to probe them in a manner reminiscent of London's Royal Court Theatre. Most of the plays denied the possibility of any solution to the Israeli-Arab problem, or suggested that should a solution be mooted it would be destroyed by dominant political elements among both peoples. Ratab Awawdeh's *Diyur Mishneh* (Subletting), (1978), describes the relationship between two students, a Jewish girl and an Arab boy who assumes the guise of an Oriental Jew, Danny. Ahmed-Danny adopts Israeli culture, and rejects both his village and his brother who attempts to return him to his roots. However, the relationship distintegrates. The girl is unable to withstand the pressure from both families who insist that the young lovers will not find sanction among either the Jews or the Arabs. Dan Ronen's

Hayom Hashevi'i (The Seventh Day), (1979) tells the story of an Israeli soldier who discovers that he is in fact an Arab boy brought up by Jewish parents. A similar case was reported in the British press in 1994: a child of Arab parents was raised by Orthodox Jews and remained traumatised by his conflict of identities.

Miriam Kainy's one-hander – the dramatic monologue, *Kmo Kadur Barosh* (Like a bullet in the head), (1983)[5] – considers the crisis of an Israeli academic whose wife leaves him for one of his Arab students. After confessing to the murder of his wife and her lover the man is removed to a mental hospital. The story is one of domestic betrayal and jealousy, the object of which is cleverly obscured in the play for it is uncertain whether the murderous rage of the protagonist, Professor Amitai Attarot, is aroused by his wife's infidelity with the boy or by Amitai's own frustrated sexual attraction to him. The political subtext of the play is constituted by the text upon which both academics are working, a poem by the medieval Hebrew poet Yehuda Halevi concerning his aspiration to reach Zion. Attarot sees Halevi's fate as a parallel to his own: 'Yehuda Halevi also drew conclusions, he went to the place for which his soul had longed, to Zion. Yes and his death? Yes even his death was such a Jewish death opposite the Western wall under the hooves of an infidel's horse, an Arab'.[6] The student, on the other hand, contends that Halevi died in Egypt, robbing Attarot of his 'Jewish' death. Attarot's final assertion in the play is enigmatically suggestive of a political statement. He turns to members of an interviewing panel in the mental hospital in which he has been incarcerated: 'Listen to me well. We will not allow some Hassan or Muhmad to destroy my life. No. I am not Yehuda Halevi. Not me. I have a state for which I went to war. Listen'.[7] The two psychiatrists contemptuously exit while he is speaking. Attarot is seeking absolution, first by calling upon the religious law (*Halakhah*) for justification and then by political sloganeering. While his final statement implies that the Arabs will be prevented from trampling the Jews to death, this appears to be ironic in the play's context of vengeful paranoia.

Yaakov Shabtai's *Okhlim* (Eating), (1979) uses the story of Ahab and Naboth's vineyard as an allegory of Israel's occupation of the West Bank and Gaza. The play is a satire on the government's manipulation of the law to accommodate its greed, and the antagonism between the political state and human morality. Hanokh Levin's post-Lebanon *Hapatriot* (The Patriot), (1982)[8] stridently criticises class attitudes and structures in Israeli society and demonstrates particular concern about the Palestinians in the Occupied Territories. With this play, set as a cabaret, and with his unique brand of visual rhetoric, Levin returns to the direct political arena where he began. The play presents a vicious portrayal of the contemporary Israeli as shallow, opportunistic and hypocritical. Its hero decides to emigrate to America and applies for an American visa; he then has to spit in his mother's face in order to prove to the American consulate that family ties will not affect his loyalty to his proposed new country. At the same time he buys land on the West Bank and assaults and kills an Arab boy in order to prove his national loyalty. He returns to his Jewish roots as a repentant, which allows Levin to satirise aspects of Jewish Orthodoxy. He also manages to compare the murdered Arab with Jewish children killed in the Holocaust. The play, however offensive, could not easily be dismissed, for many members of the audience and a number of critics not only expressed a masochistic admiration of what Levin said without necessarily liking the way that he said it, but also used the play as a basis for further attacks on their own society.

Like Nola Chilton, the playwright and director Motti Baharav specialised in social documentaries, bringing theatre to the schools and community halls. When he proposed a play to Habimah (*Azatim*, Gazans) about life in Gaza, the management refused it after some deliberation, on the grounds of lack of funding. In 1987 Baharav took his play to the Acre Festival. It depicts the encounter of four Gaza Arabs with Israeli society, and particularly the difficulties that one of them faces working for an Israeli family who regard him as less than human. Predictably, Baharav enountered many problems in the realisation of this play, not least the antagonism between the Israeli Arabs in the audience and the Gazans in the cast which, said Baharav, was worse than the antagonism of the Gazans towards the Jews. He then attempted to rescue the project by working only with Israeli Arabs. Eventually the play was performed before a predominantly Israeli audience.

These and other plays attracted severe criticism for their various political stances, the composition of their casts, their tendency to explode popular myths and their perceived naïeveté. Among the most controversial of them was Yehoshua Sobol's *Hapalestina'it* (The Palestinian Girl), (1985).[9] Utilising the device of the play-within-a-play, *The Palestinian Girl* is an elaborate extended metaphor for the political and social choices confronting present-day Israel and the tussle between conflicting ideologies. Like much of the polemical contemporary Israeli literature, this play utilises violent action to demonstrate its theme, the rape and exploitation of the Palestinian people. The central Palestinian character is a woman, Samira, whose experience constitutes the plot of the play and is realised through the device of a television production in which her story is enacted. Her television surrogate, Magda, loves David, an Israeli right-wing extremist and *Kach*[10] supporter who may or may not be an agent attempting to elicit information from her about her Palestinian comrades, and her former lover, Adnan. Sobol's play constructs an intricate portrait of Israeli society with Samira/Magda as its nucleus, a Palestinian who is abused and betrayed by her ultra-nationalist Israeli lover. Through the reactions of his characters Sobol explores the primitive sense of sexual outrage demonstrated by Jews on their discovering the love affair and Magda's pregnancy, an attitude hinted at in other contemporary Israeli literature. The notion of the re-enactment of the Holocaust with the Arabs as victims is also evident. In a convoluted, fragmentary dramatic narrative Sobol researches the complex psychology of Israeli guilt: first David assaults Magda, then he regrets the injury that he has caused her, then he loves and then betrays her. Adnan, her former lover whom she brands a 'Muslim fascist', is a Palestinian nationalist. Humiliation at his minority status has robbed him of pride and honour. The 'actor' playing him, also a Palestinian, explains the result:

You constantly live with a feeling of insecurity. You see a police barricade on the road, immediately your heart sinks ... How can an audience know that a person is angry with himself because he hid, because he was scared of the police and now he's ashamed of admitting it when it turned out he was scared for nothing, and that his fear comes from his situation as an Arab?[11]

He accuses the interior play's 'director' of concessionalism and of refusing to show an Arab character behaving dishonourably in order to prevent his being viewed as a victim of oppression. Adnan's outburst is an echo of Palestinian attitudes expressed in the Israeli press, in essays and interviews. Adnan's sense of humiliation, of dishonour and resentment at the imposition of 'the nice principles of Western culture' are similarly a reiteration of Palestinian responses as interpreted by Israeli intellectuals. In a vicious scene the Jewish lover's father, Ephraim, a veteran of the 1948 war, personalises the entire conflict with politically loaded statements to Magda such as: 'This is *my* house, do you understand?' and 'Do you think you can throw me out of here by force?' and 'If you try to throw me out of here I don't know who'll end up with broken bones'.[12] Perhaps the containment of the political conflict within the trope of individual human relationships is the playwright's response to right-wing rhetoric which normally features only the collective 'nation', 'state' and 'Judaism'.

Sobol conveys the complexity of relationships between all Israeli factions through role-play: the television Palestinian, Adnan, pretends to be a *hassid* quoting a passage from Leviticus (26, 27ff) threatening the destruction of the Children of Israel, a quotation which suits both sides, with its indication of a religiously determined destiny. Adnan's impersonation is an ironic echo of the biblical validation often summoned for certain policies by advocates of the Right and already satirised by Sobol in *Repentance*. A Jewish 'actress' plays the role of Magda, the television Palestinian girl and a left-wing 'actor' plays David, the Jewish extremist. In her passing from an English lover to a Palestinian lover and then a treacherous Jewish lover who almost takes her life and prevents the birth of their child, Magda is an ambitious encapsulation of Israel itself. In this allegorical play, the literary Palestinians are no more than devices through which the Israeli author examines *his own* profound anxieties.

Before the Intifada, playwrights had delineated the Palestinian with almost universal sympathy. A change of viewpoint during the Intifada resulted in the perception of the Palestinian as an image of frightening violence. In many cases the plays reflect the public's contradictory view of the Palestinians: while they are understood to be the victims of Israeli political policy embodied in Zionism's definition of the Jewish state, they are disliked and feared as a people. Hagit Ya'ari took an unusual approach in her examination of the lives of Palestinian women made unbearable by their men's constant abuse (*Abir*, 1992). In tone these plays resemble educational documents or statements by the authors to the public, in keeping with Jewish didactic tradition where lessons are taught through the medium of stories and fables. Content overrides form in dramatic narratives of almost primitive simplicity describing relationships between lovers or family members who exactly reflect the macrocosm of the country's politics.

A work embodying many of the attributes of anti-Occupation rhetoric, is Yitzhak Laor's play, *Ephraim Hozer Letzava* (Ephraim Returns to the Army) written in 1985 but first produced by Tzavta in 1989. Until the publication of his acclaimed first novel in 1995, Laor, a voice of radical protest from the Left, had been one of the writers most victimized by a consistent critical bias as a consequence of his political activities which, in the Israeli context, become part of the writer's persona. It should be remembered that after the publication in 1958 of *The Days of Ziklag* S. Yizhar was refused the most prestigious of Israel's literary prizes, the Bialik Prize, because his examination of early Israeli ideology was deemed questionable, if not subversive. Yizhar subsequently became a loved and respected establishment figure, and it is somewhat ironic that Laor, whose *Ephraim Returns to the Army* alludes to one of Yizhar's stories, suffered a similar fate: although he won the 1990 Prime Minister's Prize for literature, Yitzhak Shamir, then leader of a *Likud* government, refused to sign the certificate awarding the prize. This was not a mark of the Israeli political establishment's aesthetic judgement but its response to Laor's career of radical activism.

Laor was notorious for his battles with the Israeli Censorship Board although his play is less outspoken than those of established contemporaries such as Hanokh Levin and Yehoshua Sobol. *Ephraim Returns to the Army* embodies a subtle insurgency, directly derives from the situation in the Occupied Territories although it only describes it obliquely. The ideological model against which Laor's play strives is Yizhar's first story, *Ephraim Hozer La'aspeset* (Ephraim Returns to the Grassland), (1938). Yizhar was credited with the creation of the literary *sabra*, the hero of his early stories. This idealistic young Israeli constantly wages an interior war between his own needs as an individual and the requirements of his community. The situation in the Occupied Territories and the Intifada proved to be the greatest threat to his durability, for old-style romantic heroism became inappropriate in a conflict in which internal dissension shifted the moral ground.

Laor's play presents an ex-hero, Ephraim, the Military Governor of one of the Occupied Territories, who is investigating the killing of a Palestinian by an Israeli soldier. In this respect the play conforms to the tradition of the Arab-as-symbol in earlier literature in which an Arab dies at the hands of Israelis. In *Ephraim Returns to the Army* the war is no longer one of liberation and the Israeli is not a victim of foreign oppression. The burden of the play is Ephraim's confusion about his role as commander in unacceptable circumstances, and that the Jewish people, once represented by such ethical masters as Isaac Babel, H. N. Bialik, Walter Benjamin, Heine, Mahler, Modigliani, Marx and others, have now become oppressors, denigrating Jewish culture by their activities. Laor interweaves some of the archetypical attributes of the *Palmahnik* (member of the *Palmah*) with his own Ephraim, the *Palmahnik*'s qualitative antitheses: where Shaham's 'Avi'-figure was wise, sensitive and morally impeccable, Ephraim is cynical, cruel and opportunistic. Laor deliberately recalls the 'old days' with his quotations from *Palmah* literature and popular songs of the time, which he then uses to create his antitype.[13] In one scene Ephraim cynically comments to his estranged wife, '. . . the day after tomorrow they'll throw us out of here and we'll have to transport food in convoys circling besieged Jerusalem while gangs shoot at us from the fields' – a mocking reference to the siege of Jerusalem in 1948. Whereas the 'Avi'-hero was certain of his purpose, Ephraim glories in his self-confessed ambiguity.

Ambiguity in the *Palmahnik* was resolved either through the conquest of his doubting self, or through moral argument, as in Shaham's *They Will Arrive Tomorrow*. Ephraim's ambiguity masks his true nature both from himself and from the audience: he must bring the Palestinian's killer to justice or make a deal with him. He enforces punishments in his own area and sets out to find and destroy a subversive Palestinian printing press, but he has secret meetings in Athens with members of the Palestinian leadership. Echoes of Yizhar's moral odyssey, *The Prisoner* (1948) occur in the interrogation of the Palestinian in Laor's play. Ephraim's self-flagellation is savage, indicating by his reference to Shylock's famous speech in *The Merchant of Venice*, that inhumanity is the Israeli's growing burden.

While *Ephraim Returns to the Army* is not narrated from the point of view of the oppressed Palestinians, it closes with the visual image of an Arab prisoner chained to a chair, unmanned by the ridicule of a female Israeli clerk. At the end the play has shifted from the theme of individual responsibility to national morality, with its problems unresolved. We are left with the protagonist whose ideological tussle leaves him unable to do anything at all, an inertia which Laor metaphorically extended to the Occupation itself.

The political content of Laor's play is to be found less in the stage drama than in the playtext. Much of the direct political comment is embodied in stage directions which communicate the author's ideological stance to the *reader* rather than the viewer. As an ironic thrust at the censors, the stage directions deny the verisimilitude of the events on stage. Comments such as 'scenes like this do not exist in reality',[14] 'contrary to the stupid way the censor understood the ceremony',[15] and remarks about the earlier censorship and banning of the play are incorporated, in a kind of metadrama, into the dialogue. As Laor no doubt intended, the authorial comments heighten the play's realism by incorporating his own well-docu-mented experiences as a dissident into his characters' responses.

One of the most accomplished plays on the Intifada is Ilan Hazor's *Re'ulim* (The Masked Men) which achieved first prize at the Acre Festival in 1990 and was then taken up by the Cameri Theatre where it enjoyed a lengthy run. It was written while Hazor was in his first year of drama studies. Unlike Laor's play, this first full-length play directly concerning the Intifada places the Palestinians at the centre of the action. Although written by an Israeli, the Israeli standpoint is sidelined in favour of the playwright's perception of Palestinian attitudes. The play concerns three brothers in one of the West Bank towns: Naim, a Palestinian subversive, Daud a colla-borator with the occupying forces and Haled, their young brother. For once the value of the play rests not only in its plot but also on its construction. It is set in a meat warehouse against walls which are stained with blood. Gradually the story unfolds: Naim summons Daud in order to discover the truth about his possible collaboration with the Israeli authorities. A game of double bluff is played through the dialogue, with Daud evasively defying his brother and Naim offering his evidence piecemeal until it finally entraps Daud. The revelation of Daud's treachery and of the traps that he and Naim have set for each other unfold almost imperceptibly and organically, deriving naturally from the situation of the play itself, without the need for rhetoric or oratory. The tension mounts consistently, the dialogue is spare and to the point, the most powerful means of carrying the action.

This at last is a play characterised by the required 'universality', involving a situation which is identified with a particular territory but which is also relevant in many other countries that house both the empowered and the powerless. Also, the characters are well developed as believable human beings, despite, perhaps, the paternalism implied by the construction of Palestinian characters by an Israeli intellectual.[16] 'The most difficult task,' says Hazor, 'was to create the characters so that they wouldn't be artificial, to add colour to them. In this respect I took a good deal of myself, mainly for Haled who is really me or the Palestinian with whom I would like to make peace.'[17] Hazor has succeeded in avoiding stereotypes, for his Palestinians are neither pathetic, stupid nor grandiosely noble but are people with whom the Israeli audience was able to identify on a multitude of levels. For the first time the Israelis saw the 'other' sympathetically yet realistically portrayed, neither exclusively evil or exclusively good. Daud admits his cowardice and weakness, Naim is the embodiment of the terrorist until the moment of his brother's death when he is overcome by grief and remorse. Haled, who begins as a bewildered boy, grows in stature until he is able to carry out the inevitable sentence and stab Daud to death. The power shifts continuously between the two adult brothers, with one or another of them alternately in the ascendant.

The casting of Israeli actors to play the brothers facilitated the audience's sympathy with the characters, although it might have cost the play its authenticity. However, by this casting the director took a step towards demonstrating to the audience that they were watching a work of art in addition to a slice of life. A recent controversy in England initiated by the politically correct demand that Othello always be played by a black man prompted a critic to ask whether Shylock must always be played by an Orthodox Jew and to raise other anomalies of authenticity. The accuracy of *The Masked Men* lies in its setting, enhanced by the powerful strokes of characterisation and the brothers' dilemma. Their dilemma of loyalty and sacrifice glosses the material of daily reality on the West Bank as seen throughout the Israeli media. While the play makes a comment about violence, its central task is to demonstrate the destruction of all human and moral values in a situation of continuing crisis within the nation and within the microcosm of the family.

The Masked Men is an essentially *Israeli* play in its setting and language in which there are no anglicisms, only a vitreous spoken Hebrew. There is no mention of 'Jews' juxtaposed with 'Israelis', no debate about Europe or about the past. The Zionist element is implicit in the situation of the play, for the events themselves provide the ideological commentary. Above all, *The Masked Men* avoids the snares into which so much Israeli drama has fallen. Its dialogue is contained rather than verbose and over-explicit. The play makes its points through imagery, such as the blood on the wall which Haled later washes off; the knife which recurs in many plays and stories on the topic of the Intifada; excrement which points to the conditions in the West Bank towns in which the Intifada took place and also serves as a symbol for the entire intolerable situation.

In some of the political plays war and Israeli-Palestinian relations are merely implicit. Motti Lerner's *Hevlei Mashiah* (The Pangs of the Messiah), (1988),[18] was the first play to confront the issue of Israeli settlement on the West Bank. In his play the political activities of the religious settlers are touched upon delicately and tastefully rather than critically dissected. His heroes are somewhat different from the usual, being members of a family of settlers on the West Bank who are enduring the tribulations of ideological warfare with other Israelis, including the army, and the possibility of actual warfare with the Palestinians. Lerner compromises in an area that has proved troubling to most of the other political writers, that of religion. His paterfamilias, Shmuel, is a pious Jew, a member of the religious Zionist group *Gush Emunim* who quotes the biblical text as validation for the settlers' decisions and subsequent actions, but he falls short of supporting his son's solution of violence and terrorism. He concludes that rather than become murderers, the Jews must leave the terri-tories. Through a more circuitous route than that of other writers, Lerner has also reached the conclusion that the continuing occu-pation is a sign of Israel's moral regression. His settlers are predom-inantly gun-toting militants but these are balanced by his portrait of Shmuel who, while fervently believing in the ultimate right of his and his group's aims, deplores the methods by which his children set about achieving them. The play's popularity amongst the political Right in Israel indicates that Lerner succeeded in proposing some-thing more than a stereotype in the character of Shmuel.

The play's story, however, is little more than a framework for an extended political argument. The action which, with hindsight can be deemed prophetic, is set in the near future: Israel is about to sign a peace treaty with Jordan. Shmuel's son and daughter-in-law, Avner and Tirzah, have returned in haste from America where they have been propagandists for Israel. They join other members of the family including the son-in-law, Benny, a terrorist who has already served a term in prison, and Nadav, the youngest son, who is either retarded or naïve, who is building a house for himself. The news of the treaty outrages the son and son-in-law, their rage fuelled by the imminent departure of the army, leaving the settlers to face the Palestinians unaided. Shmuel arranges a massive demonstration against the government, busing in thousands of people from every area of the land. When this fails, Avner and Benny take matters into their own hands and blow up the Mosque on the Temple Mount, an action which leads Shmuel to his despairing conclusion. The play ends with Nadav's suicide, committed with an AK-47 submachine-gun.

Notwithstanding the doubts of many critics, *The Pangs of the Messiah* is more directly political than other works, offering its audience viewpoints through the characters who are little more than the embodiments of ideologies. It is entirely relevant to the issues of the time, like a gloss on the daily news 'a form of bulletin from the front lines of history'.[19] Through its characters it presents an exposition of the situation from every perspective, from the Left to the militant right wing, with every factor in the political discussion presented: ownership of the land – which has been a preoccupation of Israeli literature since the early 1960s; ideological division amongst the Israelis themselves; the inadequacies of liberalism; the role of the army; the morality of settlement; the origins of Palestinian hatred; the threat of Israeli civil war and of war with the Arabs, and the use of the Holocaust as a component of political rhetoric. Shmuel, the honest and pious Jew, admonishes his son:

It's easy to justify everything with the Holocaust. I thought our settlement here had managed to save us from our persecuted-Jews complex. There won't be a new Holocaust here ... We won't create a ghetto here. Who would come to live in a ghetto?[20]

This would be repeating a customary sentiment in Israeli litera-ture but for a few elements that redeem it, notably the two characterisations, first, of Shmuel who appears at the start to be a Bible-quoting zealot. However, his slow realisation of his sons' perfidy leads him to re-evaluate his own belief in the inviolability of settlement. Shmuel is a dramatic character who undergoes some growth, but he serves also as a symbol of classical Zionism as a flawed system whose teleological implications were largely ignored. The second character of note is Nadav, the simple, innocent son who wants nothing more than to build his house and live in it in peace. In this portrait Lerner indicates that Nadav is all that is left of the heroic Israeli of the past, ultimately victimised by hatred and violence. Shmuel remarks, referring to Nadav's construction of his house, 'Rabbi Kook says that while the pioneers building the land do not lay *tefillin* [phylacteries] they lay bricks upon the building of our holy land'.[21] Nadav and his house are poignant symbols of a paradise lost, a dream dismembered.

The play discusses organised protest, it pits political forces against each other (the Israeli army and the settlers, the Jordanian government and the settlers), and concludes with an ideological question from the settlers to the audience. The fact that Shmuel, an admirable character, ultimately sees the error of his ways, is one clear political message but it is left unresolved and undebated within the framework of the play. As is often the case in Israel, public debates took place following the staging of the play, but these did not constitute a part of the drama itself. This type of discussion sometimes transforms self-contained dramas into open-ended collections of themes for discussion.

The reviews of *The Pangs of the Messiah* exemplified some of the problems of Israeli criticism in general: its employment of unrelated criteria and its lack of political objectivity. Most critics agreed that *as a drama The Pangs of the Messiah* was acceptable, that the staging and acting were good, sometimes outstanding. Most, however – writing for centrist or left-of-centre newspapers – expressed serious disquiet at Lerner's apparent neutrality regarding the settlers and their activities. This is indicative of Israeli criticism's approach to all literature. Only rarely do Britain's eminent theatre critics indulge in this kind of stringent political comment. Their readers are not even aware of their political affiliations. In Israel, reviews of Lerner's play were politically constructed: its setting and *dramatis personae* were debated in the light of political reality, while the medium was almost wholly ignored. It is true that Lerner did not indicate whether or not he sympathised with Gush ideology, or whether he was aware of its influence or the consequences of its members' activities. The play itself gave no indication of its author's political standpoint. According to some critics it is therefore not to be classified as a political or documentary play – or indeed as a satire, an apologetic or a polemic – but as a social drama of high realism in which various family members play out their personal problems. Even so, these personal problems are strongly associated with the external political situation. The culminating deed in the play is a political one.

Many critics expressed disapproval that members of *Gush Emunim* and other religious groups in the audience appreciated *The Pangs of the Messiah* and identified with its characters. This, claims Giora Manor[22] indicates Lerner's want of honesty. However, a play's success or failure does not rest on the playwright's political sympathies and, in this case, it should not be dismissed as a failure simply because the Gush admired it. Manor castigates Lerner for revealing members of the Gush to be 'people like everyone else'. He writes: 'To understand is to forgive ... and I'm not prepared to forgive those who are bringing a catastrophe on all of us'. Manor amplifies his dislike of the Gush by using terms like 'the devil' and by invoking Stalin. He claims that realism is inappropriate in plays that satirise or demonise, and since Lerner chose realism, he obviously intended to do neither. Like Manor, Michael Handelsaltz[23] terms the play an apologetic for the Gush and accuses Lerner of irresponsibility.

During the writing of the play Lerner and some of the actors visited Ofra, the *Gush Emunim* settlement, to meet members of the Gush and consult with Gush moderates whom he acknowledged in the programme notes: 'I did not want to diminish the settlers by satirizing them. I feel that if I diminish them, I diminish myself as their opponent'.[24] There was some disagreement among members of the Gush in Ofra concerning the accuracy of Lerner's portrayal of their lifestyle and beliefs. Some claimed that he had only skimmed the surface. One, a rabbi, indicated that the playwright's own artistic integrity should supercede his attempts at even-handedness: 'This play is too proper ... from the desire to listen, to be fair, decent, you haven't put yourself or your views into it. Once I heard a section from *The Last Secular Jew* [a satirical episodic play by Shmuel Hasfari, detested by the Orthodox] ... and it had a lot of crudeness. But it was political. He put himself into it. Here the drama isn't political at all'.[25] Another commented: 'The censorship will take no notice of you'.[26] As these two laypeople intuitively understood, Lerner's attempt to be fair to all sides did not suit political drama. His play was a hybrid of political realism and family melodrama, although viewers' 'anticipated sense of the whole' prevented their seeing it in terms of the latter. On the other hand, a political work, be it fiction or drama, should demonstrate its interest in both sides, complete 'with the shabby arrangements the author despises'[27], otherwise the author will produce a polemic.

One of Lerner's major achievements in *The Pangs of the Messiah* is his shifting of the arena of political debate from the institution or the home into the street. He finds a new way of occupying urban space, one which had already been used by many European writers but not as yet in Israeli literature. In his play, the streets are controlled by protesting crowds of people; urban expanses have become political forces, the legitimate political space of the people, their battle-ground, as we have seen throughout the world. Protest is made in the open in the shared, common space away from people's homes. In Lerner's play the political conflicts are acted out, people are killed and injured on their new battleground, the streets of the developing, disputed cities of the West Bank.[28]

In this, and in similar elements, Lerner's conscious or unconscious subtext threads its way through the surface narrative, creating a palimpsest of aspiration and action. Zionism, as an outcome of nationalism, presages Palestinian aspirations for their own home-land. Nationalism itself, as a feature of modernism, grew in an urban environment, and modern Palestinian nationalism has left the Arab villages to become concentrated in the cities. In Lerner's play, both the Israeli and Palestinian struggles are focused on urban settlement, and the methods which both use to achieve their aim rely on familiar urban symbols. Avrom, the Secretary of the settlement, suggests without irony, using burning tyres and obstructive barrels to impress foreign television journalists. Shmuel's family is engaged in an evangelical mission in which his pregnant daughter's presence in the demonstration will serve as a symbol of courage and defiance. In the same spirit the mother, who is a schoolteacher, insists that the children in her charge are 'the best weapons we have'. Her daughter-in-law, Tirzah, the liberal voice in the play, responds, 'I wouldn't take pregnant women and children along simply for the television [cameras] to film'.[29] The propaganda value of placing children against armed police and soldiers was proven not only on the West Bank and in Gaza but in Soweto as well.

One text is superimposed upon another, the Palestinian strategy upon that of the Israelis. Not only are the emotional prerogatives, the religious motivation, the mode of civilian uprising the same, but similar agendas – together with the texts upon which they are based – delineate the political thinking of both factions. This makes a statement about the kindred aspirations of both sides, in this way heightening the incontrovertible tragedy of the situation. Whether Lerner intended this analogy is uncertain, but its embodiment in his text is unavoidable, lending his play a greater and more abstract dialectical weight than he would have achieved through blunt political discourse.

The example of Lerner, and many others throughout the literature, indicates that Arab/Palestinian characters do not always represent themselves or the broader conflict. They also serve to express some of their creators' inexpressible feelings. Given that the relationship of text to ideology is irrevocably part of the Jewish imagination, the invocation by Palestinian and Arab characters of Jewish eschatological[30] or nationalist[31] texts suggests that the fictional Arab is not only a symbol but the displacement by the Israeli author of a political doctrine. The writers' ambivalence towards their Arab/Palestinian characters reveals itself in their projection of sentiments that cannot be expressed more directly because of the altered perceptions of Zionism since 1948. The fictional Arab becomes their surrogate – not only one who suffers under the burden of an unattainable homeland, now unattainable to the Israelis in a different sense – but one who believes that he or she has an historically unchallengeable claim to it. Nationalistic fiction and drama suggest an authentic literary advocacy of classical Zionist ideology. Transferring the expression of ideology to their Arab characters relieves the Israeli authors of any direct identification with it. A great and complex struggle lies hidden in these texts. Embodied in the external Israeli political conflict is a subtle, concealed *internal* conflict of sympathy and rejection, the tendency to pity the underdog clashing with the writers' belief in Jewish national preservation and survival.

Overall, the Israeli political playwrights have used the theatre as a tool for the propagation of a shared political ideology. The vehicles for these statements have generally used words rather than significant events or characterisations to make their political point, with the result that they resemble interlocking slices of rhetoric or even propaganda. The documentary tradition is so deeply embedded in the Israeli theatrical culture that it has all but obscured the potential for an alternative form of political drama in which characterisation, rather than self-conscious tracts or polemics carries the message.

Athol Fugard is one writer who has been able to present convincingly the problems of victims – in this case the blacks in South Africa under apartheid – by demonstrating the specific disabilities under which they live through the individual experience of convincing characters. For example, in *Sizwe Banzi is Dead* Fugard made white audiences aware of the 'pass' [identity card] laws that were only applicable to blacks. In other plays he provided information about the effects of the various other privations of apartheid. Fugard consistently worked with black actors and writers, often within workshop productions, and for this reason his writing is convincing and authentic. The core of a political play should concern the relation between political ideas and the experience of characters who either take hold of these ideas or who, in some way, respond to them or suffer because of them. In the Israeli drama of ideas, the characters are consistently subordinated to the playwrights' didactic agenda, not least in plays which offer a critique of Zionism through the topic of Arab-Israeli relations.

CHAPTER 4

Zionism on the stage: Sobol's case

Yehoshua Sobol's conceptual methodology exemplifies the tendency in Israeli drama to use history as a resource for examining present-day Israeli society. Historical plays can be as much a comment on the playwrights' own times as on the periods about which they are apparently written. According to Herbert Lindenberger, 'A man's view of the past cannot be separated from the political and social milieu in which he works and thinks'.[1] In his opinion, modern historical dramatists, 'have been as shameless as their predecessors in reading the present into the past', and he cites Brecht as a primary example.[2]

With greater consistency than any other Israeli dramatist, Sobol provides a schematic analysis of the political and social history of modern Israel. Sobol was born in Israel in 1939. After completing high school in Tel Aviv he joined the socialist *Hashomer Hatza'ir* youth movement and enlisted in the *Nahal*, the pre-military cadet corps. Later he studied philosophy at the Sorbonne. He began his literary career in Israel as a columnist on the daily newspaper, *Al Hamishmar*, and subsequently became one of the guiding presences at the Haifa Municipal Theatre for which he wrote a number of plays. He remained strongly identified with this theatre, serving as Artistic Director until 1987 when he resigned due to the controversy over *Jerusalem Syndrome*. His writing can be divided into two distinct categories: political satires and well-made plays which present certain of his negative perceptions of contemporary Israeli society, and investigations into the aetiology of Zionism through the medium of historical texts and documents.

Sobol and Hanokh Levin are frequently coupled as representatives of their genre for their generation in much the same way as Amos Oz and A. B. Yehoshua seem to represent the twin pillars of contemporary Israeli fiction. Yet only their dissenting outspokenness unites the dramatic sensibility of the two playwrights. Sobol dissects Israeli society using historiography, biography and documents including court reports, as his sources, whereas Levin flays the community with the whip of myth and archetype. While both are rebels and have suffered from censorship, neither can be classified as a dissident. Both have their works performed in mainstream subsidised theatres, regardless of their nonconformity, and both have received important Israeli cultural prizes. Sobol has achieved some recognition abroad, particularly in the United Kingdom and Germany.

Sobol's belief in satirical theatre (like all comedy) as an effective defence against reality and a medium for actual political change may be ingenuous. Much evidence indicates that the theatre's contribution to social change is generally small.[3] According to playwright Yosef Mundi

It is clear to me that plays do not alter reality ... Not Brecht, not Ernst Toller or other German playwrights could stop the German nation from identifying with Hitler and his band. In the final analysis, in spite of Brecht's plays being staged to this very day, it was Goebbels the hack and failed playwright who succeeded in dragging the German people into total war.[4]

Susan Bennet reinforces this view:

The theatre can never *cause* social change. It can articulate the pressures towards one, help people to celebrate their strengths and maybe build their self-confidence. It can be a public emblem of inner and outer events, and occasionally a reminder, an elbow-jogger, a perspective-bringer.[5]

A good example of theatre's political inefficacy was in South Africa. During the repressive apartheid regime, when literary and press censorship was at its height, the outspoken political theatre flourished, and the most notorious political theatre space, the Market Theatre in Johannesburg, became a cultural institution. In Israel the theatres that staged controversial political material did not even forfeit their official subsidies in spite of many moves by opponents to have them withdrawn. In the years from 1980 to 1991, when more plays were officially censored[6] than ever before, even the Haifa Municipal Theatre retained its subsidy despite being in danger more than once of losing it.[7] Sobol insisted that the artist should not abandon the ideological argument even if its effectiveness is doubtful: 'I believe there is a constant struggle not only to convince your political opponent, but also to keep your own supporters from sliding towards the opponent's camp'.[8]

The burden of Sobol's early work was the material of Israel's daily press: the economy, Zionism, religion and the policy of settlement in the Occupied Territories (*hitnahlut*). He began his dialectical investigation of the founding Zionist ideology with a trilogy of conventionally structured non-documentary plays spanning the years 1947 to 1978. These and other historical dramas probe the the spiritual roots of modern Zionism, its founders, ideologues and opponents. Some of these plays are based on documents which contribute historical veracity and provide Sobol with real paradigms through which he is able to play out Zionism's countervailing forces. He not only sees history as an allegory for the present, but uses historical personalities as mouthpieces for his own philosophy, lending it an illusory authority. These dialectical plays constitute one long progressive drama of Zionism and its consequences, taken in inverse chronological order from modern Israel back through the *yishuv* of the Second *Aliyah* (1905–1914), the Vienna of Herzl and Freud and finally, with *Jerusalem Syndrome*, to the Second Temple period. In an interview Sobol confessed to wanting 'to go back to the past in order to understand what is happening here, what the hell is going on with our Zionism here in Israel'.[9] His critique of Israeli political ideology is situated within the history of Zionism and diaspora Jewry's role in the foundation of the state. His investigation resembles a continuing dialogue between the proponents of 'correct' Zionism as he envisages it, and 'incorrect' Zionism, as he deems it to have developed in Israel.

The first of these plays, directed by Nola Chilton for the Haifa Municipal Theatre in 1974 was *Sylvester '72* (New Year's Eve '72), Sobol's first full-length dramatic fiction. Originally entitled *Hamishpat Ha'aharon* (The Last Word) the play opened on 7 October, 1973, a few days before the outbreak of the Yom Kippur War. The play was postponed until the war had ended when Sobol rewrote sections and changed its title 'because I wanted to make it clear that it had been written before the war. I chose the new name, "Sylvester '72", because of its jarring resonance and the associations it arouses with the culture that developed here between the two wars, [a culture] whose most appropriate indications were New Year's Eve celebrations'.[10]

Sylvester '72 served as the opening volley in Sobol's long ideological battle. Two biblical tales, the *Akedah* and the story of Isaac and his two sons, Jacob and Esau, provide its underlying emotional texture. Confrontations between fathers and sons, sometimes with tragic results, similarly underlie other Israeli literature. The example most comparable to *Sylvester '72* is Amos Oz's short story *Derekh Haruah* (The Way of the Wind) in which the father, Shimshon Sheinbaum, a stolid, vainglorious ideologue of the labour-oriented *Hapoel hatza'ir* movement, inadvertently – yet as a result of his historically determined attitude – causes the death of his gentle, poetic son.[11] *Sylvester '72* also recalls Brecht's *Mother Courage* in its theme of war-profiteering, and, in an old man's contrived self-delusion, Pirandello's *Henry IV.*

Representing the disparate parts of the 'enterprise' and its consequences, the family in *Sylvester '72* consists of Gershon Shapira, the old father, his son, Yoash, daughter, Dina and her husband, Boaz. Gershon, a delicately comic character, is the Zionist ideologue, uttering profound truths with a sly air of mental aberration. He appears to be oblivious to the progressive distintegration of the philosophy upon which he has based his life. The play rests upon his Sheinbaum-like enslavement to the outdated doctrine of the Zionist founders, and his blindness to its consequences. In spite of his daughter's blandishments and threats, he refuses to take off the old overcoat which he once wore while making a May Day speech. Dina, who berates him for his 'spirituality' and 'lofty words', detests the coat, 'this filthy bit of history' to which he clings as if it were his only solid memorial to the past.[12]

Boaz and Dina are attempting to persuade Gershon to sign a contract facilitating their sale of his old house in one of the city's suburbs in order to build a high-rise business centre and shopping mall. They will then move to a smarter 'villa' and the old man into an old people's home. Yoash, who has been abroad for fifteen years, returns to Israel ostensibly to sign the document but actually to confront his father. An artist, part-time Hebrew teacher and *yored* (emigrant), Yoash is an enigma to a father whose imagination is circumscribed by history. Ultimately the children prevail upon the old man and, with a gesture toward Chekhov's *The Cherry Orchard*, the play ends with the sound of an axe chopping down the olive trees.

Sylvester '72 functions on two levels: the first, which was generally overlooked by critics, is a structured family drama and the second, no less significant, an allegory in which each character represents a feature of Israeli society at the time of the Yom Kippur War. All are viewed in relation to the function of Zionist theory in the Israeli political process and the practice of Zionism in the modern state. Sobol judges the founding fathers, represented by Gershon, as monstrous in their demand 'that the individual situate himself in the shadow of national events whether this means maintaining a tradition or other values.'[13] Such values and traditions oppress the sons: in *Sylvester '72* Yoash escapes to a country where they are irrelevant, while Boaz flees morally into a lifestyle which wholly contradicts them. The daughter remains discontentedly suspended between the two.

At the start of the play Gershon is clipping newspaper stories for his album, sunk in his past. He is a stereotype of the rigid father who, like the biblical Abraham, is insensible to anything but his own colloquy with God, a man who sees the world through the screen of history and a fossilised system of ideological signs. In the first production of the play, Gershon was made up to resemble Ben-Gurion. However piteous in old age, the founding fathers once subordinated their children to their intellectual authority, their moral righteousness and ideological intractability, seeking always to have 'the last word'. Yoash says bitterly to his father: 'Take your children, put them into a crucible and make the kind of children you want'.[14] Dina responds: 'He's already done that'. Yet Gershon is not just a monolithic symbol of Zionist rhetoric. He is also given to moments of self-doubt, both about his convictions and his treatment of Yoash: 'The law of the movement, values ... the words come easily out of the mouth. And inside – death. Throughout my life I haven't dared to call a child by his name. I was afraid that everything would disintegrate ... I have to say everything and there isn't time'.[15] 'What has happened [asks Israel Goor] to this veteran, the son of a generation of giants, who has frozen and petrified?' He concludes that the crisis has to do with the differing natures of the sons and the fathers.[16] The difference lies in the relationship between words and action: Gershon's eloquent speeches about roots, Jews and labour, had once been realised in practice. Now, at this juncture in Israeli history, his son-in-law accuses him of talking too much.

Having alienated Yoash by his intolerance, the hard and cynical *nouveau riche* Boaz is all that Gershon has left. Boaz is a character

frequently encountered in Sobol's plays. Critics have outdone themselves in pejorative adjectives to apply to this star of Marxist
demonology. The problem with Sobol's version of this capitalist
stereotype is that, until the very end of the play, he is not an
unlikeable character, and like many of Sobol's other villains, is the
only one possessing zest and diversity. A man who began with
nothing but now employs hundreds, including Arabs, he is gross,
cynical and self-opinionated: 'When I got out of the army I didn't
need university. I didn't have a penny to my ass, but Boaz knows
something about life! My philosophy is simple: every man has an
opening in life just waiting for him. You find it, the sky's the limit.
You don't – you eat shit all your life'.[17] Sympathising with Sobol's
negative view of Israeli materialism, the writer Boaz Evron points
out that the founding generation also lacked true *spiritual* pretensions
despite their elevated rhetoric. 'What this generation truly wanted to
achieve was conquest in every sense of the word and from this point
of view, despite his unpleasant character, [Boaz] is certainly continuing the enterprise.'[18] Evron concludes that the enterprise had
from the start intended to create the kind of power that Boaz
represents. The character of Boaz, Evron continues, reveals the
outcome of the founders' vision: domination devoid of values or any
spiritual dimension.[19]

To Sobol this character represents the ultimate corruption of the
state by materialism divorced from ideological theory. Boaz lives off
the war, he exemplifies profiteering, he cheats on his wife and
exploits his father-in-law. He expresses Sobol's deep dislike of the
resolution to the Zionist enterprise:

BOAZ Don't think it doesn't hurt me that this country is not what it used to
be. That people aren't what they used to be ... once people, old pal,
did things through ideals, faith, good for them! Now, listen, they do
everything for money. What's right is right! Money, money money ...
if I had lived then I'd scorn money. But today ... this is the reality, old
pal, and you won't change it. So I say: play the game and screw
everyone, tear the guts out of them and then – old pal – they'll respect
you and you'll be someone.[20]

Paradoxically, the old man admires Boaz's practicality, seeing in it a
reflection of the pragmatism of his own generation: '[Boaz is] a man
of superlative qualities!' he says, 'A practical man'.

Yoash is the ideological compromise, the political activist who,
after serving some time in prison, has escaped his father's fury by

living abroad. Gershon keeps a photograph of him in a black frame and claims not to recognise him when he returns, having deplored not only his dissidence and occupation but his personal rebellion. Yoash is the moral, mediating voice of the play. He and Boaz are civilian incarnations of Natan Shaham's Avi and Jonah, suggesting that these oppositional sides of the Israeli personality have existed from the beginning. Opportunism vied from the start with the moral values through which the state came into being.

Sobol's portrait of old age is accurate and acute. The old man, with his cunning lack of lucidity, is an engaging and often moving figure. For example, Boaz and Dinah tempt him by describing the glories of the old people's home. Each time they add another feature, real or invented, he continues his own fragmented inner monologue.

BOAZ It will be for your own good to go and live in a place that's suitable for you, with food and services.
GERSHON [*while paging through his album*]: Just so, just so. Oh Zilkind. Here, on wheels. A second Lassalle. You could hear a fly in the community centre. Universalists. Particularists . . .
BOAZ And you'll be surprised to hear that there are people of your own age there. Actually, we've already begun to look for a place.
GERSHON Here's Tanich'ke. A noble horse. Eleonora Duse number two. Yes, yes. (*to Boaz*) Did you know D'Annunzio?[21]

This continues for a while until suddenly Gershon asks: 'So? What's the place like?'

DINA What?
GERSHON A nice place?
DINA [*astonished*] Yes, a very nice place.
GERSHON So. Very nice. It's nice there.
BOAZ It has a garden.

After a time Gershon again escapes by returning to his album and his memories. He is both irrelevant and incomprehensible to his children, a fossil or, as many critics term him, a dinosaur. His only possible fate is to be put aside, to allow space for the generation of Boaz. It is at best an equivocal conclusion: the Zionist ideal has become fossilised and corrupted but replaced by something worse. The idealist, Yoash, who had demonstrated for Arab rights, is virtually disregarded. No extreme on its own is feasible and Sobol's conclusion is that only an ontological fusion of the three may provide the material for a functional society. Gershon and Boaz have ensured the achievement of the Zionist enterprise at the cost of the nation's mental health.

Sylvester '72 was discussed in the press almost as a political document, and in some instances it was taken seriously as a warning. It was seldom evaluated as drama – an aesthetic genre – more frequently as a political thesis. In the 1970s artists still appeared to fulfil the traditional prophetic role, confronting the nation's leaders with truths which otherwise, they believed, would go unnoticed. Critics, however, confirmed that the problems stated by 'the artists and composers' were ignored by the political mandarins. Nonetheless, this 'prophetic' feature of Israeli drama continues to distinguish it from the drama of established countries.

Together with realism, documentary drama was strongly represented on the Israeli stage from 1967 until the early 1990s. The mandate of documentary theatre is factuality, an appeal to the mind rather than the emotions. According to one of its greatest exponents, Peter Weiss, the documentary play is primarily concerned with documenting an event from authentic, factual material – letters and statistics, speeches and news reports in print or on film. However, although the facts are the proper basis of a documentary play, such a play is likely to be written as a form of protest so that 'the imaginative contribution of the individual artist [lies] in the choice and arrangement of the play's ideas'.[22] The resulting selectivity is more likely to be subjective than objective. Above all, concludes Weiss, documentary theatre 'takes sides', the playwright inviting the audience to form a partisan judgment. The problem is to keep an artistic balance between fact and fiction, truth and imagination. The value of the Israeli documentary plays therefore resides not in their recreation of a story from historical records, court proceedings and interlocutors – although Sobol in particular achieved this – but in arranging ideas with a view to provoking questions and discussion.

Israeli documentary plays, from the earliest example, Aharon Meged's *Hannah Senesh* to the modern versions (including Motti Lerner's *Elsa*, [Lasker-Schüler], are rooted in documented fact, with certain imaginative additions by the playwrights. In none of them does the focal character transcend his or her historical framework, for documentary theatre generally subordinates characterisation to message. The dramatic imagination is often hidebound not only by history, historiography and national myths but by the playwrights' functional inability to detach their characters from ideological motives. Because of the earnest intensity of these plays, characters remain little more than ciphers.

The language of the realistic and documentary plays is prosaic and unadorned. According to Arthur Miller, prose is the language of family relations while the world beyond opens the play to the void and to poetic diction.[23] Critics have stressed the absence of metaphor in much original Israeli drama, its lack of poetry. Israeli realistic or documentary plays remain linguistically in the realm of the *extended* family, the society with its common tradition and shared experience.

One of Sobol's most accomplished documentary investigations into Zionist origins is his one-act play *Leyl Ha'esrim* (The Night of the Twentieth) (1977 and 1990),[24] directed by Nola Chilton in its original production. It recounts the events of an October night in 1920 which a small group of young pioneers spend on a hilltop before descending to the settlement of Mansurin the following day. These *halutzim* are young middle-class intellectuals who have left homes and careers in Europe to make their lives on the new *yishuv*, ostensibly to realise their aspirations of an authentic life of purity within a morally elevated society it is their task to establish. The play does not, however, support these assumptions of their ideological motivation, but explores the underlying socio-psychological reasons for their venture into the unknown.

Well-documented accounts of the *Hashomer Hatza'ir* settlement – or commune – of Bitanya-Ilit, a strange experiment in almost cultic communalism, provided Sobol with the means through which to explore some of the mythology of the Third *Aliyah*, the immigration of Jewish pioneers from Europe to Palestine from 1919 to 1923. Bitanya–Ilit was one of the most interesting, perhaps bizarre, of the pioneering labour communes in the early 1920s. Located on a hilltop overlooking the Sea of Galilee, it numbered some forty or fifty men and women from Galicia who were predominantly members of *Hashomer Hatza'ir*. Their purpose was to create a new communal culture, a new, just society unrelated to that of diaspora Jewry or European capitalism. In his memoirs one of the members, David Horowitz (later the President of the Bank of Israel), likened Bitanya to a 'religious sect ... with its own charismatic leader and set of symbols ... an order of spiritual ascetics ... a monastic order without God'.[25] The Bitanya experience has been recorded in memoirs, articles, at least three novels, and in the group's annals entitled *Kehiliyatenu*.[26]

One of the characteristic activities of Bitanya was the *sihah* or 'discussion', more exactly a confessional group session consisting of monologues and near – hysterical public confessions where members bared their innermost secrets. Much of Sobol's material was drawn from the records of such sessions. His play builds on a night of *sihah* during which his seven characters reveal not only their personal secrets but also the perceived anomalies of the 'enterprise'. In fact, Sobol had little to do other than allow the characters to speak for themselves, which, according to existing accounts, their real antecedents had done eloquently. He then adapted this material to provide a critique of Zionism which was wholly fictional, for whatever the failings of the individual practitioners, the enterprise as a whole was never in doubt.

The Night of the Twentieth opens with an ideological discussion, an exchange of ideas and some fashionable banalities. Gradually the argument becomes an open confession, with the idea of nakedness both metaphorical and real providing its central image. The characters are distinctive, not entirely representative stereotypes but people with some marked individuality. Ephraim, the rebellious son of a well-to-do Viennese banker, is the establishment voice of the play, portraying classical Zionist rhetoric and historical slogans. He may represent Meir Yaari, the leader of the Bitanya group. Ephraim reinforces the sanctioned terms of Zionism for the others to question. Moshe is a more complex character, providing the idealistic as opposed to ideological value of the play, possibly the playwright's voice. A veteran of the First World War, Moshe is critical of the Zionist agenda and the focus of Zionism on nation, motherland, history and mythology. Naftali is a self-styled joker who uses self-wounding humour as an escape from his notion of his own ugliness, something of a cliché: the broken-hearted clown. Naftali forms a close friendship with Akiva which, judging by the reaction of the others, is a dark stain on the open egalitarian society of the commune. The group perceives the need to be loved personally as a sign of capitalist individualism. Shifra is violent, erotic and passionate, loved by all the men. Nehama is resourceful, self-sufficient and intellectual, all masculine qualities according to the tenets of the time. Miriam is filled with rage at Nehama's self-sufficiency, wanting a husband and child and she ultimately agrees, contrary to the collective ideals of the group, to set up home with Ephraim. These young people represent a terrible conformity, a denial of individual needs. Yet individual needs exist and their sublimation in work and metaphysical debate is clearly not effective.

Sobol suggests that this 'generation of giants' was no different from any other, that its members were confused and neurotic and had used the pioneering enterprise as a solution for personal problems. Each of his characters offers a different reason for his or her presence in Palestine and many express disappointment with the society they find there, Naftali's in particular arising from divisions even on the *yishuv*. This point is elaborated by Yehuda Yaari, Meir's brother, in his novel based on the Bitanya experience, *When the Candle Was Burning*.[27] On the other hand, there is little historical validation for Sobol's suggestion through his characters that the great national undertaking came about not as a result of any transcendent ideology, but due to the circumstances in the lives of each protagonist, such as family disputes, fear of persecution, or disillusionment with life in Europe.

The central problem of *The Night of the Twentieth* is the question of individual opposed to collective needs, including the need to love and be loved. Sobol's settlers discuss problems of egotism, the tussle between the individual and the community. Meir Yaari chronicles the creation of a brotherhood in which the relationship between members will be 'open, true and new', a spirit of 'solidarity and cooperation' in accordance with the consciousness of the youth movement and its sharp criticism of European society.[28] Secrets must be revealed, as if members of the group see themselves as a linked body of absolute fellowship, even attempting to neutralise gender differences. 'In Bitanya the communal idea went so far that sexual intercourse between two individuals was considered a despicable act of selfishness unless the two lovers later verbally shared their feelings with the entire commune at the *sihah*.'[29] In his memoirs, David Horowitz recalls that in Bitanya the criticism and judgment levelled at the individual verged on 'spiritual cruelty'.[30] The conflict between the private and the collective amplifies the play's overwrought sensibility, implicated, as it is, in love and eroticism. Sobol confirms that absolute selflessness is unattainable, that love and privacy are powerful human needs. When these needs encounter duty to an abstract ideal of community the effect is an uneasy, sometimes unworkable, compromise.

Also central to the play is the conflict between the pioneers' inherited objectives and their need to create a new and as yet untested social entity. According to Moshe, whose rhetoric provides the polemical fuel for the discussion, the group suffers under an imposed external agenda: they are divided between self-realisation and historical realisation. Moshe resists fulfilling preordained ideologies and slogans, complaining that he will not allow anyone to transform him into a manifesto. He wants only 'to live like a person with people'.[31] He claims that 'symbols' and 'myths' have replaced parental authority, becoming analogous authorities which subordinate members of the group. He no longer wants any link with history 'not Austria, not Russia, not Jewish' but only a humane society in a just world. Some of the others agree with the idea of creating a society *ex nihilo*, beginning again and renouncing Europe and European ideologies. They articulate their mythology of *galut* (exile) in terms that would not shame an anti-Semite:

EPHRAIM You all want a kind of finalised 'there is'. It will be bad for us in this country the moment we begin to live by 'there is'. We must live in constant emergence, in the tension of constant emergence ... weak fathers gave us life and hysterical mothers brought us up. This is what has rotted inside: fear of the world and a lack of security.[32]

In their perception of themselves as 'weak' they have apparently internalised the anti-Semitic Austrian philosopher Otto Weininger's malevolent charges to which Sobol was later to devote an entire play.

In his novel, Yehuda Yaari created a fictional settlement, Tel Meir, based on Bitanya of which he, and his brother Meir, were members. The settlers cleared, ploughed and drained Tel Meir amid much privation and illness. Like Sobol's group, Yaari's suffered equally from anxiety and depression: 'The Tel Meir group was always perplexed and sad. But the bewilderment and sorrow which overwhelmed us now were different and more oppressive'.[33] Enclosed by mountains, isolated and cut off and always threatened by the Arabs below, they contemplated their situation:

Unbelievable! We, the children of a wandering generation who had passed though so many countries in the course of our wanderings and who had met thousands of people on our way – we now shut ourselves up on a solitary island and regarded it as the whole world! ... A great *Why* confronted us in continuous challenge: *Why* are we ploughing? Sowing? Planting? *Why* are we living together? *Why are we living?*

Yaari's novel gives a banal reason for their angst: the dearth of women in the group. *Kehiliyatenu*, a more reliable collection of writings by the Bitanya members, offers alternative answers. It describes a *sihah*:

> A dark hut . . . the lamplight casts ugly yellow shadows over you; you sit with bowed heads, your faces are gloomy and shaking with an irritable tremor . . . Why are you so sad? Your lips are tight and your eyes those of a drunkard, and you seek something in the grey trampled dust of the floor.[34]

Kehiliyatenu reveals that stress, fear, rebelliousness and the refusal to accept reality fuelled the sense of gloom, compounded by a neurotic confinement within the community. Undoubtedly there were also undertones of sexual frustration, repression and guilt.

In his play Sobol retained the strange notions of sexuality and eroticism underlying the Bitanya settlers' philosophy. Certain ideals of eroticism became, for the repressed bourgeois diaspora Jews, a fundamental part of the ideology of social reconstruction. Eros was in fact one of the most widespread concepts in the European youth movements, derived in part from the German *Jugendkultur* (youth culture), the *Wandervogel* movement[35] (by which *Hashomer Hatza'ir* was strongly influenced) and from Freud and Buber. Meir Yaari wrote of 'the idea of the youth movement, of education and eroticism'; consequently the characteristic statements emerging from the *sihot* were infused with ideas of the collective 'erotic'.[36] There was a good deal of sexual tension in Bitanya due in part to the imbalance of men and women, and to the general air of introspection and isolation. Freedom from all normal social constraint and from institutions of conventional morality led to a confusing conflict of desire and restraint which was then sublimated into a fanciful notion of the likely political power of eroticism.

The real settlers' physical and psychological hardship generated the charged atmosphere which Sobol was able to exploit in his task of demythologisation. He utilised material from the *sihah*'s atmosphere of barely controlled hysteria. In itself it was theatrical and it makes irresistible drama on the stage. Like their Bitanya counterparts, Sobol's characters are caught at the moment between childhood and adulthood. Their projected move from the comparative safety of the hilltop to the peril of the new kibbutz down below is a metaphorical transition from youth to maturity and to action after the safety of theory and youthful debate. The young settlers are about to abandon their childhood on the mountain, although they lack full control over their own destiny.

In keeping with his methodology throughout his historical drama, Sobol anachronistically projects the pioneers' beliefs and actions onto the present day. While *The Night of the Twentieth* does question the halutzic myth and the pioneer stereotype, Sobol's primary concern is the significance of both the myth and the stereotype for modern Israel. Questions about identity and presence allude more directly to Israel than to Bitanya, and it is Sobol's stereotypical young *Israelis* who people his fictional hilltop settlement. Sobol extrapolates his own interpretation of the pioneering enterprise. With hindsight he presents his youthful 'forefathers' as incapable of answering the teleological questions perturbing *modern* Israeli society, those concerning its presence in the Middle East, its character and political future. The characters in *The Night of the Twentieth* confront contemporary Israeli questions arising from Israel's prehistory.

[The] Israelis are seeking their roots which are fused – for all the Zionists and socialists in the society – primarily in the history of Zionist and Jewish settlement in Palestine. [Sobol's] is a play about people seeking their identity written for a people seeking their identity; a play about young people seeking significance in their lives written for young people seeking significance in their lives. The hidden sting in the play is that the characters seeking significance in their lives are exactly the characters in which many of us see the source and confirmation of their lives here.[37]

Sobol's conspicuously political statements are out of place in the play, remaining detached from the integrated and carefully crafted tapestry of the *sihah*. He gives Moshe a proleptic speech about the failure of authority to consider the consequences of its policies for its citizens:

Tomorrow we'll have to go out to danger, maybe to death. The group will tell your son, Miriam, arise and go to one of the mountains and stand guard there. Will you have the strength to go on living with the group if he doesn't return? If you know that the group has never spoken to him or to you? That the people who sent your son to die have hidden themselves from you? Or perhaps we'd send him in the name of the Agricultural Centre which is dispatching us to Mansurin tomorrow? What would be the point of living? From the moment the first son is killed people will walk around here with iron in their souls, death in their spirit![38]

With some self-reflexive irony, Sobol has Ephraim complain of Moshe's 'talking far into the future'. Moshe's anaphoric oratory extends to the contemporary Middle East crisis: 'We're going to live there instead of the people who have been there until now. We're coming to take their place'.[39] He claims that the only justification for doing so would be to 'create a morally elevated society . . . a society whose motivating force is above all law. Above all religion. Above any idea, custom or tradition', an ideal egalitarian society which, he admits more than once, has no precursor in the world but must be created. Sobol appears to be denouncing Israel for having departed from this ideal text. Moshe supplies the present-day reality: if the new society is not to be just it will do no more than 'consume, be glutted, grow fat, amass property, become corrupt, disintegrate and die'.[40] The first step in this process of decline is the easy assumption of symbols, myths and slogans which impede original thought and the creation of a humane society.

Sobol's message in the play is that the group must on no account leave the mountaintop until it has achieved self-understanding, otherwise the result will be tragedy. 'We want to create a new person. For this we have to open up everything, destroy everything, come out clean. *Tabula rasa*.'[41] Ultimately his purpose is not so much to mock the muddled thinking of the Zionist forefathers but to demonstrate their lack of clarity of *purpose*. He suggests that Zionism was not a unilaterally agreed, consensual philosophy but a movement containing profound philosophical divisions. Therefore, its predominant interpretation, the one upon which the State of Israel was founded, may be fallacious. Through his skilful transposition of Bitanya, Sobol attributes the wider malaise of Zionism as a whole to the 'neurosis' of the early settlers. Early Zionism, he suggests, was realised by groups of confused, neurotic adolescents whose actions were largely sublimations of their unresolved social, ideological and sexual problems. It is therefore a product of myths and slogans, attitudes and inherited notions, removed from political reality. All this coalesced into a national mythology which ultimately shed its substance to retain an idealistic structure which was subsequently misappropriated.

Despite his fidelity, at least to the historical framework, Sobol makes little reference to the real achievements of the members of his group. In between their *sihot*, the Bitanya *halutzim* did the punishing work for which they had emigrated and to which the play scarcely alludes. In this respect Yehuda Yaari's *When the Candle Was Burning* supplements the drama's framework: he describes graphically, from

Figure 1   Yehoshua Sobol, *A Jewish Soul*, 1982.

Figure 2   Yehoshua Sobol, *The Night of the Twentieth*, 1976.

personal experience, the hardship of the life in Palestine, the heat, 'malaria, wells, serpents and scorpions', indicating that despite their romantic anxiety, the pioneers were not weaklings. David Horowitz also depicts encounters with poisonous insects and debilitating illness in his memoirs, and confirms that the urban European intellectuals were able to withstand the appalling conditions in Palestine, exhaustion and the dangers of attack. Sobol's propaganda, partly based on the comments of the settlers concerning the feebleness of the *golah* Jew, is proven by historical fact to be inaccurate. Balancing the near-psychosis of the *sihot* were the long hours of hard labour, illness and fear which, oddly enough, do not constitute the source of the Bitanya settlers' gloom.

Sobol's trilogy, *Yemei Beit Kaplan* (The Days of the House of Kaplan), (1978),[42] comprising three plays, *Habaytah Habaytah* (Going Home), *Leyl Klulot* (The Wedding Night) and *Lamaharat* (The Next Day) is devoted to the growing embourgeoisement of Israeli society. Early Israeli drama had portrayed historical events from a public, communal point of view, but in *Sylvester '72* Sobol had already rendered the political arena as the space of the family, and the trilogy continues this trend. In these plays, which encompass the first thirty years of statehood, he attempts to turn accepted ideas and attitudes on their head. His central target is the period of early statehood which has become mythologised in the Israeli conscious-ness, together with a tradition that possesses its own texts and supporting dogma.

The first and most important play of the trilogy, *Going Home* is a curious family drama which, on the surface, is a dystopian diatribe against Israel's growing materialism and consumerism. The play, set in a society which only superficially resembles that of Israel in 1947, dramatises Sobol's conviction that a society constantly at war must forfeit its founding ideology and replace it with the defective morality of wartime. According to Sobol, violence replaces values and materialism destroys the spirit. In place of the pioneers' majestic vision, which set the moral imperative at the heart of their aspira-tions, Israeli society substituted consumerism. Sobol's view of the early ideology is at times contradictory: on the one hand, he praises, in almost extravagant terms, the nationalist philosophy of early Zionism as a distillation of the best of living Judaism.[43] On the other hand, he suggests that the founding principles may not have been very strongly held, that for the 'ancestors' of the characters in *Going Home*, idealism possessed only rhetorical value.[44]

Going Home takes place on the *yishuv* during the night of 29 November 1947, the night of the UN's decision to partition Israel, with significant consequences for the future of the Jewish state. Actual recordings of portions of the discussion and vote at Flushing Meadow are used in the play. Yehuda Kaplan, a wealthy private farmer, has embarked on a mission to Europe concerning the Haganah, much against the wishes of his wife, Yaffa, a bourgeois Viennese woman. She displays no interest in his nationalist consciousness or in the significant changes about to take place in her adopted country. Her farm manager, a crude but gifted entrepre-neur, Koba Lifshitz, becomes her lover and greatly profits from the coming war. Koba (like Boaz in *Sylvester '72*), is a cynical materialist who wears tailored clothes and imported aftershave, drives a large car and talks of profit.

Kaplan returns to his house after some years abroad to discover the liaison between his wife and Koba. Her antagonism and aliena-tion ultimately provoke his return to the battlefield. Yehuda is later killed in battle, his wife and her lover indirectly responsible for his death – echoing the fate of Agamemnon at the hands of Clytemnestra and Aegisthus – and reinforcing the correspondence of Sobol's family trilogy not only to the *Odyssey* but also to the *Oresteia*.[45] Indeed, the mythological framework of *Going Home* underscores the function of myth in Israeli national history, and ideologically locates the interrogation of certain premises in Zionism. Confronted by the choice between a practical, worldly man and a mythic hero, Yaffa chooses the pragmatist and rejects the myth. Yehuda is therefore the idealised hero for which there is no place in the new state.

In his continuing examination of Israeli society's moral options, war versus profit, the common versus the individual good, Sobol has added another binary set, Zionism and diaspora Judaism. He achieved this through the character of Yaffa. Despite being Sobol's worst and most blatantly misogynistic stereotype, she is one of his most politically significant characters. First of all, the failure of the farm is the result solely of her materialism, her intellectual and moral vacuity, her sole need for instant sexual gratification. She is the very embodiment of the negative female element Sobol was to centralise a few years later through the character of Otto Weininger in *A Jewish Soul*. Second, Yaffa is not only a diaspora Jewess, but one born in Vienna, Weininger's city, which became a dominant symbol in Sobol's analysis of Judaism and the European roots of Zionism.

The secondary theme of *Going Home* – the confrontation between spiritual values and materialism in a society that has become cynical and mercenary – was a prevalent topic in the social realism of the 1950s. In an interview Sobol commented upon the social objectives of leaders of various Jewish Palestinian institutions who enjoyed an association with, for example, Lord Melchett and the British contingent in Palestine.[46] Like Sobol's Yaffa, these Jewish settlers displayed a European style of refinement, and scarcely identified with the Zionist labour hierarchy. Sobol uniquely suggests that the construction of the state was influenced more by these social elements financed by the British than by the labour movement to which many settlers paid no more than lip service. The quick and brutal growth of the bourgeoisie after 1977, he believes, had its roots in the period immediately before the establishment of the state. Sobol concludes that Israeli society admired the country's heroes but hailed the people who became rich.[47] Speaking from the platform of his own political convictions, he excoriates the notion that a financial culture associated with diaspora Jews was imported into Israel, to distort Zionism's socialist principles and determine the nature of the new state. Yaffa's corruption of the farm is therefore analogous to the corruption of the state; in addition, she neither understands nor appreciates the true male principle, the achieving, positive hero. It is possible that Sobol's plays represent a deeply rooted Israeli malaise which could, hesitantly, be called Israeli anti-Semitism. In *Going Home* – towering above the positive Israeli hero, himself a forerunner of the *Palmahnik* of 1948, and the unsophisticated socialist farm workers – is the European woman and her ugly alliance with a stereotype reminiscent of the worst anti-Semitic caricatures of international Jewry.

Methodologically, *Going Home* illustrates its propositions through familiar archetypes representing Sobol's ideological programmes: the heroic idealist, later to become the *Palmahnik*, the predatory businessman, the man of the soil, the socialist proletarian. Lifschitz heralds the time of war which – with some hindsight on Sobol's part – will determine the ultimate capitalist character of the state. Hayyim, a simple farmer with an agrarian dream similar to the utopian visions of the pioneers of *The Night of the Twentieth*, proposes the achievement of a socialist society in which freedom of choice governs:

HAYYIM Listen: here in this country every Jewish individual can find a more secure, a nicer, richer life than what he has in Europe or in America: we'll create a splendid socialist society with educational institutions, cooperatives, workers' economy and the collective economy... here every Jew will be able to choose the form of socialism he wants ...

LIFSCHITZ And if there's a Jew who wants to do business and have nothing to do with socialism?

HAYYIM Let him go to hell! We don't need merchants here ...[48]

If this play is not directly *about* Zionism, it says something about the nature of the state itself. It could be said to indicate the way in which some of the characters in *The Night of the Twentieth* have grown up in Israel, each having founded it in his or her own image. Sobol's question in *Going Home* relates to Israel's most appropriate and true image. Despite its superficiality, its serious historical distortions, its clichés and the sheer unlikelihood of its narrative, *Going Home* is an important indicator in the long journey Sobol has undertaken in his search for the roots of modern Zionism.

A peak in Sobol's continuing dialectical evaluation of Zionism is his quasi-documentary drama *Nefesh Yehudi – Halaylah Ha'aharon shel Otto Weininger* (A Jewish Soul – The Last Night of Otto Weininger) (1982),[49] which won the Meskin Prize for Drama in 1983. It features Weininger, the homosexual self-hating Jew and Christian convert, whose extreme theories were rejected by Freud and much admired by Hitler. The play is an analeptic examination of Weininger's life and thought in short scenes which mingle memory and fantasy. It is set in *fin-de-siècle* Vienna, a city suffused with psychosexual malaise, in the house in which Beethoven died which was also the scene of Weininger's suicide at the age of 23. Vienna was, additionally, composed of antinomian forces embracing every Jewish category, Orthodox and pan-Germanist, 'self-hating' and assimilated, converts and Zionists.

In one sense Weininger is typical of the literary tradition of doomed romantic heroes whose genius provokes their alienation and ultimate tragedy. In another, he symbolizes the social and ideological dualities of Austro-German Jewry. In the play he is the focal point for many of the issues of the period, both Jewish and general: the growth of modern anti-Semitism, the impact of European liberalism, the rise of Zionism and its potential effect on the Jews, and the disjunction betwen Judaism and Zionism. Although it is set chronologically earlier, *A Jewish Soul* nevertheless constitutes the progression of the debate begun in *The Night of the Twentieth*, on a level of sophistication which carries the argument about Zionism into a thesis play of Brechtian proportions. Many of its ideas are evolved from those first argued by the pioneers of the mountaintop whose origins were in the Vienna of Weininger, Herzl and Freud. Sobol's study of the contradictory character of Zionism begins in Vienna, the historical base of the young settlers' instability.

The play is loosely based on Weininger's biography and particularly on his notorious *Sex and Character* (1903), a philosophical justification of male ethical, intellectual and spiritual superiority, and of anti-Semitism. Weininger saw women as interested only in sexual gratification or procreation. Jews, according to him, believe in nothing and therefore espouse anarchy. Zionism could only come about after the rejection of Judaism since the Jews could not grasp the idea of a state. Sobol's play features Otto's 'double' who embodies both his self-loathing and his misogyny. Only at the end of the play is this alter ego revealed as feminine, the concealed female aspect of Otto which he abhors in himself, in everyone else and primarily in Judaism. Otto's 'other' examines Otto's hatred of women and Jews by transporting him to his childhood and his domineering, pan-Germanist father, and submissive, manipulative mother. According to Sobol – although challenged by a surviving member of the family – Weininger's father was an ardent Wagnerian who attempted to initiate his son into the wonders of Wagner's maniacal *Deutchtum*. Theodor Herzl himself was attracted to Wagner's music. During his composition of *The Jewish State* he writes in his diary:

I worked at it daily until I was completely exhausted. My one recreation was in the evenings when I could go to listen to Wagner's music, and particularly *Tannhäuser*, an opera which I go to hear as often as it is produced.[50]

The dominant argument of Sobol's *A Jewish Soul* concerns the very roots of Zionism, again raising the questions of the relationship between Zionism, diaspora Judaism and diaspora Jews. It begins with a summary of the Austro-Jewish milieu and continues as little more than an intricate evolution of the pioneers' *sihah*. This time the *sihah* is composed of a series of arguments between Otto and his friends Klara, a militant Zionist, Berger, an ambivalent Jew, and Hans Tietz, a non-Jewish catalyst against whom the argument unravels. Berger, who displays the reluctance of many assimilated Jewish intellectuals to identify with Zionism, complains about Herzl's 'use' of anti-Semitism which he strongly opposes. The predominant argument, however, is carried by Otto through his encounters with these and other characters. Long passages in the play feature his raving which Sobol has drawn directly from *Sex and Character*, and his theories about Judaism (some of which had appeared embryonically in *The Night of the Twentieth*).

Weininger's complex philosophical thesis compares the Jewish character to what he terms 'the feminine idea', the source of all irrationality and chaos in the world. The Aryan race, he claimed, is the embodiment of the masculine-creative principle of being, while the feminine-chaotic principle of non-being is embodied in the Jews and, above all, in Jewish culture. In Sobol's version of cultural history, the nucleus of Weininger's argument is the Jews' lack of masculine nobility: as 'psychological creatures' they are devoid of reason, capable only of emotion.

This tussle is represented in the play by Freud, exemplifying the irrational, feminine aspect of the Jews, but also exemplifying Jewish liberal humanism. Otto shows some admiration for Zionism, the rational aspect, which he characterises as 'the last remnant of nobility remaining in Judaism'. The real Weininger's admiration of the masculine principle emerged from the fertile ground prepared by Nietzsche and Darwin, and the more aggressive elements of German Romantic nationalism. Nietzsche's call for nobility was echoed in Herzl's own concept of the 'new Jew' as a man with a sense of aristocratic honour and virtue and the ability (rather ironic in view of Jewish history) to die like a cavalier. Weininger's constantly reiterated grievance concerns the lack of nobility in the Jew. Herzl, too, held to Jewish values which were in direct and deliberate contradiction to the ghetto way of life.

For Herzl, Zionism implied a radical transvaluation of Jewish concepts of honour. The traditional virtues of restraint, passivity and intellection, of the social isolation of the ghetto community, were no longer adequate in an assimilated nineteenth-century Viennese milieu.[51]

Many critics have questioned Sobol's choice of Weininger as the representative of the dilemmas of European Jewish life, since Otto's own understanding of Judaism conforms uncompromisingly to nineteenth-century formulations of anti-Semitism. Sobol does not deny Otto's anti-Semitism and presents him – as he was in life – as a phenomenon which destroys itself. Yet historical reconstruction is not Sobol's objective; rather, through his Otto, he again proposes an intricate critique of modern Israel. Otto becomes a symbol of the underlying problematics of the Zionism that ultimately created the Jewish state. Despite its long and tortuous discussions about the *nature* of Zionism which should be read in relation to Zionism's incarnation in modern Israel, the play's central proposition, unacceptable to Otto as it is to Sobol, is the *origin* of Zionism as a product of certain conditions inherent in diaspora life.

To Weininger, 'Judaism' does not signify a panoply of religion and ritual but the particular characteristics he stresses: 'female' weakness, the inability to experience guilt, materialism, lack of true spirituality (he converted to Protestantism) and lack of rationalism, all of which contradict the Zionism that he perceives as a super-rational philosophy. Sobol's Otto declares that 'Zionism will sink in the abyss of Judaism and be swallowed in it like a stone in a bog',[52] as if Zionism

and Judaism were warring antagonists. The Zionism which represents all that remains noble in Jewish life is fated to become a victim
of Judaism, its destruction leading the Jews back to their natural
state of exile. Even when historical circumstances enable Jews to
abandon the diaspora they stubbornly resist doing so. Exile is a form
of existence which suits the Jewish character, and is therefore
unlikely to change even in the event of a Jewish state. Sobol's Otto
concludes, 'There will be a need to conquer Judaism from the inside
and to be free of it once and for all'.[53] Otto embodies the very
features from which, according to him, Zionism must escape. In
addition, he is a representative of the spiritual crisis among nineteenth-century European Jewry, of the European Jew whom Sobol
appears to disdain, and also of the complex social environment in
which Zionism was born.

Despite its lengthy chunks of Weininger's philosophy, the play is
curiously inconclusive. Otto says his piece and then kills himself, and
the rest is left unresolved, with the verdict on Zionism once again
suspended. His desire is not clear: he derides the diaspora Jew but
will not embrace Zionism, even with its positive, masculine, noble
elements. Perhaps Zionism's 'masculinity' is, for Sobol, its own
principal defect. Otto's inability to accept 'mixing' extends itself to
marriage and childbirth: 'It's better not to be born than to come into
the world as the fruit of some repressed sexual nausea'.[54] It is not
difficult to see the development of these ideas in the Nazi ideology of
racial purity, its revulsion at the idea of miscegenation. If Sobol's
Otto indeed perceives in Zionism a variation of Aryanism, he
legitimises the contemporary equation of Zionism with racism. So,
through Otto's suicide, Sobol rejects even the masculine energy of
Zionism as a solution. Its strong chauvinist militarism has overcome
the humanistic, Herzl trumping Freud.

The play has been correctly seen as a critique of those within Israel's political
spectrum who believe that the solution to the problems facing the country is
military power, a kind of 'Aryan' reliance on machismo and superiority.[55]

After Weininger's suicide his 'double' lives on, dragging him into
an hysterical dance and singing: 'I love myself. As I am. A Jew, an
Aryan, a barbarian, whatever ... I love myself. I'm alive! I'm alive!
Fighting. Working. Devouring. Screwing. Singing. Dancing.'[56] The
double is a mouthpiece for Sobol's opinion of the modern Israeli, a
synthesis of Judaism and Zionism. According to Sarit Fuchs, 'The

Jewish soul, hating itself because of its weakness and exile, has given birth to a kind of distorted child: the hard, organised, opportunistic Israeli.'[57]

Sobol's conception of Zionism in the play has to be seen as provocatively reductive. His cautionary purpose is ultimately to suggest that the 'Jewish' elements have gathered the power in Israel, and that Herzl's Zionism was, from the start, either the inappropriate, 'incorrect' form of Zionism, or one that has been adulterated and remains deeply flawed.

There's a contradiction between Zionism and Orthodox Judaism. Nowadays in Israel they try to make a whole mixture, a mish-mash of Zionism and messianism. I don't think that Zionism had anything to do with messianism originally. It was ... a secular ideology, a nationalistic ideology trying to re-implant the Jews in an historical context. It's only after the Six-Day War that messianism all of a sudden started to become the expression both of Judaism and of Zionism and I think that this is our worst catastrophe.[58]

'I want to see Zionism freed from Judaism,' Sobol says elsewhere, 'When I say Judaism I don't mean the rabbinic writings but the traumatic burdensome factors in which we oscillate: blood-libels, pogroms, Holocaust. This is a destructive burden bringing revenge and hatred. I don't believe in a synthesis between the two powers.'[59]

The historical Weininger is scarcely relevant to *A Jewish Soul* for, despite Sobol's careful research, the play is not a documentary evocation of Weininger and his milieu. One has only to compare it with Herzl's *Das Neue Ghetto* (The New Ghetto), (1892), set in the same period, to see how little *A Jewish Soul* has to do with Vienna, anti-Semitism and Weininger, and how much it has to do with modern Zionism and Israel. Otto's 'Judaism' is a symbolic catchword for the Jewish tradition and psychological culture which is Sobol's principal target. He distinguishes in the play between 'universal humanistic values' and the diaspora Jewish tradition. Yet he is able to sanction Israel's legacy of *European* traditions and philosophies despite their new messiahs, including Freud and Marx, being diaspora Jews, for he admires these 'strong', humanist Jews over the 'weak' Jews.

Critical responses to *A Jewish Soul* were predictable even in their extremes. By and large Israeli mainstream critics were cautiously favourable and their reviews were accompanied by a good deal of public discussion. Some accused Sobol of anti-Semitism and self-hatred, challenging his choice of Weininger as a subject. Sobol was, however, at pains to stress his intentional demonstration of the destruction of the anti-Semite by anti-Semitism. The religious establishment petitioned the mayor of Haifa in a telegram which demanded the removal of the play which was 'dreadful in its infamy, filled with ugliness and abuse and derived, one can only conclude, from utter madness, obscenity, corruption and the hatred of Israel'.[60] A Jerusalem rabbi claimed, a short time prior to the play's Edinburgh debut, that 'if they were to put the play on abroad I'm sure there would immediately be an urgent meeting of the government regarding an increase in anti-Semitism'.[61] The matter was taken to a plenary session of the Knesset after which the management of the Haifa Municipal Theatre issued the assurance that the playtext would be modified. Two lines were excised.

The play received almost universally positive notices in Britain and Germany. Irving Wardle of *The Times* praised Sobol's 'masterly analysis of the public and familial aspects of the Jewish identity crisis in turn-of-the-century Vienna' (24 April 1983); Michael Coveney of *The Financial Times* expressed disappointment at the theoretical treatment of the subject (24 April 1983) but Jack Tinker of the *Daily Mail* wrote rapturously about the Haifa Municipal Theatre's 'great artistic achievement' which 'held its international audience in thrall' (24 April 1983). It was partly due to these reviews – and, undoubtedly to the questionable content of the play itself – that conservative Jewish leaders in Britain attempted to have the play suppressed. For the same reasons, the representatives of the Israeli government who saw it in London did so in their private capacity. This raises the problem of the political theatre in Israel, including those plays which venture into Israeli-Palestinian relations, such as Sobol's *The Palestinian Girl*, nourishing the antagonistic convictions of foreign audiences. There was a great deal of ambivalence among the Jews, Israelis and others, who saw *A Jewish Soul* in Britain, an ambivalence which had little to do with the aesthetic qualities of the play as drama. An even greater controversy within Jewish communities grew around the Haifa Municipal Theatre's tour of *The Palestinian Girl* in Germany. Israeli self-criticism creates serious dilemmas when encountered by Jews in the diaspora, rather like revealing family secrets in public.

The Israeli readers do not really enjoy their literature. They read as if obsessed; they often complain that present-day writers and poets are dangerous to the 'national morale' and damaging to Israel's self-image and its reputation in the outside world.[62]

The possibility that foreign critical articles and reviews were favourable to *A Jewish Soul* because of the sympathy of the reviewer with Weininger's anti-Jewish or anti-Zionist sentiments in the play no doubt prompted the official unease. Despite the continuing controversy over censorship which led to the abolition of civil theatre censorship in Israel in 1991, there has been little recorded discussion about the value or effect of presenting politically controversial Israeli plays abroad, whether their anti-heroes and their indictment of Israeli government policies reinforce the negative foreign image of the modern Israeli.[63] Sobol once scolded: 'There's no difficulty with my point of view. If you can't handle it – it's your problem.'[64] He recounts an incident after the first Edinburgh performance of *A Jewish Soul* when two Jewish members of the audience reproached him for staging the play outside Israel. Many more Anglo-Jews praised him for raising the subject of anti-Semitism and breaking a taboo imposed no less by Anglo-Jewry than by the non-Jews. As it happened, many of the non-Jewish members of the Edinburgh audience disclosed a sense of guilt at observing Weininger's psychological convolutions, seeing their own anti-Semitism reflected in him.[65]

The success of *A Jewish Soul* in Germany is an enigmatic phenomenon. A formal association between the Haifa Municipal Theatre and financial elements within the German theatre brought Sobol, at that time the artistic director of the Haifa Municipal Theatre, to some prominence within Germany. Subsequently three of Sobol's plays were staged in various centres in Germany, generally to great acclaim. Through their presentation Sobol appears to be seeking certain defined objectives: first, to demonstrate to the Germans the outcome of their historical anti-Semitism, second, to emphasise that the contemporary Israeli is no longer a dismal creature of the diaspora in general and the Germans in particular and, third, simply to achieve exposure as a playwright. Some of his critics differ, suggesting that the success of *A Jewish Soul* in Germany is derived from its ability to reinforce inherent German anti-Semitism. Another factor is the amazement of German audiences at seeing a play about anti-Semitism in German by an Israeli playwright.

Sobol's triumph in Germany led to a debate about German-Israel cultural links which was perpetuated by extensive press coverage. He commented:

It's clear to me that after all the debates and the censure and the demonisation that I've been subjected to I go and make theatre in a place where they want the theatre that I make ... My success in Germany has done something very good for me: it has clarified for me that art has no boundaries ... Someone said that he will not allow his plays to be shown in Germany. In my opinion, this is obeisance to the consensus. A real artist must transcend all boundaries that politicians, demagogues and various interests have set.[66]

Sobol is seen not only as a representative of the Israeli liberal conscience (sponsored, to a large extent, by German left-wing idealism), but also as a dissident whose views overcome the narrow limits of the Israeli political and cultural consensus. Yet his dissidence, as reflected in *Going Home* and *A Jewish Soul*, did not involve state interference; rather than being persecuted or even suppressed within Israel he was tolerated by the authorities[67] and mainstream theatregoers, and pilloried only by elements within the religious establishment and their supporters. However, his outspokenness and bold choice of topic and treatment have indeed invested him with some of the sparks of the dissident artist. Apart from his political views and his investigation of Zionism, he also articulates the unvoiced sentiments towards Jewish history of many Israelis who fear the label of 'self-hatred' or 'auto-anti-Semitism', a sobriquet coined by the Israeli religious Right. Selecting Otto Weininger as both a representative of and a spokesman for these concerns is perhaps extreme; yet *A Jewish Soul* has placed the issue of the Israeli intellectual relationship with diaspora Jewry in an open forum rather than confronting it by allegory as other writers, such as Amos Oz and A. B. Yehoshua, for example, have done,[68] or ignoring it altogether.

Following the success in Germany both of *A Jewish Soul* and Sobol's next play, *Ghetto*, other Israeli playwrights took their plays to Germany. Most of them discover complex ideological reasons for this foray into German intellectual society, yet there is a measure of naïveté in their efforts. Notwithstanding instances of responsive interaction, German audiences are left largely impassive in the face of Israeli confessionalism.

The Israelis tear off their shirts and the Germans remain detached. They are unable and unwilling to confront [these issues]. Sometimes they watch this self-revelation – against whose dangers they have developed a sophisticated intellectual system – with a certain cynicism. The Israelis coming to Germany don't always know how to take it.'[69]

It remains uncertain whether these Israel–German theatrical ventures represent sincere efforts by Israeli playwrights to stir German guilt, or whether they are an attempt to address some notional German-Jewish symbiosis, or give shape to an unconscious sympathy with German anti-Semitism through a transparent distaste for *golah* (diaspora) Judaism. David Witztum suggests that they are no more than a means of achieving the staging of plays which, in his opinion, would otherwise disappear without trace.

Sobol revealed an encounter with a viewer:

After the performance of *A Jewish Soul* somebody, possibly an Israeli *yored* [emigrant], said to me, 'Why do you have to show the Germans this side of us?' I exploded: 'Do you know what an Israeli Jew is today? He's a person who carries on his back and within his soul two thousand years of anti-Semitism and the need to get rid of it. He drags around with him the story of Zionism gone wrong, he drags problems of identity, of ghetto, of collaboration for survival. He's not such a pleasant creature to meet, and if you don't want to, don't invite us.[70]

He adds that Israeli members of his generation have ceased to perceive themselves as victims, just as the younger Germans no longer view themselves as the hangmen.[71] Sobol's responses and those of his interlocutors emphasise the differences in the perception of Jewish history and culture by Israeli writers on the one hand, and diaspora Jews, on the other.

In *The Night of the Twentieth* Sobol contended that Zionism is the product of thinking tarnished by self-hatred, guilt and neurosis; in *Going Home*, he presented it as the outcome of cynical cupidity and materialism, claiming that there had never been a tolerable Zionist philosophy. *Sylvester '72* tells us that Zionism is outdated and irrelevant to the contemporary reality of the Jewish state; in *The Palestinian Girl* we see Israeli institutionalised brutality in action. Nowhere does Sobol indicate what Zionism should be or should have been. His plays are essays in disillusionment and anger. The focus of his drama is still that of social realism with its constant *leitmotif*: the failure of the state to live up to the transcendental and utopian founding ideology. Instead, it is a dystopian entity, the result of a flawed and perhaps even malevolent interpretation of a philosophy, ultimately reflecting the urban European bourgeoisie rather than a socialist agrarian egalitarian society. Sobol is not the first to articulate this complaint: he is, however, the first to have done so in so accomplished and professional a manner.

CHAPTER 5

Hero's end

Sobol's verdict on Israeli society is reinforced in two plays by Hillel Mittelpunkt, one a form of thriller set in a fictitious country, and the other a form of historical documentary based on Israel's recent history. Both works mark a further step in the devaluation of the *sabra* hero and of Zionism, the ideology that gave birth to him. According to Mittelpunkt, Israel has lost sight of its goals and purpose, with power and exploitation replacing individual and collective morality. The *sabra*'s modern incarnation is a parody of the positive heroes who, in their time, captured the popular imagination and constituted an important element of the national mythology.

Alluding to a genre of 1940s black-and-white cinematic melodrama set in some exotic country, Mittelpunkt's *Ahim Laneshek* (Brothers-in-arms) (1992),[1] employs the typical clichés: sleazy cafés, prostitutes, a carnival, immense wealth in corrupt hands, hitmen, drug and arms dealing, a beautiful doomed woman, and a doctor who is unable to heal his own sickness, one in a long line of literary physicians languishing in hot alien lands. The brothers-in-arms are three Israeli ex-soldiers and war comrades now living on an island in the Caribbean. One, Mendel, an ex-*kibbutznik*, is a drugs baron, the second, Bandes, is his henchman and the third is Ganz, a disgraced gynaecologist seeking solace in the lotus land of the islands. Ganz, the play's 'hero', is the *sabra*'s murky shadow: a mercenary with a distinguished history of military service, who, after having been imprisoned in Africa, now seeks his fortune on Banzai, the (fictional) South American island. Mittelpunkt appears to have anticipated events: a case concerning similar Israeli individuals and groups in South America and Africa was publicised some time after the play had been written, but before its production.

Ganz is not entirely devoid of honour. His friend, Bandes, who saved his life in the Yom Kippur War of 1973, is under threat of assassination by the Israeli version of the Mafia, and Ganz seeks him out in order to warn him and repay his debt. Ganz is also not lacking in romance. His ex-lover, Hava, is now Mendel's wife. They resume their relationship and plan to escape together. However, circumstances lead him to return to Bandes in a final futile attempt to save him, and Ganz ultimately commits suicide. His death is ignoble: a hitman hired to kill him contemptuously dismisses him instead. Ganz's suicide is therefore a fruitless act with little of the heroic about it.

All the traditional *Palmah* qualities are perverted in the play: enterprise, courage, personal attractiveness, even honour. 'Israeli-ness' is no longer distinctive, and the men's shared nationality and army service are of no consequence. Even the hitman is an Israeli. Not only has Israel been universalised but it is transformed into a negative myth: its moral hero and propagator of the positive doctrine of Zionism has regressed to become his antithetical mythic image, the moral failure whose domain is physically removed from Israel. The brave Israeli commando is a mercenary, drug peddler and arms dealer, characterised as a 'shadow' by the hired killer. All three men scorn their roots, they have fouled their history and rejected their country. 'You and I,' one of them says, 'we stink from the same tent! The same tent, the same mud, the same shithouse!' Mittelpunkt's characters recognise that the mythology of achievement and power which vitalised Israeli culture from 1948 has been destroyed.

Mittelpunkt was able to encapsulate the despair of the post-1973 generation, a generation of lions suddenly discovering that they are no longer either feared or respected by the rest of the jungle. The core of their lives, their certainty of moral superiority clothed in justifiable power, has vanished. Israel, they realize, is a nation like all the nations, which bears particular comparison to post-Vietnam America in its disillusionment, corruption and opportunism. Zionism preached 'normalisation', the conversion of Jews from alienated dwellers in other people's homes to sovereigns of their own territory. *Brothers-in-arms* carries 'normalisation' to its most perverse extreme.

Mittelpunkt took a further step in his analysis of 1973 and after, offering the *coup de grace* in the process of demythologisation by drawing upon recent Israeli history, which was lived experience for a large proportion of the Israeli public. Whereas *Brothers-in-arms* had taken a cliché of popular culture and transformed it into a metaphor of Israeli decline, Mittelpunkt's documentary drama, *Gorodish* (1993),[2] like Sobol's plays, 'read the present into the past'. It was based on fact, the life of the Israeli general, Shmuel Gonen. Born in Vilna in 1930, Gonen grew up in the ultra-Orthodox district of Jerusalem, Mea Shearim, which is represented in the play by the constant quotation from the biblical text. He rebelled against his ultra-Orthodox upbringing and joined the Haganah to fight in the War of Independence. His performance in the Six-Day War as the youngest general in the army earned him the sobriquet 'the Israeli Patton'. His colleagues deemed him to be the natural successor to the office of Chief of Staff and, had he succeeded, he would have been the first man from a religious background to have occupied the post. After the war he was lionised and celebrated as an authentic Israeli hero. According to Mittelpunkt he was also the representative of a self-aggrandizing, corrupt and arrogant military hierarchy. After having led the Southern Command in the Yom Kippur War (1973) Gonen was charged with serious errors of judgment and was disqualified from future high military office. He resigned from the army and became a businessman and diamond dealer, travelling throughout Africa. He died in 1991.

Gorodish deflates the heroic image of the military command of the war, including that of the normative *sabra*, Moshe Dayan, military hero and Minister of Defence in Golda Meir's government. It marks a further step in the devaluing of the hero and the ideology that gave him birth. The play emerged from Mittelpunkt's 1967–70 regular army service with the Golani Brigade, keeping watch on the Suez Canal. With *Gorodish* an Israeli subsidised theatre engaged for the first time in a direct confrontation with the historical event of the Yom Kippur War through one of the characters most closely associated with it. The ghost of Gonen (nicknamed Gorodish, his original family name) still haunts any deliberations about the tragic blunder of the war of which he became, first, a symbol, and then a representative of the entire tainted mythology of heroism.

Despite Mittelpunkt's claims to the contrary, *Gorodish* was predominantly a documentary play based on recent events and oral testimony, unlike Sobol's carefully researched historical documentaries. Mittelpunkt embellished historical fact with his own glosses. Controversial historical events became a didactic analogy for events in the Israeli present. The play consequently aroused heated public controversy. It served as a further example of a play functioning as a thesis around which the debate proceeded, while the critics by and large took political positions rather than providing aesthetic criticism. Rehearsals were held in the kind of secrecy reminiscent of the atmosphere of a military operations room. Everything connected with the play was deemed to be top secret.[3] *Gorodish* begins in 1989, with the journalist Adam Baruch travelling to Bangui, the capital of the Central African Republic, to hold the first Israeli press interview with Gorodish for many years. After his disgrace Gorodish has fled to Africa to become a diamond dealer. As the ex-general, now bitter and ailing, reminisces, the play flashes back to the mid-sixties when he was the commander of the Seventh Brigade, the Israeli army's first tank brigade. In the play Gorodish is portrayed as a belligerent, sadistic disciplinarian who demands and obtains total obedience from his troops. According to Mittelpunkt's text he is corrupt, crude, brutal and, in a scene with a sculptor named Ulrich[4] in which they test-shoot rifles, something of a psychopath.

Gonen was lauded in a book by the historian Shabtai Tevet which elevated him from an army colonel to a myth and a national symbol. Tevet's 1969 appreciation (in Hebrew *Hashufim Batzriah*, which means literally 'exposed in the turret', published in English as *The Tanks of Tammuz*) painted an adulatory portrait of Gonen and acclaimed him as a new Judas Maccabeus.[5] A part of Tevet's text is quoted satirically in the play:

Six hundred and fifty kilometres from here Shmuel Gorodish is digging for diamonds. In '67, at 37 Gorodish, once Colonel Shmuel Gonen, was the new Judas Maccabeus. He was a hero, he proclaimed freedom, the entire nation loved him. Until '73 he was the good soldier, the one exposed in the turret.[6]

Later, Gorodish mockingly gives a Druze servant a passage to read: 'Exposed in the turret the battle began'. As a result of the victory in 1967 and the idolisation of the military, in the words of one of the army leaders quoted in the Israeli press, 'everyone was indeed drunk with victory between the Six-Day War and the Yom Kippur War but the difference was that from time to time we scolded ourselves and remembered that we were flesh and blood. Gorodish lived on Olympus. He thought that he was the son of the gods.'[7]

Tevet's book and certain newspaper articles, in particular those by Adam Baruch (the last journalist to have met Gonen before his death) provide some of the play's textual sources. For a while it was thought that Baruch, who appears as a character in the play, would take the part of himself but this was ultimately rejected by the director. The play deals broadly with an imagined relationship between the Minister of Defence, Moshe Dayan, and Gorodish, a relationship which sheds some light on Gorodish's rise and fall. Many of their conversations concern military strategy. In one scene, for example, they deliberate about preparations for the war, exploring the struggle for domination between the government and the military. Dayan appears as a kind of evil genius, tantalising Gorodish with hinted promises of promotion in exchange for military successes. The Six-Day War breaks out: Gorodish is prepared and brilliantly fulfils his command. Much of the discourse relating to the armoured division which Gorodish commanded has become part of Israeli culture. At the victory parade Gorodish utters the sentence which had become identified with Gonen until the end of his days: 'We looked death in the face and death dropped its eyes'.[8]

As the years pass Gorodish rises within the military hierarchy, Dayan always at his right hand, still promising glory at every opportunity. One scene takes place in Dayan's house in 1973 and includes a conducted exhibition of his famous collection of antiquities thought, at the time, to be plundered. They discuss the Suez Canal. Dayan proposes ('hypothetically') that in the event of war, an Israeli retreat from the canal could promote subsequent political gain.

Gorodish is then appointed the officer commanding the southern area and on 6 October, 1973 the war breaks out. He receives final orders concerning his strategy but his operations fail and the Israeli army is routed. His downfall follows a chilling scene in which an Israeli platoon at the canal realises it is about to be slaughtered. Pahima, a soldier, entreats the lieutentant, Carmeli, at their position on the canal shortly before the outbreak of the war: 'Come, let's get away from here ...'

CARMELI What?
PAHIMA From the post.
CARMELI Are you mad?
PAHIMA For two weeks we've been sending reports to army intelligence, someone's wiping their backsides with them ...
CARMELI It's just manoeuvres.
PAHIMA And if it isn't? We're nineteen *Freiers* [dupes], three of them are cooks, they've never fired a gun in their lives ...

CARMELI Keep watching! [*Cranking the telephone*] Ninth Battalion . . . What? What's immediate? 'Operation Dovecote' immediately? What the hell is 'Dovecote'?[9]

PAHIMA [*Puts down the binoculars incredulously*] They're going into the water . . .

CARMELI What?

PAHIMA They're going down to the water!

CARMELI Who?

[*Silence. A flash of light engulfs the position. The men are frozen to the spot and then – darkness*][10]

In 1974, after the war, the actions of Shmuel Gonen and his fellow commanding officers were examined by the Agranat Commission, headed by Judge Shimon Agranat, which was established to investigate the failure to anticipate and counter the coordinated Egyptian-Syrian attack. Mittelpunkt uses the Commission's actual findings as the text of his play's hearing, although the full account of its deliberations has not yet been released. The actual Commission laid the primary blame on the military leaders, David Elazar, then Chief of Staff, the head of Military Intelligence Eli Zeira, and Gonen. It found that in the first instance Gonen had failed to request reinforcements and that he erred in the timing of the deployment of his armour. The Commission suggested that Gonen and Zeira be relieved of their duties, and Elazar resigned. Prime Minister Golda Meir and Moshe Dayan were exonerated. In 1994 Zeira broke a two-decade silence, publishing a stinging memoir which accused the Agranat Commission of having shielded those primarily responsible for the disaster, Meir and Dayan. Gonen also attempted to counter the Commission's conclusions from Bangui where he was then living. Popular opinion claims that Gonen died three times, the first when the war broke out, the second when the findings were published and he was relieved of his military command, and the third time in September 1991 when he died of a heart attack in Milan at the age of 61. It was said that he died of a broken heart and many deem him the final victim of the Yom Kippur War.

The source of the controversy following the play was not the presentation of Gonen as a flawed hero, or the caricatures of Dayan and Meir but the play's underlying thesis – Mittelpunkt's contention that the political establishment was prepared to sacrifice soldiers in the Yom Kippur War for the sake of future political gain. Epstein, Gorodish's *aide-de-camp*, a fictional character in the play, presumably

Figure 3   Hanokh Levin, *The Child Dreams*.

the spokesman for the playwright himself, proposes that Dayan and other members of the Israeli government deliberately employed flawed military strategy before appointing an unprepared Gonen as head of the southern command a few months before an *expected* Egyptian attack. The reason, which Epstein suggests to Gorodish's defence counsel, is that by generating high Israeli casualties and offering the Egyptians a symbolic military advantage and partial victory, Dayan hoped to render both Israel and Egypt more amenable to eventual peace negotiations. In the event, he and his colleagues underestimated the strength and organisation of the Egyptian attack. Neither Israeli nor American intelligence considered the Egyptians ready for war. The Bar Lev line, a complex network of Israeli fortifications in the Sinai peninsula, was manned by no more than a small number of reserve troops. It proved to be a failure during the war in 1973. 'Every military cook knew that there was no Bar Lev line, that the positions in the canal would not hold and that the soldiers in the line were sent to their death.'[11] Former Tel Aviv mayor Shlomo Lahat, at one time Gonen's commanding officer, strongly objected to Mittelpunkt's views: 'I accept that the government of Israel might have been guilty of incompetence but I

Figure 4   Amnon Levi and Rami Danon, *Sheindele,* 1993.

totally reject the idea that it would deliberately abandon its soldiers in such a manner.'[12] The play is reminiscent of Oliver Stone's film *JFK* in its charge of political conspiracy on a grand scale.

One of the difficulties Mittelpunkt encountered in his recreation of these events was the sensitivity of those acquainted with Gonen, and of members of all the protagonists' families. He attempted to overcome such problems by a rather ingenuous denial of the play's documentary or biographical nature. It is true that many of the characters and the encounters are fictional, including scenes with Dayan and Golda Meir; also, certain events transcend any form of realism. For example, a young soldier, Friedman, who has committed suicide, haunts Gorodish throughout the play, and he is visited by a mysterious old blind woman, Um Naji, who offers advice, a type of chorus to his quasi-tragic hero. According to Adam Baruch, the play incorporates a number of genres, including realism, the thesis, and surrealism. In the realist mode Mittelpunkt not only recreates the historical characters but also offers incisive, idiomatic dialogue. In the surrealist phase, he summons Um Naji and Friedman's ghost; in the thesis phase he raises the ideological issues.[13]

In the first instance the ghost of Friedman provides a view of Gorodish's cynical cruelty in the matter of the disposal of his body, and an observation on the sacrifice of the individual soldier to the hierarchy's manipulative discipline. Friedman is more fittingly 'the biographical memory of every second Israeli, the memory which returns us to war. Its small candle remains and accompanies us in all our ceremonies amid the general understandable repression of the rest'.[14] He represents the play's topics of death and tragic fate, and the unacknowledged guilt of Gorodish who is unaware of Friedman's presence until himself reduced to a sacrifice. The equally symbolic Um Naji serves as an allusion to Brecht's *Mother Courage*, and, in her prophesying the hero's success and failure, Tiresias the seer in *Oedipus Rex*.[15] The old woman utters the most significant injuction of the play: 'Ay, ay, General, General ... you still don't see. People loved you because they saw in you everything they wanted to see in themselves and they hate you today because they see in you everything that they hate seeing in themselves.'[16] This is a transparent valedictory to the founding mythology and its central personality, the *sabra*-hero.

Mittelpunkt's purpose is embodied Um Naji's words: he attempts to interpret not only the man Gorodish but, more particularly, the time. In his words,

Gorodish is for me the most extreme sign of the period because the Yom Kippur War was born when the Six-Day War ended and Gorodish was turned into a national hero ...[17]

Like most of my generation the Yom Kippur War was for me a turning point, the beginning of disillusionment with some of the myths of Israeli society. For me this was a time when the dream of an 'imperial Israel' was at its peak and Gorodish fervently believed in it and embodied this myth.[18]

Mittelpunkt therefore takes Gorodish as the symbol of a period of national self-esteem during which the glorification of power was primary, a result of 'the national paranoias upon which the children of the *Palmahnikim*[19] were educated, and the yearning of an entire nation which in six years had established an empire to its vanity'.[20]

The outcome of the national *hubris*, as of Gorodish's own, could only be catastrophe. Also, the play provides a criticism of certain establishment figures of Gorodish's day who are still to a large extent revered in our time. It casts doubts upon the integrity and political ethics of an entire generation of national leaders, Meir, Dayan, Bar Lev (Israeli Chief of Staff, 1967–72, later Secretary-General of the Labour Party) and Ariel Sharon (the controversial right-winger who was Gorodish's rival for his post).

The staging of the play utterly contradicted Mittelpunkt's uncompromising condemnation of militarism as an end in itself, and the military establishment that misjudged events so disastrously in 1973. It was bombastic, incorporating national flags, stirring music, the kind of theatrical iconography suggestive of fascism. The result was the audience's identification with the trappings of national glory without understanding Mittelpunkt's satirical attack on it. The play is now given in schools as part of a patriotic, self-enhancing exercise and Gonen is seen as a victim of a misguided regime.

One of the central problems of Israeli drama is illustrated by this play in spite of its strong story and emotional impact. Despite his equivocation about his play's documentary nature, Mittelpunkt has done little more than dramatise facts which are already well known to the Israeli public. Consequently the Israeli audience is obliged to rely too much on its own cultural information

like a child who is told the same bedtime story night after night. The audience coming to *Gorodish* knows what's going to happen and it's impossible to surprise it with changes to the story. When, in the second half, a placard is hung on the curtain with the date 1973, you can hear the whispers of the excited viewers: 'now, now it's coming'.[21]

If the audience has no part in the 'dream of an imperial Israel' or one of national glory, peace or power, or any of the characteristically rhetorical ideologies arising from the Six-Day War, the play and the character of Gorodish are almost incomprehensible. Uncontextualised historical events in themselves do not suffice. The 'dream' referred to in the reviews is not explained in the play; the social and political background, the people's beliefs, the relationship between them and Gorodish, their changing view of him, and much else that was at the forefront of the Israeli consciousness at the time, remain beyond the play's boundaries. Mittelpunkt has rested his story on the assumption that all this is known, if not lived, experience. Baruch believes the play is directed at those groups of whom Gonen was a part, including the ordinary soldiers who suffered from the arrogance of leaders like him, Meir and Dayan, rather than to future audiences.[22] He suggests that the play will be incomprehensible to them since it is not nourished by its understanding of an individual soul or endowed with human depth. Moreover, it does not consider moral issues or a political culture external to a particular period.

This chronologically-determined play is therefore likely to mean little even to local audiences who have changed with time and events. Most critics agreed that Mittelpunkt wasted fine opportunities for strong dramatic development, sources for which exist in Gonen's extraordinary biography. On the other hand, according to Michael Handelsaltz, *Gorodish* is important as collective therapy in which the theatre reflects the public's own image.[23] If so, the play is a personal reckoning for each member of the Israeli audience, a disturbing emotional confrontation with his or her immediate past.

The reviews of *Gorodish* are as interesting as the play itself, concentrating on the political standpoints of the playwright and the critics themselves. Their reviews articulated many of the questions raised by the play: for example, did the generals indeed place themselves above law and morality? Was there any form of cooperation between the government and the army or were they rivals? If so, which was in the ascendant? While provoked by the play these are not aesthetic questions; in fact, they have little to do even with Mittelpunkt's narrative.

Shabtai Tevet unintentionally summarises a similar anomaly in the reception of Israeli drama in his attack on the play's blend of documentary and fantasy. 'How is the man in the street going to be able to distinguish in this mix of imaginings and libel between what is true and what are lies?'[24] Ben Ami Feingold censures Mittelpunkt for creating a work less concerned with Gorodish the man than with his symbolic significance for the playwright himself.[25] In this instance these and other writers have misconstrued the drama's purpose: it is not intended as a kind of television actuality whose audiences search in it for the truth. According to Peter Weiss, 'It is a matter of keeping an artistic balance between fact and fiction, truth and imagination'.[26] In this sense, as with much Israeli drama, *Gorodish* is little more than the continuation of an argument, a public *sihah*. On the other hand, this reinforces the drama's function as a continuing thesis, permitting it a dialectical voice.

In *Gorodish* fact and fiction, truth and imagination are all subordinated to the play's overriding agenda. Mittelpunkt has set out not to recount Gonen's biography or his downfall but to condemn the culture of power that arose in Israel between 1967 and 1973 with its origins in the founding ideology. This is not merely a retrospective sneer at history but a caution against the ideology of physical power as the highest value. Although, like much other Israeli drama, the play reconstructs historical events, it offers itself as a warning about the potential in the present for a recurrence of similar events through the perpetuation of military violence. A soldier tells Gorodish in the play: 'Once we believed that military strategy would be determined by political judgments; we're standing on the threshold of a period in which our politics will be determined by military judgments'.[27] In another scene, while Gorodish is making a stirring speech, a dead soldier salutes. This is a well-known quotation from the film *Patton*, ironically altered by Mittelpunkt to correct the distortion of the collective memory.

Michael Handelsaltz commends Mittelpunkt for arousing the Israeli conscience while Ben Ami Feingold censures him for using the rise and fall of Gorodish to symbolise the rise and fall of Israel's image as strong and great after the Six-Day War.[28] The other side of the political argument is represented by an article in the religious *Hatzofeh* which sarcastically deplores the sacrifice of the ex-Orthodox officer: 'He didn't sit around the campfire with the rest of the *Palmahniks*, he studied in a *heder* [religious elementary school] and in the Etz Hayyim *yeshivah* [Jewish religious academy]'. The same paper criticises the past and present governments for their willingness to sacrifice soldiers for political ends, adding 'Even today doesn't the readiness of the political establishment to sacrifice the [Occupied] Territories gnaw in our hearts?'[29] Like the reviews in the liberal newspapers, but ideologically antithetical, this article uses the play to condemn government policy past and present.

In his satirical revue *At Ve'ani Vehamilhamah Haba'ah* (You and I and the Next War), (1968), Hanokh Levin parodies a Gorodish-like general's bombast and mocks the myth of the 'few against the many'. In Mittelpunkt's play the character of Gorodish is transformed into a symbol of Israeli demythologisation which had been gaining strength since 1973. The play constituted a further step in the playwright's examination of the ultimate consequences of Zionism in practice.

CHAPTER 6

The issue of religion

There is a new custom in the land. You want to be popular – hit at the *haredim*. ... The formula for success is simple: take an anthropological section from Mea Shearim or Bnei Brak [ultra-Orthodox areas]. Display it in all its details – as voyeuristic and base as possible – add a bit of ideological conflict which in any case makes a play, rub in a little implied eroticism and lo and behold you have a certain mixture which would come out well in every *cholent* oven in Rabbi Akiva Street in Bnei Brak, even more so when it is presented on the boards of the Cameri Theatre for an audience that devours the religious every evening with a great appetite.[1]

On 14 May, 1948, the Israeli Declaration of Independence proclaimed, *inter alia*, that the new state would be 'founded on the basis of freedom, justice and peace as envisaged by the prophets of Israel'. It would, moreover, 'ensure the freedom of religion, conscience, language, education and culture'. Nevertheless, Orthodox Judaism plays a stronger part than any other religious affiliation in the political life of the country where the Orthodox political parties form one of the three major party groupings. Problems connected with their religious law and practice have divided the nation from the very beginning.

Jewish Orthodoxy and the rabbinate were not central to mainstream Zionist aspirations or to the culture of the new state, although the secular Zionists did not envisage Israel as a totally secular state. It was to be a Jewish state despite Herzl's strong advocacy of the separation between religion and state as an attribute of 'normalisation'. The structural tension between the religious and secular meaning of the 'Jewish state' became an issue only after the establishment of Israel.[2] In his play *Das Neue Ghetto* Herzl had provided an unflattering portrait of a rabbi, Dr Friedheimer. He realised, however, that it was essential to placate those religious Jews who believed that a return to the Holy Land could only be achieved through the coming of the Messiah, and at the second Zionist Congress of 1898 he supported a resolution which defined Zionism as aiming at a spiritual revival of the Jewish people, founded on modern culture and its achievements. He pledged that Zionism would not undertake anything contrary to the injunctions of the Jewish religion.[3]

While none of the Israeli religious parties have suggested that Israel should be governed according to Halakhah (Jewish law), they strongly promote their idea of a state based on the principles of the Torah and to this end they have established a network of educational institutions which they control. With increasing political power, they seek to promote legislation which preserves the status of Orthodoxy as the only recognised form of religious Judaism, and to legislate for specific religious interests, such as the Sabbath and festival observance, and *kashrut* (ritual lawfulness, especially of food). They use their political power to prevent legislation which would directly conflict with Orthodox Jewish law or interests and have, for example, succeeded in prohibiting civil marriage and divorce in Israel. The Orthodox are seen as 'flag-bearers of an ideology that wishes gradually to turn religious law into state law'.[4] Following the Six-Day War a new messianic religious element entered the arena, the nationalist *Gush Emunim* which became a recognised group (never a political party although enjoying much parliamentary support) in 1974. This group was – and still is – perceived by its opponents as a dangerous *political* faction bearing within itself the monstrous apotheosis of unchecked Zionism.

For some years the political power of the Orthodox in Israel, allied for the most part with the right wing, has been growing. Recent decades saw the rapid evolution of the messianic but non-nationalist ultra-Orthodox Jewish sects (*haredim*) usually constituted by hassidic[5] Jews, politically conservative and religiously extreme. These are often termed 'black' by their Israeli non-Orthodox opponents, because of their characteristic black outer clothing. Another comparatively recent phenomenon is the group of Repentants who are usually, although not exclusively, young, who move from various degrees of non-Orthodoxy to Orthodoxy in a spirit of repentance (*teshuvah*). Following the assassination of Prime Minister Yitzhak Rabin in November 1995, by an Orthodox student identified with the religious Right, the suppressed Orthodox–secular[6] hostility erupted into an open confrontation, fortunately confined to verbal offensives and printed rhetoric.

Amos Oz quotes a *Gush Emunim* spokesman who equates 'religious' and 'secular' as 'Jew' and 'Israeli' respectively, and refers to the battle between them:

[T]he major barricade is the one that divides the Jews from the Israelis. The Jews are those who want to live, to one degree or another, in accordance with the Bible. The Israelis pay lip service, maybe, to the heritage, but in essence they aspire to be a completely new people here, a satellite of Western culture. For many of those Israelis the Land of Israel is no more than a 'biographical accident' ... *Eretz Yisrael* means very little to them.[7]

The mutual suspicion of Orthodox and secular Israelis stems from the restless impulse of enlightened Jewish thinkers towards intellectual freedom, new ideas and modernity. On the other side stand the forces dedicated to protecting the *status quo* and often their own power as well. The conflict reached its peak during the great Jewish cultural movement of the eighteenth and nineteenth centuries, the *Haskalah* (Enlightenment). One of its influential proponents, the reformist poet Judah Leib Gordon, wrote scathingly about religious anti-rationalism, the pilpulistic (ultra-legalistic) blindness of the Jewish clergy. Joseph Perl and Isaac Erter, Enlightenment satirists, attacked the *hassidim* in lacerating satires which portrayed them as ignorant, corrupt, crude and superstitious.[8] Zionism was not kinder to religious zealotry, having risen on the barricades of post-*Haskalah* secularism and seeking to create the 'new Jew' who was free of the physical and spiritual physiognomy of his ghetto forebear.

Who was this 'religious' Jew or '*hassid*' who appeared in an unaltered guise for over a century in the secular literary consciousness? This consciousness did not ignore the nobility of Jewish religious tradition and its representatives, the great rabbinic sages of the past and present, or the pious Jews who constitute part of any community, or any shades of observance or piety in between. It was not the piety or the tradition in themselves that the secular writers disdained, but those religious representatives who positioned themselves as a bar to the community's intellectual or political development. Before political power became an issue in Israel, the Orthodox hierarchy was perceived as inimical to Jewish *cultural* development, to enlightenment and to reason. In contemporary

Israel the secular public has come to resent religiously-based legislation which conflicts with the accepted norms of a secular democratic society. At stake is the very identity, the self-image of the state itself. As far as the religious camp is concerned, increasing secularism and modernism with its trail of moral laxity threaten the substance of Jewish values.

In Israeli drama the battle lines between 'Israeli' and 'Jew' are drawn with increasing animosity. Ultra-Orthodox factions, supported by religious forces in the Knesset, constitute a strong voice of opposition to the modern theatre, and are particularly vociferous about original Israeli drama, not least of all about plays by established left-wing dramatists. Religious elements constituted the strongest opposition to the abolition of theatre censorship, mainly on the grounds of immorality and offence to the Torah. It is impossible to estimate the number of plays left unstaged due to the pressure of religious groups or following the disapproval of Orthodox elements within the Censorship Board itself, and the government. The small, but voluble and very prominent group of popular playwrights is still, even after the repeal of censorship, assailed – often without their plays having been seen or their texts read – by religious disapproval. Playwrights, aware that their drama is able to initiate crucial debates within Israeli society, often respond with exaggerated provocation. This is perhaps to draw their religious antagonists, who in Israel are political antagonists as well, into an open conflict.

Many early satires had presented the 'Orthodox' character as the introjected negative stereotype of global anti-Semitism: a black-clad zealot with a skullcap and sidecurls, venal and intolerant. In 1957 a revue, *Datiata* by Dan Ben Amotz and Dan Almagor, satirised representatives of the religious establishment including the ultra–Orthodox *Naturei Karta*. *Datikan* (a pun on the Hebrew word for religious, *dati*, combined with 'Vatican') was designated the seat of the Israeli Chief Rabbinate. The restaging of Molière's *Tartuffe* in various forms and adaptations in Hebrew and Yiddish, indicates the continuing antagonism towards the religious, the *hassidim* in particular. From the *Haskalah* the figure of Tartuffe, or at least a Tartuffe-like hypocrite, has served writers of all subsequent periods (including Sobol) in the struggle against religious intolerance. The Orthodox and, later, *haredi* (ultra-Orthodox) character is therefore a semiotic construct, a symbol of one of the most painfully and bitterly debated conflicts in Israel today.

From 1972 to 1993 at least thirty original plays (excluding satires) on the topic of Orthodoxy were staged. Many of them attempted to analyse the nature of messianism, with Zionism as its corollary. With varying degrees of explicitness they depict Zionism as a movement with the potential for generating dangerous metaphysics. For example, Yosef Bar Yosef's *Hakivsah* (The Sheep), (1970),[9] was closer in spirit to later and more aggressive plays in its depiction of the excesses of extremism, culminating in an act of archaic ritual which is entirely contrary to the spirit of modern Israel. A later play, Gavriel Ben Simkhon's *Melekh Morocco* (The King of Morocco), (1984),[10] also illustrates the danger inherent in religious fervour. It ends with an entire community facing suicide as a result of the erroneous identification of messianic portents.

Two plays by Yehoshua Sobol reinforced secular fears. In *Status Quo Vadis* (1973)[11] he opened the play with a recording of Ben-Gurion's voice reading the Declaration of Independence in May, 1948. This document became the punching bag against which many Israeli political plays built their muscle. *Status Quo Vadis* takes as its adversary the Orthodox clerical hierarchy which, Sobol claims, opposes the principles of individual freedom embodied in the Declaration. The play attacks the hypocrisy of ritual by showing, through a series of absurd episodes, the social tyranny of the minutiae of religious legislation. While his examples, selected from the daily press, interviews, sessions of parliament and court registers, are in themselves extreme, they serve as metaphors for the limitation of individual freedom by primitive and illogical forces. *Status Quo Vadis* does not discuss religious principles or attack Jewish Orthodoxy; its target is exclusively the religious *establishment*, and the political establishment as yet only by implication.

Five years later Sobol created another episodic play, partially based on the earlier material but demonstrating his view of a sinister change within the religious camp. In *Hozrim Bitshuvah* (Repentance), (1977),[12] the Orthodox are attacked not because of their increasing dominance – which is presented with some ironic humour on the stage – but because of their identification with Israeli militarism and expansionism. What in the earlier play had been represented as a powerful social force encroaching on individual liberty, was now seen as a significant *political* force, more diffuse and dangerous. The previous play's target had been the government which permitted religious coercion; in this later version Sobol and his director Ilan

Ronen turned their wrath toward the social conformity which not only permitted this coercion but encouraged it. In *Repentance* Sobol characterises the return to religion as something akin to a plague of rhinocerisation (*hitkarnefut*), referring to Ionesco's play *Rhinoceros* where people metamorphose through their absolute conformity into rhinoceroses which eventually control society. Sobol warns against the friendly or beguiling face of religion which assumes intellectual and spiritual control over ordinary people despite their own beliefs, and then manipulates them for political ends.

This play sees Orthodoxy not only as a symbol of totalitarianism but as totalitarianism itself. It presents average citizens initially worrying about the effects of religious domination. A character asks: 'Do you know what will happen if they dare to ban football on the Sabbath? Blood will be spilt!' Someone assures him: 'Don't worry. They won't touch sacred things'. While a group of men and women are chatting in their living room about the effects of the official religious policy, a visiting collector for a religious charity hands out skullcaps and headscarves and gradually trusses the people hand and foot with the straps of the phylacteries which also bind their mouths. This is neither an original nor a subtle image and the play's dialogue often verges on the rhetorical, but the situation and its implications were unique in the drama at that time. In a heated discussion about the settlements in the Occupied Territories one character asks: 'Are you against?' The other replies, 'God forbid. The question is, how do you justify it to the outside world?' 'Tell them simply: every place that the sole of your foot shall tread upon, that have I given unto you.'[13]

The principal burden of this play is in the contradiction of moral values encountered in the extreme militarism of the religious with their justification in the Bible. Sobol describes the repentance, that is, the movement of *teshuvah*, the return to Orthodoxy, in terms of popular fashion rather than true epiphany. He sees religious revivalism in Israel not as something sincerely embracing profound religious principles, but as a superficial trend even more insidious and dangerous in the short term because of its exploitation by the ruling powers.

Shmuel Hasfari's *Notzot* (Feathers), (1988)[14] (based on the novel by Hayyim Beer), attempts to achieve a nostalgic backward glance towards childhood, the time of political innocence. Such sentimental journeys are rare in the drama despite their almost obsessive prevalence in the fiction. *Notzot* deals with *haredi* life in Jerusalem in the 1950s. The messianic dream disintegrates in the face of political reality, particularly the Yom Kippur War. The play ends with the narrator, having reconstructed his life as a child, briefly referring to his work as a war gravedigger. He not only has to bury the corpses but find fragments of the bodies and put them together.

This is not to say that all plays on religious topics were disguised examinations of Zionism. There were many plays on Jewish themes which presented Judaism much more positively, portraying the ultra-Orthodox optimistically and even modernising them to the extent of dressing them in jeans. Numerous stories, including some by S. J. Agnon, were dramatised in order to redress the anti-religious balance and to provide some thread of continuity from an idealised Judaism of the past to the present time. Dramatic transcriptions of talmudic material, legends, and the tales of Nahman of Bratslav proposed the same significance to modern Jewish existence as it had possessed in the past, but their simplicity did not entirely mask the eternal tension between the old, traditional Jewish world and modern Israeli culture.

One of the most active theatre groups in Israel is the all-women Jerusalem Theatre Company, an experimental company dedicated to creating theatre with the focus on Jewish sources, Bible, Talmud, Mishna, Aggadah and Midrash.[15] The interpretation of these texts is mediated through the figures of women in Jewish history such as Queen Esther, Sarah, Abraham's wife, and Bruria, the enigmatic wife of the sage, Rabbi Meir. As a contrast to the prescriptive, well-made mainstream plays of largely polemical modern content, the J. T. C.'s plays are experimental, combining readings from the sources, songs and narrative, jazz and dialogue. They avoid decontextualisation or social and political sententiousness, presenting the stories within their own settings. Almost as a rebuke to the those playwrights who analyze Zionism through its religious offshoots, the J. T. C. avoids any religious argument, claiming that Jewish sacred literature is a cultural heritage which belongs to all of us and not only to the religious world. Rather than being detached from contemporary life, their style of playwriting suggests that the reinterpretation of biblical and other texts helps to reassess certain contemporary events, such as the Lebanon War and the post-war moral and political turmoil.

The centralisation of religious issues became one of the dominant issues of the drama in the 1980s and 1990s. Not only do these plays implicitly or explicitly reflect the struggle between Orthodox and secular in Israel, but they are increasingly based on factual documentary material. It is not yet clear whether these plays have been written in response to the growing conflict between the Orthodox, who hold the political balance of power in the government coalition, and the secular Israelis who fear their power in temporal life; whether the various religious movements are perceived as the teleological outcome of Zionism, or whether the plays constitute a cynical means towards sensationalism and controversy. The principle of any publicity being good publicity may well have spurred some playwrights to confront this difficult topic, for many of these plays became the subject of parliamentary debate and the Censorship Board's deliberations.

The 1980s saw the emergence of a playwright who viewed Israeli culture from a perspective not yet seen in the drama. Shmuel Hasfari, who for a while was the artistic director of the Cameri Theatre, is not only a man of the theatre but an observant Orthodox Jew who, as all the reviewers hasten to point out, wears a knitted *kippah* (skullcap), signifying Orthodoxy without its messianic extremes. He was educated at religious schools and studied Jewish philosophy at the Hebrew University in Jerusalem. After completing his studies Hasfari founded his own theatre group, *Hateatron Hapashut*. His list of plays is long, most of them dealing with religious Judaism or the 'religious'-'secular' confrontation. An opponent of all kinds of religious extremism, Hasfari examines Jewish fundamentalism in all its guises: messianism, religious nationalism, repentance, all the more excessive streams of Jewish Orthodoxy. He, like the members of the Jerusalem Theatre Company, has attempted to discover a meeting point between Jewish sources and the modern theatre. In his case, however, the encounter is generally ironic or satirical.

Hasfari's first major play, *Tashmad* (1982, 1992)[16] set the tone although its theme relates to settler politics as much as to religious stereotypes. The Jewish year 5744 (corresponding to 1984) is written as an acronym, *tashmad* which incorporates a Hebrew verbal radical indicating 'destruction'. The play won first prize at the 1982 Acre Festival and was revived in 1992 with no loss of its relevance. It was born out of a failed attempt to write a drama about Jacob Frank, the charismatic messianic charlatan of late 18th-century Poland.

Tashmad presents an apocalyptic scenario which takes place on the evening of the ninth of Av, the annual commemoration of the destruction of the Temple. Israel is in the process of ceding Judea and Samaria, (the settlers' names for the occupied territories on the West Bank) following an ultimatum by the superpowers. In synagogues and shelters throughout the West Bank many settlers threaten to destroy themselves if forced by the surrounding Israeli security forces to leave. This is an ironic inversion of the Massada story, for in *Tashmad* the oppressing forces are internal, rather than invading enemies. Four settlers have enclosed themselves in a bunker and threaten to blow themselves up if their demands are not met and if the Israeli army attempts to remove them. Three of the four characters are representative of streams of Jewish fundamentalism in the heart of the West Bank. Nahman, an Orthodox Jew awaiting the coming of the messiah, detests nationalism or Zionism, declaring that for him a prayershawl and the national flag are incompatible. Leibo is a *moshavnik* (cooperative settlement farmer) who works on the soil, a liberal secular nationalist; the third character is a young woman, member of *Gush Emunim*, who has brought her baby nephew to the shelter in order to strengthen the rebels' terms; and Yaakov, a repentant with a dubious past who claims to be the messiah. The conflict between the four is as complex as their psychotic struggle with the powers outside the bunker. The *sabra*, Leibo, who has served in the Israeli army, despises Nahman, the fervent proponent of messianism, because of his religious zealotry and his avoidance of military service. Yaakov the madman transforms the fast day to a festival of indulgence, mocking the naïve anticipation of the messiah who, in his distorted imagination, is himself. The situation is further complicated by a television crew which attempts to film the four protesters in their shelter.

Like Lerner's *The Pangs of the Messiah*, *Tashmad* draws upon Jewish national and religious extremism on the background of real conflict and fits well into its political framework, encompassing the settlement movement (*hitnahlut*) the increasing messianism amongst the militant Orthodox and the distorted political situation following the Lebanon War. Also, it obliquely refers to 1984, the dystopian Orwellian nightmare, through its doom-laden acronym. *Tashmad* can also be viewed as an allegory of despair at the failure of redemption. It is also a frighteningly proleptic image of the relationship between extremism and madness, and the propensity of both to lead to total destruction. In one way or another Hasfari works this latter assumption into all his plays.

In an essay on the play, the veteran novelist and ex-*Palmahnik* Aharon Meged comments that the only character likely to arouse both mockery and compassion in the audience is the 'blond, Aryan, athletic *sabra* with beautiful hands who is entirely devoid of any spiritual burden'.[17] It is he who will set the charge that will blow up the bunker and all its inhabitants. Meged's point about Leibo's spiritual poverty, as opposed to the spirituality – albeit distorted – of the three others, is an interesting one. It adds something to the continuing discussion about the *sabra* hero, the icon rendered void like Matmor's Danny Keresh, and who died, as David Grossman wrote, with the murder of Rabin.[18] Even those, like Meged, who represented him, who, in fact, *were* him, are now denying him. According to Meged, Hasfari's characterisation of Leibo illustrates his own view of a generation which lacked any form of spiritual sensibility.

Hasfari uses Jewish sources – Halakhah (Jewish law), Aggadah, Kabbalah (body of Jewish mysticism), passages of prayer, sections from the Midrash and certain mystical rituals – to good effect in his defiant theatre, and he reveals his knowledge of Talmud in *Matan Torah Beshesh* (The Giving of the Torah at Six), (1988),[19] in which the biblical Moses is erroneously time-transported to present-day Mea Shearim, the ultra-Orthodox neighbourhood of Jerusalem. Through the device of Moses's presence in the Israel of the 1980s, Hasfari is able to censure the distortion of the Torah and its values by certain religious groups. His third play, *Gisato shel Goldin* (Goldin's Sister-in-law), (1986),[20] a convoluted melodrama replete with mysteries, crime and fanaticism, contemplates the violence implicit in the phenomenon of repentance. The play emerged, according to Hasfari, from his horror at hearing several rabbinic fulminations: for example, their claim that the death of twenty-two schoolchildren in a bus accident was a consequence of the desecration of the Sabbath. Much of the play consists of quotations taken from religious repentants whom Hasfari mocks. It is an exploration of the dark powers of demented religiosity, messianism, the frightening significance of repentance as a breakdown of rationalism (even religious rationalism) which presents itself as a plague of spiritual suicide and regression.

Hasfari has a private quarrel with the ultra-Orthodox which has less to do with their effect on the body politic than on normative interpretations of Orthodox Judaism. His antagonism is therefore derived from an internal conflict of theology, ritual and belief, whereas that of the other writers is external, a *political* fear of the encroachment of the ultra-Orthodox, 'the threat of a law of darkness, a forceful return to the spiritual climate of fundamentalist Khomeiniism'.[21] For Hasfari they represent a threat to his religious principles. His *Kiddush* (1985) depicts through the inter-relationships within a claustrophobic family, the process of empowerment of the religious Zionists. The principles of traditional religious practice, such as keeping the Sabbath, are so opportunistically manipulated and abused by the parents that the son eventually abandons them, and Israel, to make a new, secular, life in America.

Hasfari's dramatic literature is particularly important for avoiding condemnation of the official religious as in Sobol's *Repentance*, or inserting himself into the minds of the settlers, as Lerner attempted to do in *The Pangs of the Messiah*. To a large extent his plays and others on the subject of religious extremism are preaching to the converted. Mainstream theatre audiences are predominantly secular, while the majority of criticism from the religious camp follows the practice of relying on texts rather than productions. Still, since he speaks from within Orthodoxy, Hasfari's views have been taken seriously by the religious establishment, to the extent that one of his satires, *Hahiloni Ha'aharon* (The Last Secular Jew), (1986), was briefly banned before being allowed with cuts. This futuristic cabaret offers a brief review of the 'unfortunate experiment' of Zionism. It takes the form of a cabaret with a master of ceremonies called Shlang. In a series of songs and sketches Hasfari offers a review of the country transformed from the State of Israel to the theocracy of Judea where Arabs and secular Jews have ceased to exist. There is no doubt that this play attacks the ultra-Orthodox and the Repentants, and contemplates the danger posed by religious zealotry to the ordinary religious and secular publics. It is also crude, its vulgarity apparently meant to reveal the naked corruption and hypocrisy of the ultra-Orthodox establishment. Prior to banning the play the Censorship Board concluded that it 'seriously affected fundamental values and the feelings of a broad public, religious and secular alike'. Hasfari alleged that the banning proved the very claims made by the play.[22]

Those who oppose him on religious and ideological grounds react more fiercely than those who question the aesthetic quality of his

Figure 5   Molière, *Tartuffe* (director Gedalia Besser), 1985.

plays. For example, a columnist, called only 'Yoav' supplies a 'recipe' similar in spirit to the one quoted above, in a long diatribe on the subject of *The Last Secular Jew.*:

Make a list of ten to twenty terms taken from the anal zone, terms of evacuation or sexual intercourse and then make sure that not one of them is missing from your stage dialogue. Add to this, to the best of your taste, somebody from a minority, from the Occupied Territories who is being oppressed under the Israeli jackboot. Season all of this with some fine young men with sidecurls and prayershawl fringes and you have a complete original Israeli play of which no important or distorted detail is missing.[23]

However sarcastic, this 'recipe' summarises many of the predominant traits of the plays concerning the ultra-Orthodox, and also suggests that they appeared in thematic groups according to sociopolitical events, again confirming the drama's documentary nature. Plays aimed at addressing anxieties within the public often appear as discursive adjuncts to significant public events.

With *Fleischer* (1993),[24] Yigal Even-Or set out to create a polemic, to weight the argument against the *haredim* and to serve a warning upon his audiences. It was a clumsy but earnest attempt through an unrefined allegory to demonstrate the effects of the ultra-Orthodox encroachment on the lives of ordinary Israelis. It is wholly contentious, a volley from the secular camp, resembling a tract rather than an artistic work.

Bertha and Aryeh Fleischer, survivors of the Holocaust, living in a secular neighbourhood, are confronted by members of an ultra-Orthodox community who are colonising the neighbourhood, and told to leave. At the start the Fleischers do not object to the new development because they see in it social and economic opportunities. On the contrary, Fleischer, a butcher, attempts to placate the new religious community by pretending to sell kosher meat and wearing a *kippah*. He does not, however, fool his new neighbours and he is required to buy a certificate of *kashrut* for an inflated sum of money. This obliges him to use his and Berta's savings. As an act of angry protest he removes his certificate of honour from the War of Independence and hangs the *kashrut* certificate in its place:

FLEISCHER I've survived the Germans and the Russians and the Poles and the partisans and the British and the Arabs so there's no reason why I shouldn't survive the Jews as well ...

As the ultra-Orthodox fill the area, the secular begin to leave.

Apart from their rabbi, the *haredim* are portrayed as ingratiating and dangerous, their behaviour a caricature and their language an unctuous parody:

HUND With the help of the Holy Name. With the help of the Holy Name, may His Name be blessed.
BERTA ... I have a headache. I'm going inside.
HUND Heaven forbid, Mrs Fleischer, it's your house. Here you are the ruler and queen.
BERTA I'm glad to know that. I'm going to put a crown on my head.

A somewhat *grand guignol* reign of terror begins. The Orthodox have eyes, spies and informers everywhere so that the secular families are obliged to work in secret on the Sabbath; religious children cut elderly people's television antennae and water pipes, they throw stones at them on the Sabbath, they poison an old woman's cats and destroy the garden that she is nurturing. Fleischer and his friend, Gershon, both ex-soldiers, are now marginalised by the violent, strong breed of religious autocrats. Gershon, who in fact is their spy, had served as an informer for the Nazis in a concentration camp during the war, a clear parallel that is renewed throughout the play.

Because of the money they have been compelled to pay to the religious, the Fleischers are no longer able to keep Shloymele, their retarded son of 30, in an institution. Shloymele constitutes a point of confusion in the play, weakening Even-Or's case for, not knowing better, he rapes a young Orthodox woman, presenting the Fleischers' religious adversaries (and the audience) with a good reason for wanting them to move away. Ultimately the couple die in a fire accidentally set by Shloymele, while their neighbour, Rosa, who has supported them in their conflict, succumbs to a stroke. The play ends with a Jobian argument, suggesting that it is as much an indictment of God as of the religious.

Rosa, an elderly widowed ex-teacher, provides the strongest articulation of anti-Orthodox feeling, fuelling the criticism that the play generates Israeli anti-Semitism. She complains that the *haredim* are stealing the country from under the noses of the general population without encountering any opposition. Her particular target is the *haredi* lawyer, Hund, and his tireless attempts to persuade her to leave. She rails against him and the Orthodox after they have poisoned her cats:

I need a gun. I must have bullets. I know exactly what to do with them. I would burn them by their beards. I would hang them by their sidecurls. They only understand power just like the Arabs. They are in their own ghetto. They only have to raise their heads – one blow and they are back in their hole like rats, like it used to be outside this country. The animals detest them with reason. A knife in the back is all they know. Today they poison cats, tomorrow people. A synagogue ... a hot, crowded smelly market and all of them screaming. A black coat in the middle of August. Who knows how many layers he's hiding under the coat. It's not Poland here. I'm not even speaking about the beard and the side-curls, if he were to do any real work for one day in his life he wouldn't dare to walk around like this. I don't know whether this is because of respect but he stinks, that's for sure.

Berta, the wife, says: 'It would be enough that he's 'black' but he's also a lawyer' to which her husband replies: 'The Jews' profession'. It is difficult to estimate the extent to which Rosa's words reflect the playwright's opinions for, when accused of anti-Semitism Even-Or rather ingenuously responded, 'It's not me speaking but the character Rosa'.[25] Nevertheless his replies to questions in interviews indicate at least some resistance to the *haredim*.

Fleischer had been on offer to the large theatres for seven years until eventually the Cameri accepted it, moving it from the Beit Tziyonei America (The American Zionist House) either because its time had come or because Hasfari was the theatre's artistic director. The play caused an almost unprecedented row in a culture of rows. Six opposition Members of the Knesset raised the *Fleischer* issue in the Knesset, terming the play anti-Semitic, anti-religious, defamatory and rabble-rousing. One of the Members (National Religious Party) had earlier requested the Attorney General to launch a criminal investigation into the play, citing Section 173 of the penal code which forbids the publication or performance of material that discredits religious faith or sensibilities. Many of the critics writing in opposition to the play, in addition to the MKs, had not seen it but were appraising it according to the text. The *haredim* also examined the play for illegality which they did not find. The furore led to the reopening of the question of censorship, the reason being the Cameri's public subsidies primarily from the Ministry of Education and Culture and the Tel Aviv Municipality.

The debate encompassed the issue of freedom of speech, but a freedom with varying interpretations. For example, one of the religious Members of Parliament, Yigal Bibi, declared his support for a proper argument and freedom of speech, 'but freedom of speech should not be identified with the anarchy of speech particularly when it becomes racism and self-hatred'.[26] The problem in Israel is not one of self-hatred but, on the contrary, hatred of an entity which can be defined as an 'other', far removed from, and threatening to, the perceived self.

An Orthodox newspaper, *Yom Shishi*, claimed that the Orthodox in *Fleischer* are negative stereotypes while the playwright has used every device possible to favour the oppressed secular family: they are old, they are survivors of the Holocaust and they have a retarded son. In fact, Even-Or to an extent attempted to redress the balance and mitigate his hostility towards the *haredim* by making his secular characters, his putative heroes, utterly insufferable. Fleischer and his wife Berta are dishonest, Fleischer sells pork, his memories of the past are tinged with contempt for himself and his generation. The *haredi* rabbi, on the other hand, is portrayed as a gentleman, courteous and dignified, with the performance of one of Israel's finest actors, Yossi Yadin, doing much to add depth to his character.

The 'secular' columnists accused the religious of fundamentalism and the Orthodox accused the 'secular' of irresponsibility and perversion, calling for a renewal of censorship or some legal form of interference. A moderate concluded that 'when an objective viewer of an Israeli play reaches the conclusion that if he wants to save his life he must go and burn down a religious neighbourhood one must then read the writing on the wall'.[27] Two members of the *Likud* prepared to lead a public debate about the theatres' utilisation of public funds for 'extremist' plays. They, too, discriminated between freedom of speech and the taxpayer's right to withhold support from 'extremist' statements. Michael Eytan MK declared, 'there are expressions in the play in which, if you had to exchange the word 'Orthodox' (*haredi*) with the word 'Arab', there would be a cry to the heavens and the play would not have advanced beyond its first performance'.[28] The Mayor of Tel Aviv wondered with weary irony whether the Cameri had not actually called upon 'these religious gentlemen' in order to create a furore and bring audiences into the theatre. One of the liberal weekend newspapers confessed that the play appeared to be an instigation to violence against the religious. A religious spokesman questioned the nature of original Hebrew drama, claiming that even 'rubbish' from abroad would be preferable to it. The furore regarding *Fleischer* led to a further parliamentary argument about the function of the playwright, one formulated according to the MKs' own political views. When a parliament undertakes to prescribe the playwright's agenda and defines the role of the artist in society, freedom of speech is seriously threatened and censorship becomes possible once again.

The playwright defended himself by denying that the play was racist and claimed that comments overheard in the streets confirmed that that the play expresses the sensibilities of a large proportion of the non-Orthodox community. At some performances the audiences cheered at many of the more rabid remarks, laughed and shouted words of agreement. When Fleischer declares, 'Those people, just lay a hand on them and the government will fall' there was a sigh of agreement from the audience, 'a silent amen from the depths of the heart.'[29] However, during one performance a woman shouted to Yossi Yadin, who played the rabbi, 'I wish you would die'. This was not a condemnation of the rabbi as a character but of the actor playing him. While Even-Or claims to support neither religious nor secular fanatics and to be free of partisanship, he admits that his purpose in this play was to arouse the public and to warn them that the events of the microcosm should not be permitted to extend to the macrocosm. The play consequently becomes a totally political instrument.

The *haredim* must not steal the country from us and the secular should not, through sheer confusion, reach the point of terrible hatred for them. They must stop sweeping everything under the carpet, they should look at themselves in the mirror and see the dangerous polarisation, the two camps ... it can happen that soon the war with the Arab countries and the Palestinians will come to an end and then what? Then we'll wake up to a war of the Jews. The destruction of the Temple, so they say, happened not because of the Romans but because of Kamtza and Bar Kamtza [internal Jewish dispute]. We must not refuse to see that Kamtza and Bar Kamtza are living among us again ... [30]

Even-Or declares, further, that the 'secular' must fight for their beliefs and their values as the ultra-Orthodox do for theirs. His views are echoed by a popular columnist, Hirsch Goodman: 'Continuing to wear blinkers and pretending there is not a problem is not a solution. It is a quick way to an inevitable conclusion that the ultra-Orthodox see very clearly and we fail to recognise'.[31]

The press played its part in intensifying the row: *Ma`ariv*, for example, ran a photograph of Shloymele raping Hava with the caption: 'A temporary victory for the secular in *Fleischer*'.[32] Almost with one voice the reviewers for papers with a religious alignment alleged a clear comparison in the play between the *haredim* and the Nazis. For example, after being offered assistance by the rabbi for his move from his house, Fleischer says bitterly 'I once saw how courteously and honorably they turned Jews from their houses – in cattle cars'. The reviews demonstrate that the inaccuracy of factual statements about the play, its plot and its staging, is in direct proportion to the emotional agitation of the reviewers *on both sides*. Their reviews are manipulative, politicised and tendentious; one, for example, speaks about the 'retarded child' as indicative of the playwright's excessive sympathy for the Fleischer family. It omits the inescapable fact that the retarded 'child' is thirty years old and guilty of rape. Another example is a long, confused, angry sentence, referring to culture and art: 'The fact that the state assists and partially supports a play like this, that the Ministry of Culture, yes, the one that contains those who wish it to remain in the hands of Shulamit Aloni,[33] gives assistance to a theatre in order to allow it to present Nazi plays like these on its stage"[34]

Public discussions took place after two of the performances. These were less an exchange of ideas than a 'squaring up of unbudgeable opposing sides.'[35] The argument transcended the play and its egregious qualities, moving into the general religious–secular discourse, an argument in which the play is almost irrelevant except as a motion around which the debate raged. Critics saw themselves as warriors in the ideological war, taking issue with the ideas in the play rather than with the play itself. Even Michael Handelsaltz, a perceptive and sober drama critic, was driven to rhetoric by the play. After condemning Even-Or's crude emotional manipulation through utilising the Holocaust and mental retardation, Handelsaltz warns that 'those who speak in the name of the religious whose feelings are hurt by this play might do well to ask themselves what it is that arouses the secular public, the makers of the play and its audience to feel as they do about the religious community'.[36] Sarit Fuchs, also usually even-handed, rejects complaints that religious feelings have been wounded; in her opinion, it is not their faith that is being criticised but their actions.[37] Other reviewers cross their professional boundaries when, for example, a writer protests that Fleischer was not alone in suffering during the Holocaust, for many religious Jews were also victims; or, from the other side, that ultra-Orthodoxy 'is a system that from an historical point of view actually caused a demographic reduction of the Jewish nation'.[38]

In summoning the spectre of the secular community's fear of the *haredim*, *Fleischer* and other plays on the topic of religious culture fulfil an important ideological function regarding Israeli identity. This is an increasingly potent topic on the Israeli stage. Playwrights do not explicitly declare the reason for their anti-*haredi* bias whether, in their opinion, *haredi* dogma represents a distortion of Zionism or a threat to personal freedom, to the liberal basis of normative Judaism or to the future of Israel, or all these. On one level it seems to be no more than a question of representation, the extent to which the ultra-Orthodox are perceived to be the representatives of Israel. If so, this might justify the accusations against the non-Orthodox of 'self-hatred' or anti-Semitism: distaste for the so-called 'blacks' suggests distaste for the stereotype of the Jew, a stereotype with which the secular Israeli fears being identified. On a deeper level extremist Judaism is a threat to freedom, it creates an 'atavistic fear in the face of unknown forces'.[39] The religious and secular are respectively designated as 'black' and 'free'.[40] If nothing else, these plays seem to confirm that 'Israeli' is one thing and 'Jew', something else.

The aesthetic value of the play is of less importance than its message. The viewer seeks 'at least an echo of the doubts that are perturbing him in terms of social identity'.[41] The rhetoric of Amir Oryan's review is as fiercely one-sided as that of the pro-Orthodox critics, to the extent that he fails – as do the latter, for their own purposes – to see the character Fleischer's own faults. Oryan adds a dimension to the allegorical aspect of the play by viewing the son, Shloymele, as an ugly mutation of the *Palmah* hero and therefore of Zionism, a blind power like Dr Frankenstein's monster or a *golem* that has been harnessed by the Orthodox, for the rabbi takes in Shloymele after the death of his parents.

The critical rhetoric raging around *Fleischer*, expressed almost exclusively in the Israeli press, became too hysterical to be of value as a serious assessment of a dramatic work. 'Secular' critics produced more recognisable theatre criticism, although they too were not averse to taking ideological sides. Many of them praised the production and the acting, and the more well-disposed conceded that these elements improved the play. Most agreed that it is over-melodramatic, relying on emotionally-charged issues such as the retarded son, the Holocaust and Rosa's personal tragedies.

Even as an imperfect melodrama, however, the play raises important questions. It may treat its themes inexpertly – the issue of freedom of choice, the separation between religious establishment and state, democratic pluralism, Zionism and the image of the state – but it served to intensify the argument and keep it at the forefront of the public's attention. Its importance was reinforced by its reception by the audiences. Attendance figures proved this play to have been highly successful, with 56,264 spectators having seen it. It was nominated as one of the top ten most successful plays of 1993 and 1994, with only a little over 50 per cent of the total audience identifying with the secular characters. Yet religious spectators reported that they sensed such hostility and even hatred directed at them that they felt inclined 'to take off their skullcaps.'[42]

In *Sheindele* by Amnon Levi and Rami Danon (1993)[43] there was no obviously tendentious objective. Levi, a journalist who has studied life among the *haredim* for over a decade – his research resulting in a factual full-length account of their lives[44] – intended to examine an incident of internal conflict. The play revealed the dynastic and power struggles within the *haredi* community and within the family, the accreted customs of different groups, the effect of halakhic rule on women's lives, the relationship between the individual in these communities and the community itself. There was little in the play to create revulsion in the audience, certainly no more than could be derived from a story about any closed community. Had it been a foreign ethnic group, for example, a similar story might have aroused astonishment and perhaps distaste, but not the antagonism that emerged against the ultra-Orthodox community, anticipated by the critics and the play's opponents.

Sheindele is intended to be seen as a foretaste of the situation that would arise were the Orthodox ever to achieve a political majority, and Israel become a *de jure* theocracy. The play was based on a case, widely reported in the Israeli press, concerning a young ultra-Orthodox woman, Hendele Feinstein, who was divorced against her will. Her husband subsequently remarried but Hendele, refusing to accept his decree of divorce, would not remarry. She therefore became a self-created *agunah*, a woman neither married nor, in her own eyes, free to marry. The play tells the story of Sheindele, the daughter of a powerful rabbi, now deceased, and his formidable, property-rich widow, Feige. For ten years Sheindele has been married to Yoelish, a brilliant rabbinic scholar. The community's rebbe (religious leader), sends Yoelish to take control of a famous *yeshivah* in America for two reasons: the first is Sheindele's barrenness which prevents Yoelish from fulfiling the commandment 'be fruitful and multiply'; the second, which is less pious, is that the rebbe wishes to leave the dynastic succession open for his own son, the less favoured Yosl. In doing so, he antagonises Feige who takes her revenge by banishing forty-five American families from the community, even digging one of them out of his grave and reburying him under the rebbe's house. The rebbe, unable to persuade Sheindele to divorce Yoelish, invokes the halakhic rule whereby the signature of one hundred rabbis will secure a divorce despite the wife's opposition, and allow the husband to remarry. The play ends with Sheindele's madness: she appears barefoot and bareheaded before the rebbe, ranting about the body beneath his house.

Sheindele fulfils the drama's educational function by attempting to teach the audience something about the religious communities, but it is scarcely an accurate portrait. In a work based on the abuse of power within a significant community in Israel, Levi's and Danon's characters are no more than stereotypes which prevent the play from achieving emotional depth. Reviewers, aware of the importance of the issues involved, concentrated on matters of thematic truthfulness rather than on the quality of the play or the production, although this was discussed. The two playwrights claimed that everything in their play had either happened or could have happened,[45] but without supplying an emotional peg on which to hang the action, the play has no greater value than a televised documentary. *Fleischer* did not propose to reproduce an event but it aroused a strong response in the audience. *Sheindele* was to a large extent a series of tableaux which neither instigated an argument nor required an emotional response.

Levi and Danon portray the *haredi* world as dominated by male laws enforced by the men and helplessly entrenched by the women. Without exception, the play's female characters are prisoners, even the rabbi's widow who is bound to her dead husband's *herem* (ban) against Sheindele's moving to America, and young Rochel, Sheindele's friend, who suffers from acute anxiety of no specified cause. At the core of the play is the problem of the status of women in a community ruled by Halakhah. Both Sheindele and Rochel are powerless, unable to take personal decisions, Sheindele (like the real Hendele) remaining at the mercy of the rebbe who has sent her husband away. Sheindele's mother, although dominating, is bound by her dead husband's ruling about America, and forbids Sheindele to join her husband there. Yoelish himself does nothing at all. Sheindele's barrenness renders her a non-person in the community: a childless woman is without quality, particularly in a prominent family. She is therefore useless, no more than an object to be utilised as a tool in the dynastic struggle. By emphasising the inferiority of women in halakhic law, the play also emphasizes the unbridgeable gap between ultra-Orthodox culture and that of normative, non-Orthodox or secular society.

Sheindele's transformation at the end from a subservient, passive young girl to an angry, vengeful woman standing dishevelled and wanton before the rebbe redeems the play with a moment of good theatre, while losing all verisimilitude. At this point Sheindele becomes a little like a Jewish version of Ibsen's Nora, suddenly discovering a certain individual power rather than passively remaining the property of a man.

The play could perhaps have incorporated a version of tragedy, having as its subject a society in which the individual confronts an utterly intractable system; however, there remains only the possibility of tragedy, attempted too late with Sheindele's rebellion. Her brief escape on her own to Nahariya offers possibilities which remain unexploited and we retain only outward events rather than inner development. Arthur Miller discloses the crucial element of the playwright's internal vision in his discussion of Ibsen's *Hedda Gabler*:

Ibsen's focal point of attack, his contemporaneity, was rebellion against small-town narrowness, smugness, the sealed morality whose real fruit was spiritual death. But we cannot bring *his* context to *Hedda Gabler* any more. Society, conditions, have melted away and she lives autonomously now, a recognisable neurotic who transcends her historical moment. The journalistic shell of a play – its reflective mirror surface – is its moral part without which it could not be born. But its transcendency springs from the author's blindness rather than his sight, from his having identified himself with a character or a situation rather than from his criticism of it.[46]

Unfortunately *Sheindele* allows for little but the reflective mirror surface.

At the same time, the fact that *Sheindele* and *Fleischer* were produced in the same year and that Hasfari's work has enjoyed popular success for some years, indicates that there is a continuing need for plays on the topic of the religious-secular *kulturkampf*. The transfer of *Fleischer* to a central mainstream theatre signifies a certain dialectical trend within the society. The question is whether the plays establish an anti-religious mythology, whether they merely supply the audiences with the sensationalism they require or whether they contain a more profound, unstated agenda. If these plays express apprehension and constitute warnings these are not only of the *haredim* and their lifestyle, but of the extremes to which Jewish self-realisation may ultimately lead.

Few critics were able to take *Sheindele* seriously, despite the seriousness of its intention. One of those who did, Daniela Fisher, rejected the claim that the characters were stereotypes and affirmed that they allowed audiences 'a peep into the *haredi* community.'[47] On the other hand, the play was compared first to a soap opera, then to a Mafia family battle.[48] Others condemned its banality, superficiality and lack of real characterisation, pathos or profundity. Despite the play's basis of fact, an Orthodox reviewer concluded that the playwrights are so unenlightened about religious life that his daughter was not offended by *Sheindele* because she could not recognise in it anything of her world.

The framework of protest need not be as culturally defined as *Fleischer* and *Sheindele* to be effective. Modern Hebrew writers have always reworked their literary tradition to provide themselves with new spiritual and cultural definitions. In Israel not only their own but foreign canonic literature is appropriated and then reinterpreted to suit new cultural purposes. The usual 'channels of decoding' vary from culture to culture, the result being a variety of culturally determined readings and responses.[49] For example, a group of African writers seized on Shakespeare's *The Tempest* as a way of intensifying their demands for decolonisation within the framework of the dominant culture. Israeli playwrights, like the Africans, practise deliberate interpretative 'error' by which they generate 'an *alternative* orthodoxy responsive to indigenous interests and needs'.[50] Protest through an established work becomes a matter of focus and interpretation.

The Cameri's production of Shakespeare's *The Merchant of Venice* in modern dress (1994) served as another link in its chain of anti-Orthodox plays, a part of the *Sheindele* and *Fleischer* cycle. In this version of the play Shylock is transformed into an armed West Bank settler. The villain at the heart of the religious–secular dispute is not the *haredi* but the religious Zionist.

Figure 6   Poster for Shakespeare's *The Merchant of Venice* (director, Omri Nitzan), 1994, showing Yossi Graber as Shylock.

The play, directed by Omri Nitzan, was set in a warehouse filled with merchandise. Despite Nitzan's claim that he had set out to present both sides of Shylock's character, the visual aspects of the production subverted his intention by immediately indicating an anti-Orthodox bias. Where the text of a play is already known to the audience, the *mise en scène* will be interpreted against that knowledge. In the case of Nitzan's *The Merchant of Venice*, they could immediately decode his various visual signs. Dress, posture and body language established the contrast between the homosexual Antonio, his friend Bassanio, and Shylock. The costumes offered a variety of non-verbal signs, metonymically making the distinction between the diaspora Jew and Gentile or the ultra-Orthodox and the secular Jews in Israel. Antonio and the other young men were fashionably dressed as prosperous urban yuppies while Shylock wore a grey business suit and a homburg, clothed, according to one of the reviews, like a Tel Aviv pawnbroker of the 1950s and 1960s.[51] This corresponds to the image the *sabras* would have held of the diaspora Jew at that time.[52] At the start of the play Shylock is presented as a clean-shaven gentleman who wears a small *kippah* under his homberg. At the end he appears as a religious fanatic bent on revenge: he wears a large white *kippah*, he has grown a beard and his face is ferociously angry. The veteran actor, Yossi Graber, made of Shylock a vengeful militant with enormous, maniacal eyes.

Much of the criticism of Nitzan's production of *The Merchant of Venice* was defensive, as if the play had indeed been *written* by a *haredi-*hating secular Israeli. Few attempts by directors throughout the ages to soften the caricature of Shylock the Jew have succeeded. He is an anti-Semitic stereotype, despite his eloquence, and if the play offends the Israeli audience it should perhaps be stricken from the repertoire, like Wagner's operas. Once the play is given, however, protest against the text is inappropriate for it does not reach audiences and critics as a surprise, certainly not in Israel where the play has had numerous productions over the years. Audience, director and actors are partners in a contract with the theatre that has selected the play for production. Viewers expecting anti-Semitism are obliged to calculate their own strategies of response to it and to each new version of the play.

Some viewers are not able to do so. Shmuel Schnitzer exemplifies the indignation aimed not only at Nitzan's production of *The Merchant of Venice* but also at the text. He begins his essay by accusing the Israeli audience of being mesmerised by the name of Shakespeare to the degree that they fail to recognise the play's anti-Semitism. Instead of being offended and insulted when a Jew is spat upon, kicked, robbed of his daughter and then choked on the cross, his possessions divided amongst the Christians, they laugh. 'This mockery of Jewish honour and the mockery of truth achieve a commendation on the part of the audience who, it seems, does not listen to the text offered to it and does not understand that Shylock the oppressed, the mocked and degraded, the robbed, is us'.[53] Further, writes Schnitzer, the image the Nazis apportioned to the Jews is a direct progression of Shakespeare's view of Shylock. Schnitzer does, however, admit that the character's psychological and ideological change of focus is dependent upon the interpretation, but concludes that Nitzan's version could be seen as an anti-Semitic Israeli production of an anti-Semitic play.

Nitzan clearly chose to interpret the character as one of the protagonists in the Orthodox-secular *kulturkampf*. In his production the famous monologue is not highlighted but subsumed into the action. The ultimate humanity of Shylock, if it exists at all in the play, is not attempted. Shylock's essentially comic stubbornness, which Schnitzer excuses as 'human zealousness', becomes religious extremism which places the play within the *realpolitik* of modern Israel. As Shylock is transformed from a quiet gentleman into a religious zealot, he removes his hat and dons his white skullcap and prayershawl. At one point he aims an imaginary machine-gun at the other characters, to complete the image of the angry settler. Schnitzer comments that for the sake of political authenticity Nitzan sacrifices the elements in the play that transcend the clichés of anti-Semitism. His views are echoed by the Israeli historian Shelomo Zand:

'We are left with a totally anti-Jewish play, an impression which the moments of an almost-pogrom do not alter. It seems as if Omri Nitzan deliberately wanted to make a connection between a Jew without protection in a hostile society crying "pour out your wrath upon the nations" [Jeremiah 10:28] and between "pour out your wrath upon the nations" of a Jew armed with a rifle running amok in Hebron'.[54]

The point of these reviewers is that we should not include every religious Jew in the category of fanatic or militant.

Zand alleges that overt anti-Semitism is erupting in Israel.

Certain members of the public have in the past called for the hanging of the ultra-Orthodox from telephone poles and a well-known left-winger has claimed that when he sees them he understands the Nazis' actions. This play spreads oil on the fire of hatred. The stereotype of the corrupt ultra-Orthodox will penetrate the hearts of the audience and this is how it began in Germany.[55]

He then offers a warning about the rise of neo-Nazism in Israel. Other critics also experienced a sense of unease despite their agreement with the production's sentiments. Some newspapers ran pictures of Graber as Shylock, looking murderous and wearing his large *kippah* while running his fingers across the blade of a knife, ready to plunge it into the Gentile's chest in order to claim his pound of flesh. Zand accused the Cameri Theatre of 'expertise' in the appropriation of the theatrical image of the '*yehudon*' (a pejorative term for a European Jew) and mentioned *Fleischer* in this regard.[56]

It is difficult to determine the nature of the Israeli public's 'horizon of expectations' with regard to this play. Even approved readings of it leave the public with the matter of anti-Semitism and Shylock's demand for his pound of flesh. Nitzan's rendition *justifies* the loathing of the Jew, allowing the liberal, secular Israeli audience to endorse the traditional anti-Jewish bent of the play. Nitzan himself is unequivocal about the purpose of his production: to raise questions about extremism in Israel. Like many others, he sees the Hebrew theatre as a document, for he expressed the hope that the play would lead to public discussion and 'touch the open nerves of the Israeli public. This is [the theatre's] function'.[57] Everything that Shakespeare presents in *The Merchant of Venice* is 'tied to our reality, to our inner world. I have put on this play as if it were an Israeli play ... it has a specific relationship to religious fanaticism'.[58] However, when asked whether his Shylock is intended to recall Baruch Goldstein, Nitzan replies that the association must be the viewer's.

Shylock does not reject the notion of an eye for an eye. There is no place in him for compromise. It can't be a good Jew who wants to cut up flesh. I think Shylock is a bad Jew who's hit upon a fanatical situation. It's impossible to speak to him about mercy or pity. He's also a terrorist and a madman because he insists that they understand him. There's no symmetry with Israeli reality but there are associations. I understand the process Shylock undergoes as a kind of Orthodoxy that moves towards extremism; religious fanaticism without any compromises.[59]

As with many discussions about the nature of *The Merchant of*

Venice, Nitzan becomes confused in his own argument. He claims that there is no danger of its arousing anti-Semitism in Tel Aviv as it would abroad. 'What we can do is only return to the place in which this play will serve as a mirror.' Yet if Jews see themselves in the mirror of an anti-Semitic play, this is indeed anti-Semitism. It reflects them as Shakespeare saw them. Nitzan's somewhat obscured point is that this image of Shylock is the mirror image of religious extremism rather than of the average Jew or Israeli.

CHAPTER 7

The political uses of the Holocaust

In Israel not even the Holocaust was spared enlistment into the arguments about Zionism. The Israeli literature on the topic has become a means for advancing the debate. It is a small, but significant, body of literature, the reasons for its sparseness open to conjecture. Generally they seem to converge on two possibilities: methodological constraints on the authors and the demands made by the founding ideology.

We, the audience in Israel, have had a problem from the start relating to the subject generally and its staging in the theatre in particular. Our attitude to the presentation of events from the Second World War and the destruction of the Jews through art generally and on the stage in particular is very complex.[1]

There is also the question of the moral seemliness of creating art about the Holocaust at all, whether memory and history should be transformed into creative art. We must transmit memory', writes the Israeli novelist Aharon Appelfeld, 'from the category of history to the category of art'.[2] On the other hand, Claude Lanzmann, director of the film *Shoah*, argues, 'The Holocaust is above all unique in that it erects a ring of fire around itself . . . Fiction is transgression. I deeply believe that there are some things that cannot and should not be represented'.[3] He therefore denies the possibility of any but documentary representation of the Holocaust. Arnost Lustig writes:

While history, philosophy, psychology or sociology each stands alone, literature includes all of them and re-creates all elements into its own literary amalgam, out of which comes something that exists nowhere but in literature.[4]

Either way, there has been a *crisis* of representation brought about by many generic, aesthetic, epistemological and ethical difficulties peculiar to Holocaust literature, for example, its exact status within generic categories, its reception and evaluation, and the feasibility of its composition. The ethicality of creating this literature is a subject which provides the substance for a continuing debate too extensive and complex to summarize. Not least of all is the problem of language: the horror of genocide remains outside its boundaries to the extent that 'silence' has become, among other things, a theoretical construct to indicate various experimental means of language use. George Steiner and others have demonstrated the inadequacy of language to convey the concentration camp experience, and survivors repeatedly emphasise their inability to find the means to communicate it. Primo Levi, for example, affirms that 'our language lacks words to express the offence, the demolition of a man'.[5] Paul Celan has striven to reinvent or reform language in order to establish a new lexicon of meaning and, failing that, to find a medium for conveying silence. Jerzy Koszynski's novel *The Painted Bird*

explores "the new language of brutality and its consequent new counter-language of anguish and despair". The boy protagonist of the novel suffers a period of muteness before being able to speak and bear witness. His struggle against speechlessness signals the author's effort to forge a "new language" for Holocaust narrative.[6]

It is not only language that presents an obstacle to communication and understanding, but the tension between the nature of life within and outside the concentration camps deters writers from exploring the nature of the victims' experiences. As Levi commented, even after the war, when the full atrocity of the camps had been exposed, no one wanted to listen to survivors.[7] Similarly, Appelfeld:

And just as the [survivor] witness could not continue to stand in the space of this terror, neither could the Jew who had not experienced it. A kind of secret covenant was created between the survivor witness and the one to whom, as it were, this testimony was directed, a covenant of silence in the path of which many misunderstandings have accumulated.[8]

Appelfeld alludes to the methodological difficulties inherent in breaking the silence, implicitly asking whether it can be done at all. The Israeli poet Leah Goldberg questioned the ability of fiction in particular to convey the truth:

Somehow, when a person who has experienced either the most terrible or the most elevated things tries to convey them in the form of a play or a story he makes a separation between himself and the experience so that its telling becomes a kind of pose. More than once I've had the opportunity to read the works of people from there, from the death camps, and it was impossible not to sense a kind of sham in their words because in addition to talent courage is also required ... For that reason we very often find more life in diaries and letters ... words that don't pretend to be art ...[9]

Ideological tension provided a further impediment to the creation of literature in Hebrew about the Holocaust. During the 1920s and particularly the 1930s, when Hebrew literature was shifting its centres of production and diffusion from Europe to the *yishuv*, the condition of European Jewry was not unknown, even though the *yishuv* Jews were accused of being 'passive and neglectful of events taking place in Europe'.[10] Hebrew writers commented upon their own helplessness in relation to these events but their ideological disconnection from the diaspora was already implicit in their physical relocation to Palestine.

Why did the Zionists in Palestine fail, on the whole, to express strong solidarity with their brothers in Europe? The reasons were ideological and not merely psychological. Zionism was a revolution in Jewish life, and the Jewish tradition of lamenting collective persecution, which Zionism considered a poor substitute for action, was one of the cultural tendencies they wanted to reform. At the time of the Holocaust Ben-Gurion did not believe it possible to do anything practical to save the Jews of Europe and what was not practical did not interest him.[11]

Ben-Gurion and other Zionist leaders, including Weitzmann (themselves immigrants) treated the diaspora with disdain. Ben-Gurion 'regarded the Holocaust as the ultimate fruit of Jewish life in Exile. As such it represented a diaspora that deserved not only to be destroyed but also forgotten'.[12] To add insult to injury,

[T]he historical interpretive scheme of the *yishuv* reflected negatively on the moral character of the victims and survivors of the war by suggesting that their fate was due to the sin of having made excessively naïve assumptions about the future of the Jews in the diaspora that prevented them from emigrating to the Land of Israel before the war.[13]

Although the *yishuv*'s stance vis-à-vis the Holocaust is still a source of debate, it seems that in order to assuage their sense of guilt, many immigrants to Palestine 'began blaming the victims for marching to their death like sheep to the slaughter'.[14] Later, Israeli responses appear to have incorporated guilt, denial, distaste, rejection and a sense of literary impotence. Alan Mintz suggests that shame rather than grief and the shock of loss resulted in the 'conspicuous avoidance' of the Holocaust in their literature.[15]

Zionism could not assimilate the Holocaust in its scheme of national rebirth and the creation of the New Jew except by discovering a *national* significance to it. Appelfeld cites the humiliation induced by the the *yishuv* generation's simplistic historical formulas: exile was to be followed by redemption; Zionism would redress the problem of assimilation; the pioneers were wise, contrary to the dangerous naïeveté of the diaspora Jews. National revival was the important consequence of suffering; associated with this was the idea of cause and effect, the 'festively adopted' conviction that mourning is followed by celebration. 'In fact,' Appelfeld continues, 'it is practically a law ... that on the ashes of one period will rise another'.[16]

Already well equipped with a pre-existing system of linguistic and metaphysical signs, the Jewish historical imagination was able to integrate these structural processes. The Holocaust was therefore utilised as yet another symbol in the process of national revival and in the establishment of a pride of national achievement. Israel was indeed *geulah*, salvation. The least uncomfortable method by which the Holocaust could be incorporated into the national consciousness was to retreat from its horror 'into the comfort of facile explanations'.[17] Heroes of resistance during the Holocaust were celebrated as a 'bridge' leading to the revival of the nation of Israel. The rest were relegated to *galut* (exile). 'The Holocaust seemed to affirm what Zionist education had claimed, that the future belonged to the national revival in the Land of Israel. Jewish life in exile could lead only to death and destruction'.[18]

Classical secular Zionism had always been equivocal about East European Jewish culture which the Hebrew novelist Hayyim Hazaz, had identified *inter alia* with a world of 'oppression, defamation, persecution, martyrdom'.[19]

The very image of the 'ghetto Jew' represented the essence of what was corrupt and soiling in Jewish life ... European Jewry was thought to be destined sooner or later either to wither or be swept away... The dominant emotion elicited by the Holocaust among the *Palmah* writers was shame: shame over the impotence of the *yishuv* to affect the loss of their murdered brethren, and shame over what they perceived to be the submissiveness of European Jews in their extermination.[20]

The notion of 'lambs to the slaughter' became the prevailing image of the diaspora Jews to the *sabras*. This idea of fatal submissiveness was at best strange to the generation of fighters and heroes, and at worst contemptible. For the *sabra* it was difficult to dispel the deeply held conviction that *galutiyut* (diaspora life) signified nothing but fear, weakness and humiliation. 'Weak fathers gave us life and hysterical mothers brought us up. This is what has rotted inside: fear of the world and a lack of security'.[21]

This attitude, represented as political justification in Sobol's *The Night of the Twentieth*, was explicitly expressed in the early literature, and not uncommon outside it:

Generations of youngsters had been brought up to believe that the existence of the diaspora was not only a catastrophe but a disgrace. Jewish victims of Nazism were often thought to have gone 'like sheep' to the slaughter. I remember a Hebrew textbook, widely used in Israeli high schools until at least the late fifties, which included the following analysis of the Hebrew poet Bialik's great lament on the Kishinev pogrom of 1903: 'This poem depicts the mean brutality of the assailants and the disgraceful shame and cowardice of the diaspora shtetl'.

In this odd text, the words 'disgraceful', 'shame', and 'cowardice' were the key terms that pointed to the heart of Zionist education. In the shifting moods of remembrance and rejection, younger Israelis were at first torn between anger and shame at having such a cursed past.[22]

In Yigal Mossinzon's *In the Wastes of the Negev* Avraham proclaims:

I at any rate won't be a refugee! Enough! I won't live in a strange house! I won't wander the byways! We're fighting a war for Jewish independence – and we'll achieve it with less blood than is spilt – for nothing – in one Polish *shtetl*. For nothing ... I could have been in Warsaw, unarmed! To be slaughtered like a sheep! Today I have weapons, not many, but I live in hope that the ship will come. Cannons will come, our planes will fly in these skies – and until then, fight, don't give them any respite, know that this is the first time it's not for nothing. I want to appear in my Danny's eyes as a person who has fought and not as a miserable refugee who has run away from his country. This is the only soil that doesn't turn us into refugees and beggars.[23]

Optimism, achievement, men and machines deployed in the heroic struggle – these are the most decisive contrast to 'lambs to the slaughter', the Polish *shtetl* and the unwelcome negative image of diaspora life.[24]

Some of the most canonic Hebrew writers held negative views of European Jewry. For example, the novelist and playwright Yehudit

Handel offered her appraisal on a national television programme in 1989:

If I'm to be blunt there were almost two races in Israel. There was one race of apparent sons of gods. These were the ones who had the honour and privilege to be born in Degania, in Shehunat Borokhov, Givatayim, and apparently I belong to these sons of gods. I grew up in a working-class neighbourhood near Haifa. And then there was – it's possible to say it – an inferior race. People we looked at as inferiors who have some kind of blemish, a hunchback, and these were the people who arrived after the war. I was taught at the school for workers' children, that the ugliest thing, the most lowly thing is not exile [*galut*] but the Jew who came from there.[25]

Segev also quotes Leah Goldberg, herself born in the Ukraine and an immigrant to the *yishuv* in 1935: 'This people is ugly, miserable, morally equivocal, difficult to like'. The Israeli writer was expected to discover in the new immigrant-survivor someone more than an unfortunate refugee living off his or her wits but this would be a task requiring 'a massive effort'.[26]

Israeli denigration of the diaspora (*shelilat hagolah*) incorporated distaste for the living conditions of East European Jewry, for their 'perversion' and 'moral corruption'. They seemed to the young Israelis to be even more wretchedly offensive in their tragedy. In their essays, school pupils exposed their alienation, their lack of spiritual identification with the victims, their determined refusal to tolerate any form of negativity. The Holocaust was portrayed as a Jewish disgrace.[27] The role of 'other' was primarily assigned to the diaspora Jew 'who would stubbornly stick by the notorious strictures of traditional Jewish identity without perceiving the new light of resurrection coming from Zion'.[28]

At the time, Hebrew drama supported these views; it failed to reflect the shifting opinions among *yishuv* emissaries and the Israelis about the qualities and abilities of the survivors, or to see them as 'human material of the most desirable kind' as did Jewish officials in the 1940s. Commentators noted survivors' organisational talent, strength, vitality and initiative which contrasted with negative expectations of them.[29] Ben-Gurion amended his own pessimistic view:

I found to my astonishment – it would be difficult to say to my delight, because there are manifestations of corruption – that there is less corruption than is likely under the circumstances. I found that, despite everything, people are healthy, both in the physical sense and in the spiritual sense. The majority are precious Jews, precious Zionists with deep Zionist instincts, ready to undergo again all troubles – if this is what Zionism requires – with fervour for the unity and the survival of the Jewish people.[30]

Although many instances of survivors' heroism and battlefield experience were known at the time,[31] the drama almost entirely ignored them. One canonic exception was Aharon Meged's *Hannah Senesh* (1958), a glorification of heroism which employed the traditional terminology of myth and martyrology, appropriate to the historical selectivity of the time. Generally, however, the drama's negative attitude to diaspora Jewry served its need to create a myth of itself as a mode of positive propaganda, to entrench Zionism's charter of redemption.

Few plays of the time placed the Holocaust at their centre. the most prominent being Natan Shaham's *Heshbon Hadash* (A New Reckoning) (1954), which dealt with the problem of Jewish collaboration; Leah Goldberg's *Ba'alat Ha'armon* (The Lady of the Manor) (1955), which presented an interesting attempt to synthesise the best of European culture with the brightness of Zionism and Israel; and Moshe Shamir's *Hayoresh* (The Heir) (1963), which debated the juxtaposition of German blood money and Israel's spiritual and historical heritage. These topics recur in Ben-Zion Tomer's *Yaldei Hatzel* (The Children of the Shadow) (1963), one of the most important plays on the topic of the Holocaust, concerned with the nagging questions of German *wiedergutmachung* (reparations), collaboration, Israeli identity and the absorption of refugees into the new, ideologically sabraised society.

Another reason for the limited Israeli literary response to the Holocaust was thought to be due partly to the Israeli writers' involvement in historical events of their own – the War of Independence and nation-building – followed by their need to define a separate identity, and their confrontation with new social and political pressures. Also, the survivors forced the native-born Israelis to encounter a past that many of them had not yet wholly relinquished, and reminded them of their own narrow avoidance of the catastrophe. Generally the survivor, who contradicted the ideal of a positive hero, was not desirable as a character in the narcissistic literature of the 1950s. In the drama of the 1950s and 1960s survivors are portrayed almost exclusively as people striving to forget their past, a metaphor for the playwrights and their society.

After the disaster of the Yom Kippur War perceptions of the Holocaust changed. Israelis came face to face with their own vulnerability and for the first time they identified with Holocaust survivors as people whose resistance was constituted by their very survival. After the *Likud* had gained power in 1977 the Holocaust was sometimes crudely manipulated and used as a political instrument. It became customary for Prime Minister Begin to invoke the death camps to justify his political policies – by reinforcing the perception of the Jews as eternal victims and the Arabs as Nazis. It was difficult to distinguish between memory and propaganda in his rhetoric. On the other side of the political spectrum, memory of the Nazi genocide led to increased controversy over the Occupied Territories and an examination of issues relating to Israel's new image as conqueror and ruler of over a million Palestinians.

At the end of the decade of the 1970s, for all or any one of these reasons, Israeli society began to view the Holocaust as an integral part of its own history. For the first time it was able to comprehend Israel as a collective phenomenon incorporating all of its political and historical elements. From that time the Holocaust became an essential component of public and artistic life in Israel,[32] transformed from a topic to be avoided or denied to one which had, for one reason or another, increasingly come to represent Jewish fate. Personal memories and testimony realised through artistic media became as legitimate as official national memorials and commemorations. With the new perception of the Holocaust came the realisation that traditional toughness, of muscle and weapons, celebrated in popular culture as well as in 'high' literature, was no longer the sole manifestation of courage and heroism. In a sense the hero was reborn, a more equivocal, less obvious hero. Once the nature of the brawny *sabra* of 1948, the *Palmah* hero, had been reassessed and ultimately perceived as either myth or metaphor, the implicit and often explicit accusation of 'lambs to the slaughter' was questioned, with the result that the earlier disparaging manner of presenting survivors was redressed. The drama reflected this re-evaluation, with playwrights proposing an altogether altered understanding of Jewish history, heroism and survival.

Danny Horowitz's *Tcherli Katcherli*[33] (1977)[34] was the thematic prototype for much subsequent drama. Its extravert style disguised a profound self-appraisal through which it confirmed the Israelis' coming-to-terms, their acceptance of the Holocaust, however unwillingly, as a component of their history and not solely the experience of the Jews 'out there' in the diaspora. For this reason, rather than its dismantling of the hero, the play achieved great acclaim and was awarded the Best Play prize for 1978.

Tcherli Katcherli is not 'about' the Holocaust in the sense that the Holocaust as an historical event constitutes its subject matter. Rather, it demonstrates the dominance of the Holocaust in the cultural development of Israeli society after the Six-Day War, and the society's gradual growth away from a consciously forged, doggedly-held heroic archetype to a more realistic social construction. The play demonstrates a process of maturation: the hero in his most superficial, stereotypical incarnation grows to be psychologically equipped for introspection and some self-criticism after the Six-Day War, and is ultimately able to amalgamate the 'other', the diaspora Jew, into his cultural identity. In the play the *sabra* figure is a symbol rather than a delimited myth. He represents the youthful Ashkenazi élite whose cultural influence in Israel far outweighed its size. Horowitz delineates their evolution from the golden youth of the pre-State period to their maturation and consequent assumption (according to the play) of a persona far more authentic and suited to the changing times.

Horowitz achieves this by an ingenious method of fragmentation in which the hero seldom appears whole but is constituted by the sum of his parts: synecdochical objects, types of clothing such as the shorts worn by the young Israelis during the 1940s and 1950s, popular children's games, food, activities, ideas, period-specific language including slang, historical characters and events, allusions to literary works and their authors, folksongs and folkdances. These elements contain metaphorical significance although the differences between metaphor and myth have become blurred. Nevertheless they make of the play an important cultural document. The Holocaust is interwoven with all these pieces in complete scenes or in fragmentary pictures, like flashes on a movie screen.

Horowitz's dramatic style calls upon another amalgamation, in this case of the many genres utilised by Israeli theatre over twenty years: documentary drama, allegory, political satire, and a mixture of devices: dramatic monologue, dialogue, poetry and rhetoric. The play is composed of forty short scenes, the majority of which are contextualised in the printed text by means of a statement and in the staged play by changes of speaker. Each actor represents one or another of the manifestations of the *sabra* in his society from the 1940s to the time of the play's composition.

Despite its polymorphic structure, the play progresses through a distinct historical continuum. While events follow in apparently chronological order, the play is not a history of Israel or of the Jews but the careful probing of the nature of the *sabra*, Tcherli Katcherli, in relation to his people's history. Woven throughout the historical presentation is the Holocaust, seen always as an active factor in the present and therefore external to the more-or-less diachronic history. Well-known metonymic signs of the Holocaust are shown: the words over the entrance to Auschwitz, the photograph of the old man whose beard has been cut off by laughing SS officers, and the photograph of the frightened little boy with his hands up in the air. The Holocaust appears first as an event beyond the *sabra*'s experience, an event whose victims he at first denigrates according to the spirit of the time. Horowitz places him and the State of Israel in opposition to the old man and the little boy. The play is therefore as much about the Holocaust in Israeli society as it is about the society itself.

As the *sabra* stereotype wanders through his incarnations, he carries with him changing images of the Holocaust, beginning with a a sense of affront that it should have happened simply because of a 'cut penis', an ironic *reductio ad absurdum* throughout the play. Forceful visual images of the two victims underline Tcherli's vow of 'never again'. He responds with a need to exact revenge, or at least to perform an action of resistance or opposition. Later, after the Six-Day War, he experiences the discomfiture of realising that the method of his revenge is reminiscent of the crime itself. Finally, he refers, with loaded irony, to the domestication of the Holocaust within the society, to the Holocaust-as-kitsch, a possible money-earner, one of the many displacing methods of absorbing its enormity within Israeli society.

Tcherli's initial affirmation of the active and practical New Jew defines the equivocal response of the *yishuv* to the suffering of European Jewry. The child in the photograph reinforces this response. To the practical man of action, the personification of the Zionist movement, the solution was simple and practical: get out of the picture. 'Warn everyone that they won't see you in the picture again.'[35] Ultimately, according to the *sabra*'s oversimplistic formula, the boy will go to Israel. Whether Horowitz is exercising the irony that defines the entire play or whether he is suggesting that the ultimate aim of the victims of the Holocaust was to settle in Israel, is up to the viewer to decide. While not necessarily historically accurate, the victim's projected future in Israel is an affirmation of Israel for the Israeli, the accepted juxtaposition of suffering and *geulah*. In the elevated, poetic language that typified the early literature of the state – especially that of S. Yizhar who appears as a character in one scene – the speaker in *Tcherli Katcherli* contrasts the life 'here' of openness, light and nature with the 'there' of cellars, thick walls, Yiddish, persecution and gold teeth (the first linkage in the play of the diaspora Jew and gold).

The play is a construction of texts, visual, musical and verbal, as if Tcherli himself is no more than a textual collage. Throughout, he calls upon examples of the popular culture and serious literature of the time, as well as the canonic Jewish literature of the past. Notions of the inseparability of literature and life in Israel are corroborated by a dialogue with Yizhar in which he is implicitly indicted as a representative of the *Palmah* generation. He is the creator and spokesman of the political stands which required 'demythologizing' by the younger generation. Creative literature studied in the schools served as an ideological force, filling a propagandistic role throughout the young Israeli's education, in accordance with Ben-Gurion's views about the functionality of literature. The scene with Yizhar, and the many literary allusions throughout the play, conform that in Israel the writer bears some responsibility for the creation of cultural mores and political ideologies.

Always in the background as a form of annotation to the present, the Holocaust intrudes on Tcherli's self-definition as 'anti-crema-torium'. His is the lightness and freedom of smoke, not the ashes of the dead. Yet the word `ashan (smoke) is one of the most frequent semiotic evocations of the Holocaust. The *sabra*'s freedom is moderated by the collective memory. 'Gold' appears again in a scene of joyous self-affirmation: 'Clean, I'm clean, purer than gold'; again the language subverts the tone: the word used is not *zahav*, 'gold' but *ketem paz*, 'fine gold'. Since *ketem* is also a stain, the scene may be referring to the controversial question of the reparations which could hardly be ignored by anyone writing about the 1950s.

In the ensuing scenes the tone changes once more: the bloodlust, represented by a finger on the trigger, leads to a sense of unease. The play examines the War of Independence from a moral viewpoint, the clash of human values with the exigencies of war. Images of killing in war and the memory of children in the gas chambers are mingled, as if the soldier is unsure whether his present action is an appropriate reponse to the Holocaust or merely reminiscent of it. According to Ziva Ben-Porat, the distinction between the fighters' 'no option'[36] (*ein brerah*) response and their pleasure in killing is blurred by the sexual terminology of the scene.[37] It is at this point that the question of humanitarian values is introduced through more direct images of the Holocaust, striped pyjamas, smoke and ashes, bereaved mothers, gas showers. At the same time, the speaker uses all the ambivalent euphemisms of war and conquest: 'face to face battle', 'territory cleansing', 'purification'. These and the insertion of the German words, *rechts* and *links* already points to what was to become a recognisable literary analogy between the Israeli army in the Occupied Territories and Nazi Germany.

The play's focus gradually shifts to the growing crisis which defined the period immediately preceding the Six-Day War. Then 'Tcherli Katcherli the Second' makes his appearance, a personality lacking the endearing characteristics of his forebear. He is an ex-soldier exulting in the much criticised 'festival of victory' following the Six-Day War. The Holocaust remains in the recesses of his consciousness, justifying his present self-aggrandisement but suggesting for the first time his rather abstract self-definition as a moral victim, the casualty of a political situation out of control.

The gulf between the '*Palmah*' and later generations is stressed by Tcherli the Second whose moral deterioration increases when he becomes 'Tcherli Katcherli the Third'. This is a university graduate and professional whose aspiration to live well is realised by diaspora means: gold. Tcherli has now allowed himself to become incorporated into Jewish history, but this accommodation is equivocal, based as it is on nothing but materialism. Gold, he says, will be his strength, as it always was, an assumption, finally, of the stereotyped diaspora Jew into the Israeli persona. Tcherli indicates that while his acceptance of *golah* is uneasily achieved, it is underlined by his determination that the Holocaust will never again take place. His new rapacity represents an ironic contradiction of Zionist Socialist philosophy, the advent of Sobol's Boaz and Kobi Lifshitz, the *geldmenschen*, in Israeli society. The *sabra*'s view of the diaspora, perceived through the medium of Tcherli the Third and allusions to gold throughout the play, is still largely negative. Moreover, Horowitz's references to the diaspora are no longer intertextual or allusive as are those located in Israel; he ignores diaspora Jewish culture to focus bitterly on gold, the most stereotypical or 'mythological' of diaspora phenomena.

The new *sabra* questions his own image. Will he trivialise the Holocaust by placing the photograph of the little boy on a keyring and then mass produce it? This question carries a warning: the photograph which was shocking and dreadful to the first Tcherli is now reduced to kitsch. Jewish history is demystified. The new Tcherli is a despairing, empty character, middle-aged and embourgeoised, aware at last of his obligations to history. At the end of the play he is unsure of his identity or his name, in his own words he is 'perhaps lost',[38] the summary of the generation suffering the aftermath of the Yom Kippur War.

Critics write glibly about Israeli society's 'coming of age', its absorption of the Holocaust into the fabric of its societal consciousness and self-identification. Horowitz himself claims, 'if it is necessary to shape the first axiom of our existence in Israel we must go to the Holocaust and understand its projections'.[39] But the drama alone among the literary genres reveals that this 'absorption' does not settle easily within the Israeli body politic. Playwrights – who have been much more politicised than fiction writers from the start, and have less opportunity for narrative development – relate to the topic with greater ambivalence.

The 1970s and 1980s saw a uniting of the collective consciousnesses, as we have seen from *Tcherli Katcherli*, a link forged between survivors and the rest of Israeli society. For the the new generation of writers the event had altered its focus. They had not – as adults struggling to fashion an identity in the new state – encountered the survivors *en masse* soon after the Second World War, living and fighting side by side with them a matter of months after their arrival in Israel, as the 1948 generation had done. They were able to 'alter' the Holocaust imaginatively, allowing it to assume the proportions of literary tragedy rather than face the unendurable revelations of history.

A positive outcome of this reordered approach to the Holocaust was laying to rest once and for all the accusation of 'lambs to the slaughter'. In the 1980s plays attempted to correct the perception of compliance or weakness by demonstrating that there had been a variety of Jews in the concentration camps, and not only the victims who conformed to the martyrological typology entrenched by historical responses to catastrophe. Yehoshua Sobol objected to the sentimentalisation of victims because it proposed another method of dehumanisation. He and other playwrights attempted to correct the perception of the *golah* Jews by suggesting that they were no different from anyone else, neither exclusively good nor exclusively bad, heroic or cowardly. Difference was no more a guarantee of salvation than martyrdom would have been. Also, the 'lambs to the slaughter' image was altered of necessity because the Second Generation, which had grown to maturity, was struggling to come to terms with their parents' experiences.

The value of Motti Lerner's *Kastner* (1985)[40] resides not in his recreation of events from court proceedings and interlocutors – although he achieved this to some extent according to the principles of documentary theatre – but in provoking questions which to this day remain unanswered. Lerner did not fulfil all of Piscator's injunctions concerning documentary theatre: his staging owed little to mixed media, there were no projections, slides or mechanical devices, only a complicated variety of small sets and narrative spaces signalled by different doors. However, his play did employ a sequence of brief narrative episodes: in 49 scenes, a prologue and an epilogue, Lerner recounts one of the most pivotal event in the life of Dr Rudolf Israel (Reszö) Kastner (then Secretary of the Hungarian Zionist Organisation) which took place in Budapest in 1944.

Hungarian Jewry was largely an assimilated community, with the Orthodox and the Zionists constituting only small sections within it. The Zionist Organisation, which was aligned to the Labour Zionists, neither represented nor influenced the Jewish community as a whole. With the advent of the Nazis in Hungary in 1944 it was almost impossible to establish an effective Jewish underground resistance movement since many young Jews had been drafted into labour units in the Hungarian army, and there was no help forthcoming from the largely anti-Semitic Hungarian population. However, the small Jewish underground was able to smuggle Polish Jews into Romania and Austria and save at least 100,000 in Budapest itself by means of forged documents. In 1944, towards the end of the war, Eichmann was still dutifully fulfilling the demands of the Final Solution and deporting as many Jews to Auschwitz as its crematoria were able to process. After Rudolf Hoess had complained that Auschwitz was becoming short of gas, Eichmann demanded that he throw the Jews directly into the ovens.

When Otto Komoy, the Chairman of the Hungarian Zionist Organisation, refused to deal with the *Judenrat*[41] Kastner, by all accounts an unimpressive personality, offered his services as mediator. He began negotiations with the Gestapo in Budapest with Joel Brand and others. Brand was a member of the Jewish Relief Committee who had been active in the conveyance of Jews from Poland to Hungary and Romania. The negotiations involved the ransoming of Hungarian Jews, first for dollars, then for trucks, foodstuffs and arms. The Nazis agreed that, for a payment of two million dollars, Hungarian Jews would not be ghettoised or sent to concentration camps. The negotiations were tortuous. The official Jewish agencies in Western Europe and the United States were powerless to raise the money on their own, and the Allies were at best uncomprehending, at worst obstructive for political reasons of their own. Eichmann yielded nothing, ultimately breaking every promise and, by May and June 1944, he was deporting 20,000 Hungarian Jews a day to Auschwitz. Altogether 800,000 were murdered. Kastner was able to secure 1,685 visas for a list of Jews who then left Hungary by train, and he was thought by some to have been involved in saving a further 195,000. Kastner's intermediary for the financial arrangements was SS officer Kurt Becher. After the war he testified at Nuremberg in Becher's defence. Becher was freed.

In 1954 Kastner was living in Israel and had achieved prominence both in government circles[42] and as the editor of a Hungarian-language newspaper. Malchiel Grunewald, a refugee from Vienna who had strong links with the Israeli Right, publicly accused Kastner of abandoning Hungarian Jewry and collaborating with the Nazis. Grunewald claimed that in March 1944 when the Germans, along with Eichmann, had occupied the previously independent Hungarian state, Kastner had wilfully refrained from warning the Jewish community of their certain fate despite his detailed knowledge of the massacre of five million European Jews. Further, according to Grunewald, his silence had facilitated the organisation of transports to Auschwitz while achieving his own rescue and that of his family and friends aboard the special train. This charge led the Israeli government to sue Grunewald on Kastner's behalf on four counts of criminal libel. The judge found that the charges of collaboration, 'indirect murder' and Kastner's postwar testimony in favour of Becher were proven and therefore not libellous; the fourth count, of sharing plunder with a Nazi, was found to be libellous and Grunewald was fined the nominal amount of one Israeli lira. The judge, Benjamin Halevi, a supporter of the Irgun,[43] accused Kastner of having 'sold his soul to the devil', a phrase which plagued him for the remainder of his life. Kastner was murdered in 1957 by three people widely believed to have had acted on behalf of elements associated with the Herut[44] party. Kastner was posthumously cleared by the Israeli High Court of all charges of collaboration,[45] but remains an example of Israeli demonology.

The controversy about Kastner endures to the present day, indicating that the affair has transcended its historical limitations and remains pertinent to the present Israeli situation. During the trial itself, the line of demarcation between memory and politics was not blurred but simply disappeared'.[46] Underlying the dispute was the fact that Kastner was a Labour Zionist, supported by the Zionist-Jewish Agency establishment, and those accusing him of collaboration were the Revisionists who denounced Ben-Gurion, the Labour leader, for failing to assist Kastner in his efforts to barter for Jewish lives. Shmuel Tamir, Grunewald's Counsel and a supporter of the Israeli Right, later Begin's Minister of Justice, described Ben-Gurion as 'the Minister of treachery and corruption' and accused him of direct complicity in the extermination of the Jews in Europe.[47] He argued that Kastner's collaboration with the Nazis was like the collaboration of Mapai with the British in Palestine during the Mandate. An entire mythology arose as a result of the trial which itself was an excuse for party political confrontation and the reiteration of old enmities by Mapai and Herut. Tamir reinforced Grunewald's claim that Kastner had been aware of the annihilation of Hungarian Jewry but concealed it from the Jewish community in order to obtain his train. The trial became a trial of Mapai. Forces represented by the Revisionists, who prized Jewish rescue through resistance and underground activities, accused the Labour Zionists, led by Ben-Gurion, of collaboration with the Nazis for ideological reasons of their own. In fact, the Israeli right-wing attempt to discredit certain Jewish community hierarchies in Nazi-occupied Europe had its roots in earlier political struggles within the Zionist movement and on the *yishuv.* Tamir did not deny the

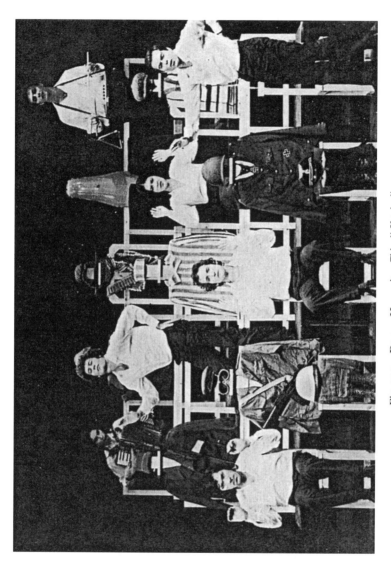

Figure 7   Danny Horowitz, *Tcherli Katcherli*.

assumption that controversies surrounding the activities of the *yishuv* leadership interested him more than the quarrel between Kastner and Grunewald.

The spotlight of the trial (which affected the general election in 1955) was therefore directed at the quality and character of early Zionism. This allowed Lerner (and later Sobol in *Ghetto*[48]) to add another dimension to their study of events during the Holocaust: a debate about the official Jewish bodies who bore the responsibility for creating and *defining* the State of Israel. There is an undoubted connection between the rise of *Likud* and the increased interest in the Holocaust during the 1970s which unleashed the barely suppressed enmities at the base of the Zionist enterprise.[49]

The so-called 'Kastner Trial' itself represented a manipulation of Holocaust memory for party political ends. Lerner's *Kastner* used the Holocaust not to recapitulate party enmities, but to question the image of the Israeli, the New Jew, in the context of contemporary politics. In production, the play led to a reprise both of the Kastner-Grunewald controversy and the Mapai-Herut (Labour-Revisionist) conflict. Lerner crystallised the debate through his Kastner who represents neither directly, only the argument for negotiation rather than armed resistance as a means of saving lives. Counteracting the strong and well documented evidence against the real Kastner, Lerner attempts to redress the balance by presenting him as a man driven by the desperate plight of the Hungarian Jews to shed his pride and honour and initiate the sinister negotiations with Eichmann and his lieutenant, Herman Wisleceny.

The play is loosely structured in the form of a trial, opening with the indictment spoken by Kastner's adversary, Grunewald, and ending with Kastner's defence. Each short scene presents its own witnesses and evidence, with the audience serving as the jury. At the conclusion the crucial questions remain unanswered: did Kastner deal in Jewish blood in grandiose negotiations with the Nazis, or was he a hero who rescued as many Jews as possible? Was he a romantic innocent who was outmanoeuvred at every turn by Eichmann, or a clever opportunist who rescued only his family, friends and Jewish 'prominents'? Lerner stated in an interview that his intention was to portray Kastner as a man confronting existential dilemmas and adopting life as the highest principle, surmounting national honour.[50] As with Gens in Sobol's *Ghetto*, the line between the

Figure 8   *Arbeit Macht Frei*; table laden with food.

pragmatism employed in the life-saving effort and self-interest was frequently difficult to distinguish in the chaos of the time.

Lerner indicates his departures from historical fact in his preface to the play. Maintaining a surprising neutrality, given the subject matter, he avoids a psychological analysis of Kastner, concentrating rather on the practical dimension of his activities. However, Lerner makes it clear that he challenges the perception of Kastner's absolute evil which was – and still is – widely promoted despite his later rehabilitation. His Kastner is an enigmatic figure who literally sups with the devil but never abandons his obsessive mission to save as many Jewish lives as possible. He persists with his negotiations and risks his life by defying Eichmann; he alienates his wife, Bodio, his mother and, in his single-mindedness, members of the Jewish leadership. He fraternises with Wisliceny and, in one scene, seems to be pimping for him. At the end of the play he refuses a visa for the leader of the Orthodox Jewish community in Budapest (Phillip [Pinhas] von Freudiger, who later testified at the trial), since the fateful train is full. Apparently it was incidents such as this that earned Kastner the sobriquet of collaborator and led to accusations of personal partisanship in his selection of people to be saved aboard his train.

Within the limitations of the genre, Lerner glosses well-documented facts by focusing on Kastner's obsessiveness which he establishes from the start of the play. He avoids speculation about Kastner's personal agenda. His Kastner is convinced that any physical resistance to the Nazis means certain suicide in the conditions of the time. To start with, Lerner neither indicts Kastner nor supports him; his attempt at objectivity or neutrality rests on contrasting a negative view of him with a positive one. The audience swings from sympathy to aversion, from irritation at Kastner's ingenuousness to admiration of his persistence and courage. Ultimately, however, Lerner's objectivity gives way to a gradual exculpation, confirmed by Kastner's speech at the end of the play which reads like the defence's summation.

Your honour, the only ghetto in all of Europe whose inhabitants remained alive was the Budapest ghetto and this was despite the absence of activities which you might call 'heroism'. The ghetto was saved thanks to the connections I made with Hermann Kromey and with Kurt Becher of the SS and with their help I got four additional trains to go to Vienna and I was able to stop the killing in Bergen-Belsen and Theresienstadt. Because of these connections the prosecution called me 'the Nazis' greatest merchant'.[51]

According to Peter Weiss, the selectivity involved in documentary drama is far more likely to be subjective than objective, leading to the problem of untrustworthy documentaries. Documentary can never be fully authentic, Weiss continues, 'since to meet the limits of the stage, the material must be pruned, an inevitably subjective process'. Above all, documentary theatre 'takes sides'. Weiss concludes: 'The playwright chooses his subject for this kind of treatment because he wants to invite a partisan judgment.'[52] Lerner, perhaps deliberately, obscures his own judgment. His Kastner emerges as a naïve figure, well-meaning, committed and vain, remaining the Nazis' pawn. He is constantly astonished by Eichmann's treachery:

KASTNER But sir, we had an agreement. There is a signed contract. We organised lists according to your directives. We paid. Now you come and tell me that the agreement is nullified? It's impossible to go on like this, sir.

EICHMANN You're too tense, Kastner. You, of course, will want to leave. To Theresienstadt, I suppose? Or perhaps you'd prefer Auschwitz?

KASTNER I won't fall for threats sir. Whatever is waiting for me at Auschwitz is waiting for me behind that door.

EICHMANN Don't put it to the test, Kastner.[53]

When Kastner expresses his amazed disbelief that the Nazis are capable of grand deceit, and lays the blame at the feet of the *Hungarian* government, Freudiger says of him: 'This man is lost'.

Apart from Kastner himself, most of the other characters are two-dimensional or stereotypical. Even Joel Brand, the true hero of the story,[54] emerges as a weak, cringing character, entirely overshadowed by Kastner. Eichmann is not portrayed as supernaturally evil but as menacing, ironic and imbued with undeviating disdain and contempt for the Jews. The remainder of the characters are representatives of the various formal political factions operating within the official Jewish world: Mapai, General Zionists, Revisionists and the religious Agudat Yisrael.

As a creator of documentary drama, Lerner asked crucial questions. One of these concerns the curious inadequacy of the *yishuv* in the matter of assisting the European Jews. The second question concerns those Jews who were viewed as having gone 'like lambs to the slaughter' by the activist Revisionists and the Irgun. Lerner refutes this assumption by suggesting that the Nazis misled the Hungarian Jews, with Kastner's unknowing help, into believing that they were about to be rescued, thus forestalling any resistance or attempts at escape. Lerner's play repudiates this persistent accusation of Jewish compliance and instead proposes the rescue of Jewish honour, even through the distasteful bartering of Jewish lives for cash and supplies.

In accordance with the refutation of the 'lambs-to-the-slaughter' image, the Jewish characters in *Kastner* are not portrayed in a wholly positive light. There is constant disagreement within the community; Kastner is somewhat disdainful of the Orthodox, claiming that 'Freudiger will save only his family and a few more religious families close to him. Freudiger is not able to take part in real, inclusive, rescue'.[55] Lerner cites other squabbles among the Jewish leadership, hurt feelings even *in extremis*, interests to be protected. He demonstrates that a desperate situation arouses the worst in almost everyone, bickering, suspicion, accusation and double-dealing. The play includes a reflection on the Hungarian-Jewish bourgeoisie who, even towards the end of the war, persisted in the belief that the Germans would respond to gentlemanly behaviour.

The true value of *Kastner* is not in the well-known story it tells or in Kastner himself but in the issues which transcend the play itself. It contributed to the process of Holocaust acceptance within Israeli society as an historical component of its own as well as of European Jewry, narrowing the gap between 'them' and 'us'. It portrayed the Hungarian Jews as a group with which the Israelis could identify, not exclusively the unilateral 'lambs to the slaughter' with their eyes turned heavenward. Of equal significance was its attempt to alter the accepted meaning of collaboration and heroism and attack the Israeli mythology which saw the Holocaust as proof of the correct choice made 'by *sabra* heroes such as King David, Samson and Judah Maccabee, over the diasporic intercessionary path of the Jew Mordechai'.[56]

In effect both Lerner and Sobol are trying to revise our thinking about collaboration and heroism against a forty-year-old history of Israel celebrating and the glorifying the deeds of such national figures as Hanna Senesh and Mordechai Anielewicz, leader of the Warsaw uprising. Naturally it is always easier and simpler to make national heroes out of brave soldiers than morally ambiguous ghetto leaders like Gens and Kastner.[57]

Lerner defends his treatment of Kastner by emphasising the very absence of mythological or archetypal attributes in his character, and by admitting that Kastner seems an unlikely 'hero' for the Israeli public to admire:

We have grown up on the myth of Massada, the myth of heroism and suicide heroes. Dudu, Jeremy [the Paratrooper], Meir Har-Tziyon, Mordechai Anielewicz. Kastner is a hero who remains alive at any cost. He does not appear to be a hero in our eyes. He was a go-between, he was 'protected', haughty, a bribe, a negotiator, buying and selling, a man who never held a gun in his life ... not appropriate for an heroic myth ... We can't continue to nourish 'suicide heroes'. Perhaps this was essential in Jewish mythology on the way to [the establishment of] the state, but to go on clinging to that mythology is suicide. Look at where it's leading us. Kastner believed in negotiation because to him human life was the highest principle.[58]

He adds: 'Why should national honour interest me? Can one live off it?' Through his character of Kastner, Lerner suggests that heroic

Figure 9   Yehoshua Sobol, *Ghetto*, 1984.

physical action may not be the only criterion for the definition of heroism. His Kastner therefore serves him as a political metaphor on a number of levels. Lerner's play is an historical account of an event within the Holocaust and, at the same time, an implicit criticism of Israel's policies of might. If not an analogy, the play is at least a warning to Israel that negotiation may ultimately serve far better than the exercise of force.

The issue of collaboration, still regarded as 'an open wound' in Israel, constitutes a fundamental topic in the play. Many playwrights have grappled with it, the three most prominent plays preceding *Kastner* being Natan Shaham's *Heshbon Hadash* (A New Reckoning) (1954), Tomer's *Yaldei Hatzel* (The Children of the Shadow), and *Mishatfei Pe`ulah* (Collaborators) by Dov Tzahor (1974). Shaham's play, written during the Kastner trial, examines the guilt of Jewish collaborators and the right to judge, punish or forgive them. Tomer presents a member of a *Judenrat* who is his own harshest judge but is ultimately forgiven by a young Israeli. In Tzahor's *Collaborators* one of the characters describes any attempt to bargain with the Germans as collaboration with the devil whilst another Kastner-like figure argues that any attempt is better than none. Both Kastner and Oskar Schindler, in their literary incarnations, appear to have been men of similar character, arrogant, opportunistic, womanisers and rogues but the real Schindler, being a Nazi himself, could not be accused of collaboration. Kastner, a Jew, having achieved as much as Schindler in harsher circumstances, is disgraced as a collaborator.

The story of Kastner served as the basis for two non-Hebrew language plays. East German Heinar Kipphardt's *Joel Brand, Die Geschichte eines Geschäfts* (Joel Brand, the History of a Business Deal) (1965), on the subject of the Hungarian 'deal', accuses the Germans of the destruction of the Hungarian Jews. However, in his minutely-researched documentary play he also denounces the Jewish organisations and leadership, including Chaim Weitzmann (later Israel's first President), that failed to reveal any objective understanding of the events in Hungary, and the British, particularly Lord Moyne, who obstructed the Brand enterprise. The more extreme of these plays is *Perdition* (1987) by the English playwright, Jim Allen which was to have been produced in London by the Royal Court Theatre Upstairs. This play, which fits the category of 'untrustworthy documentaries', caused an unprecedented controversy in Britain.

After representations from official Jewish bodies, Jewish historians and other prominent Jewish figures, as well as a deluge of public argument, its performances were cancelled. The debate included reservations by leading Anglo-Jewish historians, including Sir Martin Gilbert, about the accuracy of the historical references made in the play. It incorporated arguments about the relationship of anti-Semitism to Zionism and of the Zionist establishment of the time to the Holocaust, and it of course raised the problem of censorship. Over a period of three months the argument generated over 150 articles and letters in the press from correspondents within Britain and abroad, including many notables and some defenders of Allen who proclaimed themselves to be 'anti-Zionist Jews'.

Perdition is an anti-Zionist and anti-Israel tract based primarily on anti-Zionist sources, and it includes a barely veiled hint of Holocaust revisionism despite its dedication which reads: 'To the Jews of Hungary who were murdered by the Nazis at Auschwitz'. It argues that the Zionist leaders in Hungary allowed themselves to become 'the Zionist knife in the Nazi fist'. According to one of the play's leading characters, the Jews of Hungary 'were murdered not just by the force of German arms but by the calculated treachery of their own Jewish leaders'.[59] The play's critics did not dispute the validity of the issues posed by the Kastner case but were troubled by the uses made of it by Jim Allen and British left-wing anti-Semitism. They claimed that he had wilfully distorted both fact and interpretation in order to draw conclusions about the entire Zionist movement and the character of the State of Israel, and that his selection of events from the historiography of wartime Europe was consonant with his rejection of Israel. The historian David Cesarani reported that *Perdition* 'does satisfy all criteria by which anti-Semitism is normally recognised'.[60] The fundamental problem of the play, which is an anti-fascist polemic, is that Allen uses Zionism rather than Nazism as his exemplar of fascism and the analogy of Israel rather than Nazi Germany in his warning about the future revival of global fascism. 'I see the play as a small contribution to rescuing the Jews from Zionism. It's a very pro-Jewish play.'[61] Allen also makes the historical connection between Zionism and Nazism based on 'blood and land' which Sobol has agonised throughout his drama. He employs the same device of utilising the past or manipulating Jewish history to serve the political purposes of the present. For this to be done inside Israel is sufficiently controversial, but outside Israel it becomes an even greater threat to Jewish self-confidence and the Jewish self-image.

CHAPTER 8

The Holocaust as political analogy

During the 1980s there was a change in the drama's conceptual approach to the Holocaust. Plays no longer centralised specific Holocaust-related problems or even individual experience; instead the Holocaust became a significant semiotic element in the recognition of the political discord encompassing Israeli society. Reconciling Zionist ideology and the Holocaust occurred, through the eyes of the drama, by the most subversive means possible: the analogy of fascism, associated in the main with Nazi ideology, and the Israeli occupation of the West Bank and Gaza. This was at best a cautionary device, at worst bitterly polemical. It became a commonplace, almost a fashion, among left-wing Israeli playwrights, at least two of whom, Sobol and Hanokh Levin, won major national prizes. Needless to say, it provoked controversy:

We are already paying the price of this obstructive fashion, this perverse and vulgar fashion with a loss of a sense of discrimination, a muddling of terms and a blurring of important boudaries, in the ugly and distorted system of sensitivities and a language which has been corrupted beyond redemption.[1]

Not only 'fashionable' writers combined the Holocaust with distinctly Israeli problematics. In September, 1988, an article in the daily newspaper *Davar* described the right-wing *Moledet* party as 'the new Nazi party' since it used the word 'transfer' when discussing the removal of the Palestinian population. A short while later, an opposition election advertisement in *Ma'ariv* suggested a link between the ruling *Likud* and Hitler, an advertisement for which the paper later apologised. The words of a popular singer encapsulated the political self-indictment: 'We'd better begin preparing a glass booth for ourselves in which we'll sit when they judge us on what we have done to the Palestinian nation.'[2] The most damning statement was made by the popular left-wing novelist, A. B. Yehoshua who was quoted in *Newsweek* as saying that he could understand how the Germans in the Second World War could claim to know nothing about the Holocaust since many Israelis refused to read newspapers or watch television, therefore finding it easy to separate themselves from events taking place fewer than ten kilometres away. Yehoshua was the first theoretically to utilise the Holocaust as a comparison.

[I]n our collective and personal unconscious, whether we like it or not, it isn't the picture of the French in Algeria or the British in Kenya but of the Second World War and the Holocaust (and let's not forget that the Holocaust was not only about gas chambers but also the humiliation and torture of individuals, old people, women and children) which are the 'founding visions' upon which we have been educated and which we have assimilated into our being.[3]

Throughout the 1990s both the Left and the religious Right appropriated the terminology of Nazism: the Left, to characterise official policies relating to the Occupied Territories, and the Right, to demonise their political opponents, particularly Yitzhak Rabin and his government.

By their comparison between fascism and Israel's activities in the Occupied Territories, the playwrights place the Holocaust within a recognisable and universal political context, as a symbol of totalitarianism everywhere rather than the outcome of a unique hatred of the Jews. Perhaps this conflation is the reason for the growth of drama on the subject in the late 1970s and 1980s. It has another, perhaps unintended consequence: with compassion constantly directed at the Palestinian victim rather than the historical Jew, victimhood is transferred and the Jew is seen by the drama as strong, not a weak lamb; even the characterisation of oppressor is better than the historically accrued self-image embodied in the notion of 'a lamb to the slaughter', the consistently negative image of the diaspora Jew. 'Lambs to the slaughter' had no place in a society widely perceived, from within and without, as powerful and fearless.

Yehoshua Sobol proposed a similar analogy, of fascism and the more militant manifestations of Zionism, in a play which depicted a series of events in the Vilna Ghetto during the Second World War. His *Ghetto* (1984),[4] the first of a trilogy of plays about the Holocaust, is based on the diary of events in the ghetto kept by the former director of the Grosser Library of Warsaw, Hermann Kruk, from June 1941 until July 1943. *Ghetto* is the only play written by a native-born Israeli about the Holocaust in its own time, portrayed from within rather than by allusion or symbolism. While Sobol does, as always, use hindsight to adopt a moral stance, he also attempts to recreate the plight faced by a specific group within the ghetto.

We have built up a series of myths and comfortable versions of what happened in the ghettos and camps, a version which makes a great event out of certain facts of armed resistance, but which imposes a silence on something that is surging and burning, sobbing in the depth of a collective soul. It was trying to make the surface but was constantly suppressed.[5]

Sobol is referring to the Israeli tendency to glorify victims who took up arms, while ignoring other forms of resistance. He also advocates an honest confrontation with the hitherto repressed knowledge of the Holocaust.[6]

Documentary drama is at best able to reproduce historical events for an audience whom the playwright wishes to educate or inform. Yet there is something contradictory in the notion of documentary theatre, with its psychological objectivity and overtly political agendas, being employed for a topic as complex as the Holocaust, even in the form of a fragment of its history. *Ghetto* is therefore a hybrid: structurally a documentary drama in the Brechtian tradition, replete with songs, banners, choruses, dancing and cabaret, all centred on the theme of mass extermination which, for the first time in Israeli drama, is depicted on the stage. Within the carefully researched documentary and its Epic Theatre realisation, however, is a tragic narrative of aspiration, courage and human endurance, represented both realistically and symbolically.

What I tried to show in *Ghetto* was that the Jews in Vilno tried to resist the Nazis, not by using force against them but by resisting spiritually and morally, by trying to survive not only as living creatures but mainly as human creatures ... I think that's why they created the library and had all the cultural activity in the ghetto. For years this was not mentioned here in Israel. The consensus was that most of the people went as sheep to the slaughter whilst there was a minority of heroes who stood up and resisted the Nazis gun in hand ... [R]esistance in the ghetto represented a very small minority, less than one per cent of the population.[7]

Sobol praises those who survived the other way, morally and culturally, and who demonstrated a different kind of heroism. He reports that the people who called themselves 'second-class survivors', that is, those who were not involved in armed resistance, felt that justice had been done to them for the first time through the play.[8]

The Vilna ghetto, which existed for little more than two years, had a thriving cultural life consisting of theatre, music and various educational events. At its head was Jacob Gens, originally the chief of the Jewish police, a Revisionist, and believer in productivity as a means of saving lives within the ghetto, who was antagonistic to the Jewish underground, deeming it a danger to Jewish lives. He could have escaped with his Lithuanian wife but he chose to remain with his people and was murdered by the Nazis in 1943. He was a puzzling man, disliked and distrusted by the ghetto inmates who suspected him of collaboration, judging him as harshly as posterity has done. Hermann Kruk was the ghetto's librarian and archivist. A Bundist – that is, a Jewish socialist who considered Yiddish to be the language of the Jewish people – he was antagonistic to Gens's Revisionist nationalism and his eagerness to promote Hebrew in the ghetto. A certain Weiskopf (whose first name is not supplied either in in the diaries or in the play) was an entrepreneur who ran a succesful tailoring industry in the ghetto. In the play he becomes rich and ostentatious, evolving from a ghetto tailor who seeks to ensure the survival of those in his employ, to a rapacious businessman for whom money is the only goal, the Boaz-Lifschitz character reappearing yet again. The German Commandant, Hans Kittel (Kittel in the play is a composite of a group of men in control of the Vilna ghetto) was an actor, musician and aesthete and at the same time an appalling sadist – even among an assembly of sadists – who had controlled and demolished other ghettoes before his arrival in Vilna.

By the summer of 1943 the Nazis had annihilated three quarters of the Jewish population of Vilna. Among those remaining in the ghetto were a band of actors, singers and dancers who were able to sustain a programme of drama and cabaret productions. The Vilna ghetto theatre was an extraordinary phenomenon which, in its first year, put on no fewer than 111 performances. By the time the ghetto was liquidated in September 1943 the number of performances had doubled.

Set in the Vilna ghetto between 1941 and 1943, Sobol's *Ghetto* charts the multipartite relationship between Kittel, the *Judenrat*, Gens, a group of theatrical and musical performers, and a number of other individuals carrying out their specific functions within the ghetto. While historically based, these are at the same time broadly representative of various social and cultural strata within the East European Jewish communities of the time, and symbols of ideological strands within both German and Jewish culture. In the play *Haya*, a young singer, has stolen a few ounces of beans. Instead of killing her, Kittel, who is attracted to her, as he is to music and art, decrees that she must repay the value of the beans in a performance which he will judge. Upon this rests the creation of a musical entertainment for him, and under his direction, just as he directs the inmates' real lives. Meanwhile Gens contrives to save as many Jewish lives as possible despite risking the taint of collaboration.

With its music, songs and spectacle, produced with a cast of forty at London's National Theatre, fewer at the Haifa Municipal Theatre, *Ghetto* is a play of truly Brechtian proportions, paradoxically incorporating some exuberant echoes of the classical Yiddish theatre. British critics questioned the play's overwhelming spectacle as an 'excess of conscious theatricality' in the context of the Holocaust;[9] 'Its sheer theatricality, its sense of artifice and spectacle, occasionally overwhelms the human and the individual';[10] 'There are moments in this brilliantly staged evening when you question its very theatricality and musical accomplishment. At times the spectacle and music seem diverting for their own sake, and anything that diverts attention away from the underlying horror of the experience cannot help but seem questionable.'[11] In its German version, directed by the German-Jewish director Peter Zadek, it became 'a Holocaust musical at whose peak there is an orgy on the stage during which [the singer], a microphone in her hand, sings Jewish songs. Sobol: "This was the most beautiful production of *Ghetto* I have seen." '[12]

Ghetto's most sensitive agenda is concealed within two more easily accessible themes: first, the nature of the ghetto's Nazi and Jewish hierarchies and the relationship between them and second, the idea of spiritual resistance to oppression. This, indeed, is the point registered by the reviewers of the British productions in 1989 and 1996: the vibrant life of the spirit in unimaginable circumstances. Sobol's point is that art, and specifically theatre, can simultaneously provide spiritual comfort, defiance and communal solidarity, a fundamentally political assumption.[13] Of course his realisation of this assumption in *Ghetto* is greatly ironic, cast in the form of an entertainment about an entertainment taking place within the framework of genocide.

At the same time, Sobol demonstrates the diverse strategies utilised to deny or escape reality as much for him as a playwright writing about the Holocaust as for his performers in the Vilna troupe. First, he uses the surrealistic device of a character operating a marionette to express opinions that would bring certain death it uttered by an inmate of the ghetto. This also serves Sobol well in overstepping the circumscribed historical boundaries. *Ghetto*'s marionette is a fitting image for the manipulation of every individual element within Hitler's grotesque and monstrous theatre. The second strategy is the diverting task for the ghetto dwellers of producing the entertainment; the third, the Jewish songs themselves, deeply moving expressions of despair, suffering and hope which remain safely organised and contained within accepted structures. Through its songs the interior 'play' illustrates the emotional impact of the historical cataclysm.

Sobol attempts to construct a play out of the Vilna Ghetto's activities that fulfils his own decrees concerning the task of theatre: 'A theatre that did, as the slogan testifies, what theatres should always do: defy reality, affront conventional taste, challenge hypocrisy. The forbidden game, the thing one can't help doing because one should not do it'[14] This political conception accommodates Sobol's discursive and provocative kind of theatre derived from Brecht, Toller and Piscator, but it does not suit the underlying aims of the Vilna inmates in the deadly grip of the Nazis: they defied reality, certainly, but there was no conventional taste to affront in the world of the ghetto nor hypocrisy to challenge. These are precepts which fit the normal social hierarchies of an establishment and its antagonists; of conservatism and radicalism in societies in which political theatre serves a discursive function, and which are not facing certain extermination.

The ghetto theatre's production is, therefore, a starting point rather than the main focus of Sobol's play. Despite many scenes about the 'entertainment', and the performance of songs actually composed in the ghettos of Vilna and elsewhere, he pays greater attention to the wider issues, and to the psychological choices facing the ghetto's inhabitants and their oppressors: for example, the tailor Weiskopf becomes the ghetto capitalist; Gens adopts a policy of pragmatic accommodation with the Germans and acts either as a collaborator or a saviour, a judgment left undecided. Kruk, a supporter of the underground resistance, produces a poster proclaiming 'No theatre in a graveyard' (a statement made by the real Kruk in his diary). He records the events in the ghetto but refuses to participate in its administration, claiming that saving books instead of lives promotes the continuation of Jewish culture. Kittel is an enigma rather than a beast. He venerates art and plays the saxophone, weeps with emotion after listening to Haya's song and permits the ventriloquist Srulik's excesses. Through Kittel's character Sobol addresses the naïve and sentimental question of art and atrocity, the moral value of art.[15] 'By demonstrating how easy it was for a man to be both a misty-eyed Mozartian and capable of gassing people, the Holocaust notoriously put paid to the idea that artistic sensibility and virtue have any necessary link.'[16] Kittel's strutting through the play with his two black cases, one containing his saxophone, the other a sub-machine gun, supplies Sobol's comment on this question.

Kittel offers a provocative justification for his demand that the Jews set up a theatre: 'This painful cross-fertilisation – German soul with Jewish spirit – where will it lead us? ... This intimate contact between us, this painful but so fruitful mixing of the German soul and the Jewish soul will still lead to greatness.'[17] This would seem to be an implausibly encouraging comment in the circumstances, if Sobol had not intended it to be ironic. In the end Kittel, with his fine artistic soul and his two black cases, murders every Jew in the ghetto after treating them to fresh bread and jam.

In many ways also a derivation of the *sihah*, *Ghetto* proposes ethical dilemmas which it does not attempt to answer. It questions the morality of setting up a theatre 'in a graveyard'. In fact, Kruk's dictum raises ethical and aesthetic questions about the function of art, particularly art concerning the Holocaust. The play addresses questions of conscience, and the problem of collaboration of which Gens was, and still stands, accused. In the play he ends his rhetoric of justification by proclaiming: 'in order to allow Jews to remain with a clean conscience I was forced to wallow in filth and to function without a conscience'.[18] He reiterates one of *Ghetto*'s central propositions, one which considers the nature and integrity of survival rather than survival itself, and by implication, the nature of heroism. Some inhabitants of the ghetto ask whether it is better to join the partisans and fight with arms or to resist as a group within the ghetto itself. Gens responds to Weiner, a doctor:

You obviously don't understand what the Germans are doing to us. We may not express resistance to the Germans only and solely through arms like the underground working in the ghetto ... the Germans are carrying out a war of extermination against us, not only of our bodies but of our spirit as well. The are trying to penetrate into our souls. They shoot their bullets into our flesh and they are trying to shoot into our spirit ... we must wage a war of the spirit against them ... Millions have already been murdered. They won't kill us all. They will lose the war. But they can conquer us in spirit, permeate us with their death-sickness.[19]

This speech is made in the context of a selection Gens is compelled to make in apportioning insulin to a group of diabetics. He decides to choose the strong for the life-saving medication and to sacrifice the weak. His rousing speech therefore assumes an ironic overtone.

Woven into the play is the problem, always an undercurrent in Sobol's drama, of the nature of diaspora Jewishness. Kruk comments on what he terms Russian-Jewish self-hatred which, as a Bundist, he is unable to understand. He gives examples of the brutality of the ghetto's Jewish police who are as sadistic as the Germans, and the leaders of the *Judenrat* who mingle with the Germans and use Jewish prostitutes. Kruk believes that these phenomena reveal the depths of Jewish self-loathing which induces them to abnegate themselves to the extent of assuming other, even German, identities. Sobol's idea that not everyone went to their doom like lambs to the slaughter may be more positive.

Sobol's depiction of the theatrical and musical activities in the Vilna ghetto, and the discussions about art and survival, serve only one level of the play's purpose, that of spiritual resistance as a form of heroism. On another level the play is a metaphor for the ideological conflicts characterising Israel of the 1980s, particularly Israeli interpretations of Zionism. This was largely for Israeli, rather than international, consumption. *Ghetto* is not therefore an entirely historical drama, for historical events are not its main concern. It should not be seen only as an example of documentary theatre, despite its fidelity to documented fact. The political argument dominates the playtext. The secret of the play's successful Brechtian stylisation – that the alienation effect should be produced paradoxically by a theme of intensely human potency – is precisely because that theme is not paramount. Sobol subordinates the historical material of the Holocaust to an analysis of Zionist ideology through the interplay of representatives of various strands within the Zionist movement. For example, Kruk fiercely opposes the theatre's performance on moral and ideological grounds:

KRUK   You, the Jewish police, the *Judenrat*... you're free to spend time with the Germans. The workers' union in the ghetto has decided to respond to the invitation with a complete ban. Not one of us will go to this vultures' concert.
GENS   I'm telling you this: the workers' union is disbanded. It's not legal.
KRUK   It's the only organisation in the ghetto that has been elected democratically. Are you building a nation here? You're building yourself a kingdom and this theatre is going to be your Versailles. We won't have anything to do with this revisionist farce.[20]

The real and often startling subtext of the play, which was largely eliminated in its British and German productions, places it squarely with other examples of the Zionist critique which dominates Sobol's earlier plays. Sobol's articulation of the problem renders the play chilling not only in its content but in its psycho-political implications. While he denies the allegations of a comparison between the Nazi past and the Israeli present, he suggests, once again defining Zionism by one of its most militant components, that the Jews have internalised totalitarian persecution to such an extent that when they cease being its victims they victimize. He quotes an essay by Martin Buber, *Sie und Wir*, written a year after *Kristallnacht*, in November 1939, reporting that some Zionist Revisionists postulated a certain virtue in Nazi ideology as being effective for a nation in a state of crisis. Sobol adds, 'What was bad about the Nazi ideology, of course, was that it was directed against Jews. Apart from that unfortunate perversion they shared its belief in a policy based on national egoism.'[21] He suggests that this 'policy' possesses a clear potential within Zionism. Also, he emphasizes a curious synthesis of opposites in German and Jewish culture and history. Even Buber speaks of the 'particular collaboration of the German spirit and the Jewish spirit, the *DeutchJudentum*, as it was expressed in the cultural inheritance of German Jews.'[22] Following the Berlin performance of *Ghetto*, Sobol suggested, in the context of a discussion about Israeli politics, that many extremist Israelis were influenced by Nazi ideology and the 'egoistic' chauvinism about which Buber had warned.

If a day comes when we adopt Hitler's god here in Palestine and only change its name into a Hebrew one then we are lost. Well, what I think now happens in Israeli society, at least with the extremists, is exactly this.[23]

According to Sobol, Israeli extremists have already 'adopted Hitler's god'. He added in another Berlin interview: 'I don't want the Germans to feel guilt, but responsibility. What the Germans did to us explains what is happening with us in the present'.[24] In part, despite his energetic refutations, *Ghetto* is an investigation of this phenomenon.

In this regard, the most revealing section of the text is the discussion between the Bundist Kruk and Dr Paul, the Nazi historian of Zionism, played by the same actor who plays Kittel, suggesting two conflicting sides to the same character. In addition, they are the embodiments of two principles recurring in the play, the German will to death and the Jewish life-instinct, rendered always as *hiyuniyut*. Even Kittel, the master of death, exalts *hiyuniyut* before destroying it. To Dr Paul, the Jews are a people in whom the death-instinct is entirely absent. Through his intense devotion to Zionist scholarship Paul is able to see the dangers which Zionism faces should it ever achieve autonomy:

PAUL Permit me to say to you [Kruk] within the swinishness and brutality in which we find ourselves, that my acquaintance with you is to me like a breath of life. Therefore it is doubly a pity for me that you do not undestand what is happening with regard to your own history. You have chosen the diaspora and you have abandoned the future of *Eretz Israel* to people like Gens who will not refuse to receive the control from our hands or from the hands of anybody who will give it to them.

KRUK Here in the ghetto but not in *Eretz Israel*!

PAUL Permit me to disagree with you.[25]

Paul's arguments gradually assume the tone of political propaganda when he describes the activities of the Zionists in Palestine. 'They try to be too much like us,' he adds, 'caricatures of us.'[26] He believes that the essential humanism of both nations (Kruk) has been desecrated by extremism (Gens). Only in connection with growing Zionist militancy and militarism does he speculate about Germans' *thanatos*, the death instinct – opposed to the vitality (*hiyuniyut*) of the Jews – in the Jewish soul. Without much equivocation, therefore, Sobol implies the evolution of Israeli political power from the Nazi ideological model. Significantly these ideas are expressed by a German character who has visited Palestine and regards himself as being able to pronounce on both cultures. Paul is therefore a mixture of spirituality and pathology, an ironic product of the grotesquely projected symbiosis between the German and the Jew.

Gens is, for Paul as he is for Sobol, the archetype of political obduracy in any future Jewish State. Gens articulates the metaphorical sense of Israeli enclosure that is, the notion of Israel as a ghetto and he also provides a self-referential glance at Sobol's dramatic motivation. Through and around this enigmatic character Sobol expresses some of his most conspicuously political ideas and articulates his fears regarding the future of Zionism in Israel. Gens emerges as a man of contradictory passions, responsible for the fate of his people yet oddly removed from their daily concerns, overpowered by his own rhetoric, which on one occasion at least sounds suspiciously like a Sobol satire on current Israeli criticism. Gens is infuriated by a song calling for an uprising and he demands that those responsible create theatre,

but not theatre like this which rubs salt on the wounds and incites rebellion. Is this what we need now that the situation is finally peaceful? Jews, there's nothing to be afraid of. The ghetto is more secure than at any other time. Is this the moment to call people to rebellion? Create theatre – please. But theatre that will make people happy. The public must be calm, disciplined, it must work. You want to create satire? Go ahead. Make satire, but good satire.[27]

Sobol ridicules the self-styled ultra-nationalist: 'If there is anybody with a national feeling in the ghetto, I am that person. I am the patriot and the nationalist and the real Jew'.[28] Gens goes on to make some extraordinary proclamations concerning the use of Hebrew in the lives, culture and education of the ghetto dwellers: 'We will introduce the subject of Palestinography ... We will organize an evening of Bialik in blue and white. Teachers who are not sufficiently nationalistic will be removed from the educational organisation. I want to hear someone say anything against this. [To Kruk] Do you have anything against this?' Kruk replies: 'It's a pity Dr Paul isn't here. They have succeeded better than they can imagine'.[29]

Sobol's satire is aimed at classical Zionism as he sees it, with its symbols and icons and its totalitarian potential. Throughout his drama he appears to see this excessively nationalistic aspect of Zionism, represented in *Ghetto* by Gens and the *Judenrat*, as an unwanted accretion upon profound and meaningful truths.

If *A Jewish Soul* was well received in Germany and Britain, *Ghetto* could be hailed as an international hit, staged in various cities in fourteen countries and in twenty-seven languages between 1984 and 1989. It was one of the few Israeli plays to break through the local confines of the Israeli drama and certainly the first to achieve international acclaim. Productions differed in diverse countries and German cities. In London, for example, the final scene, the last appearance of the theatre troupe, was rewritten: in place of a dance of discarded clothes, members of the troupe metamorphosed into little Hitlers, to the music of Beethoven's ninth symphony.

Unlike the Israelis, only a few foreign reviewers perceived the other, subtextual theme in the play. For example, Keith Gore writes, 'I was progressively irritated and alienated by *Ghetto* as we seemed increasingly required to subscribe to a message addressed to present-day Israel'[30] 'Sobol was born in 1939: the question haunts the Israelis of his generation as it haunts the glittering action of this play. For behind *Ghetto* is the entire questioned identity of the Jewish people in the post-Holocaust age.'[31] 'Sobol is writing as a modern Israeli and partly seeking the Zionist future in wartime Lithuania. Vilna thus becomes a Jewish microcosm showing separate factions emerging through the common task of survival.'[32]

Ghetto was staged by the German director Peter Zadek in Berlin in 1984, receiving the best play award in Germany for that year. It was shown, in addition, in Cologne, Dusseldorf and Hamburg. One of the most positive reviews appeared in the *Frankfurter Allgemeine Zeitung*, according to which the attempt to combine a ghetto operetta with mass murder proved to be informative and persuasive.[33] The critic of *Die Deutsche Zeitung* suggested that in the face of the new wave of anti-Semitism the play and its producer should have avoided certain emphases. Perhaps one of these was the Yiddish-accented German adopted by the actors, encouraged by the Israeli director of the Dusseldorf production, David Levin (brother of Hanokh). A left-wing German newspaper, *Konkret*, accused Sobol of anti-Semitism because he portrayed the Jews as objectionable in the Nazi context. Sobol responded by reproving the journalist for using the image of a morally unimpeachable Jew as a tool in his quarrel with the Right. Gunther Rühle, the director of the Frankfurt Theatre, deemed Sobol's play more anti-Semitic than Fassbinder's controversial *Der Müll, die Stadt und der Tod*.

It is difficult to determine the exact reason for *Ghetto*'s success in Germany. The most facile is that it sustained the Germans' inherent anti-Semitism. Another is the German audiences' renewed amazement at seeing an Israeli play about the *Holocaust* in German. Discussions with the audience following one of the Berlin performances revealed that the play had provided them with a form of private catharsis, particularly since German productions of *Ghetto* centred on the Holocaust alone, entirely eliminating the dimension of Israeli political criticism.

The play failed in the United States. Frank Rich, the formidable critic of the *New York Times*, damned it as boring, a trivialisation of the Holocaust and a near-counterfeiting of the nightmare of the century. Michael Handelsaltz attributed this failure to the play's aesthetic limitations. He added that Jewish audiences expect a play concerning the Holocaust to be something of a religious experience and they resist being faced with difficult questions.[34] This was the case to a certain extent in London where many members of the audience regarded *Ghetto* as a commemorative ritual rather than a theatrical event. People who rarely, if ever, attend the theatre sat through the play as if they were participants in some transcendental experience.

A measure of the play's international success may be due precisely to this inability to confront it as a work of art. Either critics have no methodology of evaluation, given the subject matter, or those who attempt to criticise it do so with apologies: 'The difficulty for the reviewer (at any rate this one) comes from the feeling that any reticence with respect to what is shown on the stage may suggest a lack of sympathy with those whose suffering is portrayed'.[35] 'There are, very occasionally, plays and productions which make criticism seem impertinent.'[36] 'Joshua Sobol's *Ghetto* is a dramatic event that overwhelms the emotions and defies criticism.'[37] These critics and some members of audiences apparently equate criticism of material relating to the Holocaust with anti-Semitism, despite Sobol's challenge to them within the play itself.

Arbeit Macht Frei in Todland Europa – an extraordinary postmodern multimedia event for which the proper designation can only be a 'happening' – was first presented at the Acre Festival in 1991. The event blurred the boundaries of artifice and reality and dared to do what no theatre in Israel had previously attempted. A passage through *stations-tableaux* from historical events to the Palestinian–Israeli conflict, the play not only presented physical artefacts, newsreels, television films and photographs from the Holocaust but also compelled immediate responses to them from its audiences. It presented the Holocaust 'analogy' in its most graphic and unmistakeable form. In Acre each performance admitted only fifteen viewers who moved with the actors from the Centre for Theatre in the Knights' Hall into the various venues constituting the locus of the play. It was 'total theatre' during which the audience not only followed the actors but entered into discussions and ate with them.

From the start of the Acre event, when the fifteen ticket-holders were ordered to stand to one side, the tone of the evening was set. Travelling on a minibus, the action – the actors and the audience – reached the venues comprising the 'setting' of the play, beginning with the museum dedicated to the ghetto fighters. Smadar Ya'aron-Ma'ayan, playing a guide named Zelda, led the audience through the museum, recounting details of the history of Nazi Germany as they moved along, so that the audience, at the same time a theatre audience and a group of visitors to a museum, found their own sense of reality blurred, particularly when suddenly called upon to answer questions. The bus journeys included the screening of films about the Holocaust and aspects of Israeli culture. Another 'guide', the Israeli Arab actor Khaled Abu Ali, discussed the Polish anti-Semitism that had facilitated the establishment of death camps in Poland. Once again Jewish passivity is alluded to, the lambs-to-the-slaughter argument although, as Abu Ali reminded the audience, there had been instances of Jewish resistance.

The audience, sometimes on foot, sometimes by minibus, moved from venue to venue, each place darker and more claustrophobic, and at various points they encountered discarded clothing, watched on television monitors a Jewish woman undergoing the tattooing of her concentration camp number, walked through a reproduction of the entrance to Auschwitz bearing the motto *Arbeit Macht Frei* beside an Israeli flag, heard Nazi and Israeli songs being compared, conversations about the 'selections' in the camps and the significance of Zionist and Jewish history. At one stage Abu Ali appears, serving the audience coffee and cake while complaining that he has been beaten, and then, as a Palestinian, he offers some autobiographical facts. The 'play' ends with a surrealistic, raucous, almost sadomasochistic orgy during which members of the cast successively place themselves in degrading and undignified positions, naked, suspended by their legs, ridiculously garnished by foodstuffs, uncomfortable and debased.

They were themselves, humbled, naked and actually sacrificing themselves like scapegoats on the altar of the experience. It's true they were stilll actors in an artificial theatrical framework which they had created and to which they had brought the viewers, but their exposure and their humiliation were so acute that it was almost impossible to contemplate.[38]

Since this *was*, after all, a theatrical performance the audience was powerless to intervene, to protect the actors or to intercede for them, but sat in silence, watching. The orgy owed something to the decadence of prewar Germany and it served as a trope of modern Israeli materialism, but its point about the nations of the world as onlookers in the face of the annihilation of European Jewry was well made. The viewer was a watcher and a collaborator at the same time.

The theatre here did not 'deal with' the topic of the Holocaust and did not 'express' its views about it. It did not 'say' anything about the Holocaust or in memory of it, and did not 'say' anything about the power of theatre.[39]

What *did* it say? Apart from its condemnation of Nazism, it attempted, with intermittent success, to make many statements about Israeli politics and the Occupation refracted through the prism of Holocaust awareness. This was uncompromisingly Israeli theatre which reflected local attitudes to the Holocaust, viewing it from within the Israeli consciousness. It held a mirror up to the society, all the while importuning the audience to an increased awareness of events in the Territories. Every theme touched upon by earlier drama found its place in this play: the effect of the Holocaust on Israel's international relations, particularly on its relationship with its neighbours; the nature of the licence afforded by Holocaust memory in Israel's dealing with others; the exploitation of the Holocaust in Israeli right-wing rhetoric; the contributions of the Holocaust to the creation of the collective Israeli identity.[40] The play did not shirk current issues: the vulgarisation of the Holocaust within Israel (alluded to in *Tcherli Katcherli*), rituals of public remembrance, Israeli children's grasp of the Holocaust, and the nature of contemporary Zionism. The Nazism-Zionism 'analogy' constituted a potent subtext to the play. In a sense the audience was 'softened up' by the visions of the Holocaust to contemplate Israeli political reality and to see the Palestinian, played by an Israeli Arab, as a victim.

In this play and others similar to it, victimhood is transferred from Jew to Arab. Successive generations of Israelis have laboured to interpret Jewish victimhood. The question now is whether they project this victimhood onto their literary Arab/Palestinian characters. Israelis are victims no longer despite the tendentious manipulation of the Holocaust by some political leaders and religious militants. With the shedding of their own victimhood the Israelis have achieved a sense of positive selfhood. At the same time the writers demonstrate real political anxiety: positive selfhood incorporates the moral responsibility which the nation has struggled from the start to fulfil. *Arbeit Macht Frei* indeed concludes with an image of the dehumanisation and degradation of the Jew, but the Arab is also dancing naked on the table amid the remnants of a meal, entreating the audience to beat him and proffering a bottle opener on a rope around his neck for thirsty (or 'indifferent') viewers to open their bottles of beer. The play's ultimate excess – the portrayal of one of the actresses sitting naked in a tub, forcing food down her throat and spreading it over her body – indicates a kind of self-loathing as Jew, as Israeli and as victim.

Arbeit Macht Frei was taken to the Berlin Festival in 1992 despite protests in Israel from those who claimed that the play 'washed dirty Israeli linen in public', considering it particularly inappropriate for Germans to witness the laundering. Others argued that the play would assist the Germans to salve their own consciences, or that it reinforced the global view of the Jew as eternal victim, or that it would reveal the Israeli as a racist and that everything was 'mixed together in an eastern salad, seasoned with a mental *tehina, humous* and parsley to the point of degradation, defilement, the loss of structure and total humiliation'.[41] Leading members of the Berlin Jewish community and the Israeli diplomatic establishment stayed away. The play – which was given in simultaneous translation into German – crossed into forbidden linguistic, historical and semiotic territory in Germany. It bewildered the audiences, constituted in the main by young middle-class Germans, with a few foreign visitors including, at one performance, the director Peter Brook. In Germany the thirty people permitted to attend each performance were transported through the city of Berlin by bus. The event began at a museum which had once been Gestapo headquarters; from there the audience was driven to the suburb of Wannsee, some thirty minutes from the city centre, to the villa where the Final Solution to the Jewish Problem had been plotted, now a memorial to victims of the Holocaust.

Although the progress of the evening did not differ substantially from that in Acre, the context effected a vastly different ideological perspective. The play's potency was heightened by the venues, by the German language and an audience with a cognate and yet conflicting collective memory, the perpetrator confronting the victim. As in Israel, Smadar Ya'aron-Ma'ayan played Zelda, a guide leading her charges through the history of Nazism represented by the metonymic objects most closely associated with the Holocaust: yellow stars, articles of clothing and horrifying photographs. The group then moved on to the east of the city, to a brewery that was originally the headquarters of the East German Secret Police, the Stasi. There they were led, through narrow, dank, badly lit tunnels, into the cellars where the remainder of the performance took place. On television monitors they watched cuts from Lanzmann's *Shoah*, other films about the Holocaust, about Hitler, and interviews with kibbutz children regarding their own awareness of the Holocaust. National commemorations – *Yom Hashoah* (Holocaust Day) in Israel and the memorial day to the German resistance – were compared. From this point, to the audience's growing bewilderment, the show moved ideologically from Europe to Israel. When the Israeli national anthem, *Hatikvah*, was played the Germans immediately rose; as they did so the strains of the anthem melded into *Deutschland Über Alles* which is banned in Germany. The audience did not know whether or not to remain on their feet and some sat down. Later, as part of the action, members of the cast questioned the viewers about their awareness of the activities of members of their families during the war. They received polite but evasive replies. The action moved to another room representing 'Zelda's' house in Israel during the 1950s, where she and her neighbours discussed their difficulties as Holocaust survivors and revealed their ambivalent attitudes toward the Arabs.

In Israel the following scene had portrayed a soldier swapping stories with the audience as if at a celebratory dinner on the evening of *Yom Ha'atzma'ut* (Independence Day). In Berlin the character was an expert on international terrorism, a consultant to the government who invited his colleagues to dinner. He was played as a brash, macho and racist Israeli, the least appealing incarnation of the *sabra*. The audience was confronted by a table laden with Israeli delicacies and invited to eat. According to the Israeli critics who were present, the German members of the audience ate with gusto and enjoyed their meal while the Israelis in the audience could stomach nothing. Critics suggested that the Germans were not competent to grasp the Israeli discourse embodied in the experience. Meanwhile the Arab actor, Abu Ali, spoke of the genocide of the Palestinian people. Finally the entire group moved to a location decorated as a disco where the orgy as in Acre took place.

The German critics misunderstood the play, seeing it only through a general and rather more conventional ideological perspective, and their reviews revealed many factual inaccuracies about the play, about the Holocaust and about Israel. It was in Germany that members of the audience availed themselves of the bottle opener and drank Abu Ali's beer. 'It was painful and beautiful,' wrote a German critic, 'the shock had an effect and it was essential, like the provocation and the breaking of taboos in order to mourn.'[42] After the performances the cast held discussions with the German audiences, 'the children of the victims and the children of the murderers' in the words of a columnist, but the Germans were not forthcoming. It seems that the writers' political mediation of the Holocaust material prevented the German audiences' comprehension of the play's implications. Yet Thomas Lachmann, a young theatre critic who had expressed anti-Israel views during the period of the Intifada, declared his ambivalence:

Our shoes are covered in mud, bits of rice and gravy clings to our clothes. I stand in the street. The director David Ma'ayan wanted to give us catharsis, to the Jews and the Germans. I refused. When they played the national anthem I sat down. I didn't reveal my name to the interviewer. I didn't jump onto the table to beat the Arab even though he invited me a number of times to do so. With all this, I had never before been seduced by actors from a foreign land to peer so deeply into their bare soul – which is our twin soul.[43]

The questions to be asked are why the Israeli artists should want him to and why the necessity for this twinhood with the Germans; why indeed do the Israelis wish to be understood by the Germans, not only through the medium of this event but by means of other plays as well. Their implicit comparison of themselves with the Nazis implies the need for punishment. The attribution of their own brutality to the German model had already been stated by Sobol. Like him they proclaim their oppostion to Israel's treatment of the Palestinians, together with their awareness of their own impotence. What emerges from *Arbeit Macht Frei*, particularly in Germany, is self-flagellation rather than the theatrical arraignment and punishment of the Germans. The intensity of accusation directed at the Germans, Israelis and Zionism – which deeply moved the Israeli audiences – appears to have left the Germans' consciences unraised. The response of Israeli critics was more varied: some expressed themselves moved and overcome by the experience, others detested the mélange of Holocaust and Israeli politics. Whatever the reaction, *Arbeit Macht Frei* took the drama of the Holocaust into political realms previously untried by Israeli drama.

In the 1980s many plays incorporated the topic of the Holocaust peripherally, with playwrights viewing it as a phenomenon which conditions generations of Israeli lives. Most notable of these is Yosef Bar Yosef's poetic *Hagigah Shel Horef* (A Winter Celebration), (1992),[44] which suggests that human fulfilment will always remain elusive in the post-Holocaust world. Plays of varying standards were produced during this decade, some containing some form of personal or political agenda, others which exploited the Holocaust for sensation or bias. Michael Kahane's *Harikud Shel Genghis Cohen* (The Dance of Genghis Cohen), (1984), based on the novel by Romain Gary, depicts the relationship between Genghis Cohen, the ghost of a Holocaust victim, and the ex-SS colonel who murderered him. This haunting of the now respectable German stresses the impossibility of freedom from the Holocaust for both victim and oppressor, and the victim's potential for becoming the murderer's nemesis. In addition to its comment on the Holocaust, the play was seen in Israel as a symbolic confrontation with the complex relationship between ruler and ruled, especially after 1967.

German reparations appeared as a theme in a number of plays including Hillel Mittelpunkt's *Makolet* (Grocery), (1982) and *Kiddush* (Blessing) by Shmuel Hasfari, (1986). Yosef Mundi's *Leilot Frankfurt Ha'alizim* (Frankfurt's Happy Nights), (1987), reiterates many themes relating to the Holocaust's pertinence for Israel. At the centre of this play is Willi Wolff, a Holocaust survivor, now the patron of a string of sleazy nightclubs throughout Europe. His Frankfurt club is almost bankcrupt due to the spread of Aids. While he reagards himself as a sensitive man and a lover of art, his specialty is sadomasochistic pornography and, in the face of financial ruin, he begins drug trading. Into this milieu walks Didi, an ironic portrait of the *sabra*, a tall, good-looking, muscular young man from Israel in whom 'there is nothing of diaspora',[45] seeking a job. The play charts the attempted corruption of innocence and becomes a rather heavy-handed indictment of Europe's corruption of the Jew and the European Jew's of the Israeli. In the end Didi proves himself to be incorruptible and leaves the club. Woven throughout the play is the demand that Israel recognise the role played by the Holocaust in its own history.

WILLI You're runing away because you're afraid of the truth.
DIDI Which truth? [He stops]
WILLI About the Holocaust.
DIDI I look forward, I build the future for myself.
WILLI And what about the past?
DIDI It's yours, not mine.
WILLI [*coming closer to him*] You're mistaken, it's yours as well.[46]

Later Didi, a throwback to Mossinzon's Avraham, says: 'Unlike you, we would never have let the Holocaust happen. We would have fought'.[47] His views on Europe are stereotyped, perhaps ironically so, directing his aversion at its rottenness and estrangement from everything that signifies Israel's purity. Mundi establishes a saving undertone of irony by having Didi angrily leave the club not however, to return to Israel but to move on to the United States in search of wealth. As in Levin's *The Patriot*, the Israeli is compromised by greed and corruption.

Mesibat Purim shel Adam Ben Kelev (The Purim Party of Adam, Son of a Dog), (1981), a dramatisation by Yoram Kaniuk of his novel *Hayehudi Ha'aharon* (The Last Jew), is set in a psychiatric institution and deals with the separate madnesses of the Holocaust and the State of Israel. The central character, who has survived by pre-tending to be the camp commandant's dog, explains to the audience that schizophrenia is an effective means of enduring post-Holocaust life. Kaniuk revises topics which frequently recur in Holocaust drama, one being the Holocaust as an unhealed wound within the survivor's soul and that of every Jew. Kaniuk's second theme is, again, the 'analogy' which proposes a Holocaust of another kind as the potential consequence of Israeli politics. Kaniuk's emphasis in the play on psychosis and characters who pretend to be mad as a means of survival, refers to the basic absurdity of Israeli life:

Where else can you find a man and a woman who have lost both their families in the Holocaust building a new family in Israel, only to lose their first-born son in the 1967 war and their second in the 1973 war. You don't need to be Sartre to realize that you live here in the midst of a vicious cycle.[48]

For him madness is the most appropriate trope to indicate the impossibility of organizing experience for a society which has emerged from chaos and disintegration.

The reason for the Israeli playwrights' rehearsal before foreign audiences of local political problems is plain. The darker and more enigmatic phenomenon, their need to stress these issues primarily to the Germans, leads to less confident speculation. Whatever the reasons, the dialectical nature of the plays, including those which refer to the Holocaust, demonstrates that the writers are still in possession of that moral subtext which has defined Israeli literature ever since Yizhar's 'The prisoner' (1948). The constant return to the *moral* feasibility of conquest and occupation is a positive reminder for Israeli audiences that it is not only *realpolitik* rising from Zionist dogma that underlies political discussion, but also an ethical debate. Whether this or any other political or philosophical agenda is *appropriate* in the context of plays about the Holocaust remains an open question.

CHAPTER 9

Metaphor and mythology

The shift from dogmatic idealism to political criticism is frequently enclosed within structures which are neither documentary nor satirical, but in wider symbolic or mythical formulations and in terms borrowed from world culture. A number of Israeli playwrights, including two of the most prominent, Nissim Aloni and Hanokh Levin, have framed their political message within more poetic, visionary structures. Aloni, in particular, has succeeded in defining the Israeli political self through a non-Jewish, non-Israeli image. One extreme in Hebrew drama has been a parochialism devoid of an intellectual argument transcending the local and temporal; the other extreme is Aloni whose intellectual canvas is dazzlingly extensive. Born in 1926, he is chronologically a member of the *Palmah* generation, but philosophically he is widely divergent from them. Although his thinking was not influenced either by the kibbutz or the youth movement, he conformed to the general mood of his generation by calling for a war of the sons against the fathers:

the fathers taught the sons to fight a war against an external enemy for the sake of creating a new reality but they didn't teach them to fight the real war for the sake of this reality – the war against the fathers and their realised ideology.[1]

Aloni was also responsible for occasional outbursts that coincided with the prevailing post-war mood in the Israel of the 1950s. In common with some of the most prominent spokesmen of his generation, he voiced the problems connected with the transition from wartime to political independence. Because of his references to the *ivriyyut* ('Hebrewness') of Israel, some associated him with the Canaanite movement which touched most of his contemporary writers even without their formal adoption of its ideology.[2] The Canaanites were members of an Israeli political movement of the 1950s which promoted the idea of 'Hebrewness' in place of 'Jewishness', that is, they favoured the total separation of native-born Palestinian Hebrews from the diaspora Jews. They sought to eradicate all links between the diaspora Jews and the emerging territorial Hebrew nation. Yet Aloni elevated parochial concerns to the level of myth, achieved for the Hebrew theatre the 'universalism' long demanded by its dramatic criticism.

In common with many of his Israeli contemporaries, Aloni contributed material to satirical revues, in his case for the popular group *Hagashash Hahiver*. As a serious dramatist he initially experimented with Jewish cultural material, including the Bible, as an allegory or a source of cultural archetypes. Like Sobol, he used Jewish history as a means of examining contemporary social issues. His later plays abandoned this Jewish textual framework in favour of European literature, mythology, folktales, legends and history. His plays sometimes exhibit vaguely Israeli settings although the place names have little relationship to reality. Topics, some associated with tragedy, recur in his plays: the killing of the father by the son, the death of kings, the figure of a clownish, weak or grotesque king, nostalgia for a glorious past, the search for a killer, a Pirandellian world of role-play, masks and dissimulation. In the list of his major and constantly reiterated themes a relationship, vastly allegorised, to Israel can be discerned, a deeply subtextual restatement of Israeli literature's most obsessive preoccupations. Aloni cloaks them in magic so that his plays, like all great drama, exist on several levels at once.

Apart from his first play, a biblical-historical drama based on the conflict between Rehoboam and Jeroboam, *Akhzar Mikol Hamelekh* (The King is the Cruellest of All), (1953),[3] his plays' strongest connection with Israel rests in the metaphorical nature of the 'self' that they project, a young man who destroys an older patriarchal figure. This conflict has lain at the core of Jewish literary consciousness from the time of the *Haskalah*, the Hebrew Enlightenment, and was adopted by Israeli literature from the start.[4]

There is an eternal war of which no generation is free, the war between the sons and the fathers ... There are wars of greater or less bitterness, but a complete absence of this war testifies only to a complete or partial deterioration of a generation. Governments and lifestyles last for a long or a little time but the war of the sons against the fathers is one that invests all these systems with a new, fresh spirit or undermines them or causes their destruction.[5]

Despite the reiteration of this and other themes which have become almost hackneyed in Israeli literature, we should not devalue the real problems of Aloni's generation. The clash between the European founders, with their idealistic visions of a future in Palestine powered by the best of European and Jewish culture, and the culturally Israelised sons, is deeply rooted within the Israeli sensibility. This conflict has supplied Israeli literature with its most potent symbolic partnership, the father and the son, which appears in numerous guises throughout the fiction, poetry and drama. A father-son conflict frequently revealed itself in other modernist literature as well, particularly during the period of German Expressionism, albeit for different reasons and from different social derivations. In some Expressionist dramas, for example, 'the father symbolised all the forms of repressive and insensitive authority which had to be smashed if the son were to realize himself'.[6] This has a less brutal analogy in the Hebrew literature of the time: yet while the Jewish fathers' influence was grounded elsewhere than in interwar industrial power, it was no less repressive for that, with the inevitable consequence of a spiritual rebellion by the sons. Controlling, traditionalist fathers were frequently functional in the lives of the defecting Jewish intellectual sons, the new 'apostates'.[7]

In contemporary Hebrew poetry the figure of the dead father as *revenant* haunts the son, visiting him in dreams with a reproach for his desertion of Jewish tradition and his faith, implying that the son has killed him by renouncing his cultural world. The *Haskalah* author M. Z. Feierberg formulated this cultural betrayal through his indictment of his apostate hero for 'murdering everything inside him: himself, his father, his father's fathers, his entire people'.[8] A generation later the guilt has intensified. By creating a secular society with its representative the New Jew, the Israelis turn their backs on the patriarchal figure, symbol of authority, identity and traditional Judaism. To them, therefore, the primordial murdered father is not a legendary Greek king but a cultural father whom they have destroyed by betrayal, abandonment and, finally, rejection. To palliate their guilt, the sons justify their actions by means of a twofold accusation levelled at the father: weakness on the one hand, and violence, on the other, both symbolised by the primal story of the *Akedah*.

Aloni proposes the inevitability of the act of patricide: 'The fact of a man being a son to a father is a trap from which it is impossible to escape. What is there for a son to do in life other than kill his father?'[9] Yet Aloni alone has specified the Oedipus myth rather than the *Akedah* through which to trace this cultural tale of love, murder and guilt. His Oedipal metaphor is extended in his dramas, where the guilt of patricide destroys the son as well.

Aloni's central image, a king deposed or killed by a son, is redolent of his perhaps unconscious preoccupation with the nature of authority. The titles of his plays indicate his persistent interest, if not obsession: *The King is the Cruellest of All*, *The American Princess* (Hanesikhah Ha'amerikait), *The King's Clothes* (Bigdei Hamelekh), *Napoleon – Alive or Dead* (Napoleon – Hai o Met), and *Eddie King*. Kings are fathers or rulers destroyed by the sons. Even in those of Aloni's plays which avoid reference to monarchy in the title, a son kills his father or a father figure. Moreover the king or father is a grotesque figure, his spiritual distortion the reason for the son's compulsion to usurp him. Another incarnation of his metaphorical father possesses a special resonance for Israeli society, the father as a buffoon-king symbolising authority become grotesque, idealism reduced to the ridiculous, power to comedy. Aloni demonstrates leadership to be pathetic and inept, the leader to be a figure whose incapacity for compromise echoes the defeated romanticism of his, Aloni's, generation.

Aloni's deviation from the Israeli dramatic norm of realism rests not only in this scheme of filial rebellion and usurpation but in the non-naturalistic structure of his plays which are a mélange of modernist styles and resonances combined with extraordinary stagecraft. His theatre is not exclusively Epic Theatre, Symbolism, German Expressionism or the Absurd but a combination of them all, a distillation of a variety of European theatrical trends prominent since the beginning of the twentieth century. It is also highly literary, based on an intricate network of intertexts, rewarding the reader of his playtexts as much as the viewers of his productions. Each of his plays is written within the framework of a fable, classical myth, fairy tale, card game or legend. Each one draws from diverse theatrical traditions, the carnival, the cabaret, the *commedia dell'arte*, operetta, television and opera.

Aloni is not alone in his choice of European classical mythology through which to mediate experience. Sobol had utilised the *structure* of a myth, the *Oresteia*, in his trilogy *The Days of the House of Kaplan*, and a few Hebrew poets also took Greek myths as their narrative roots in addition to their Hebraic sources. Their use of Greek mythology is self-consciously literary since its archetypes are imported rather than native to the local culture. Aloni's choice of particular myths and European tales, such as Hans Andersen's 'The Emperor's New Clothes' and non-Jewish phenomena such as the tarot pack in *The Gypsies of Jaffa* (Hatzoʼanim Miyafo), is a matter of express artistic need. It suggests, in the first instance, radical discontinuity with his own traditional past. He has selected universal paradigms instead of being confined only to Jewish tradition, in 'a nostalgia for world culture', to use Mandelstam's phrase.[10] Aloni's use of non-Judaic sources offered him a means of making significant statements without having to depend on a single cultural or religious order. The artistic problem, as always in Jewish culture, entails a philosophical and religious one.

Second, by his recourse to these sources, Aloni implicitly identifies Hebrew literature as being of European descent. This complies with his need to alter his traditional contexts. Third, Aloni shifts the context of the Hebrew language away from the sacred literature of the past. The shock of the language encountering an alien cultural system, in Aloni's case often doubly alien due to strange geographical settings, becomes an ironic comment in itself. Aloni's choice of classical myth appears then to be less a matter of assuming the myth's non-Judaic 'nuclear idea' than relinquishing his own traditional sources.

Aloni's second play, *The King's Clothes*, (1963),[11] at last introduced the entity the Israeli critics had been seeking, the 'universal' play, into the Hebrew dramatic repertoire. It was an allegory which bore little relationship to Israeli life or Jewish history but which was derived from Hans Christian Andersen's 'The Emperor's New Clothes'. By taking the Hebrew theatre beyond its territorial borders and out ito the modern technological world, abandoning overt 'national' characteristics, *The King's Clothes* set the tone for Aloni's subsequent drama. It explored beneath a surface which had until then served as the only material for original drama in Israel. *The King's Clothes* took a further step in Aloni's use of satire to combat the corruption of power, which he had already investigated in *The King is the Cruellest of All*. It satirises the ridiculous in society, the lies and dishonesty of public life, politics and art, of official institutions in any newly established bureaucracy, and the degeneration of idealism and its objectives. Despite the play's non-locatable setting, Aloni draws on his best-known model, Israeli society of the 1950s.

His third play, *Hanesikhah Ha'amerika'it* (The American Princess), first produced at the Onot Theatre in 1963 and renewed for Habimah in 1982 with additional characters and dialogue, is his most virtuoso work. It was written for only two onstage characters, with other parts played by offstage voices speaking through loud-speakers. Its complicated story owes a good deal to the myths of Oedipus, Persephone and the Fisher King, as well as to fairy tale. Boniface Victor Felix von Hohenschwaden is the king of Greater Bogomania, an absolute monarch and chronic philanderer whose wife, Cecilia, died some years previously after having gone mad. The king has been exiled for twenty years in a South American country, living in poverty as a teacher of French. His son, the Crown Prince Ferdinand, shares his banishment and his whore. Boniface spends his days in fantasies about his past and hopes for his restoration to the monarchy. Into his life comes Dolly Kokomakis, the self-styled American princess originally from Bogomania, who once loved him. She is a typical Aloni creature of fantasy, someone who could not possibly exist. She sends Boniface a tape recorder with which to record his memoirs and then dispatches a film producer to make a film about him. Ferdinand agrees to play the part in the film of his father in his youth, to marry his 'mother' and conceive himself. He is then to play himself and, according to the dictates of the script, to kill his father, now played by the king. During filming Ferdinand 'shoots' the king and then discovers to his horror that live bullets have replaced the blanks and he has indeed killed his own father. The Oedipal story being enacted in the lives of father and son reaches its tragic culmination through the film about their lives, a fiction. Life is driven by art in a feat of transformational theatre where threads of reality and fantasy intermingle like the themes of a fugue.

With the revival in 1982 of *The American Princess* the critics again questioned the play's relevance to Israeli society. Setting the story in a foreign land did not eliminate the possibility of Aloni's judgments being closer to home. 'The deep structure of the play is the one revealed there in South America, in the fate of the exiled king and his son but which returns him to what is close and known.'[12] Set at a distance from Israel the play holds a mirror up to Israeli society, reflecting a commonplace in the literature of Aloni's generation, the breach between the Zionist ideal and its realisation within the autonomous state. The Zionist founders had played a vital role in

Jewish history; once fulfilled, however, their 'dream' was driven to the margins of the society's real needs. The result was a generation caught between their fathers' romantic aspirations and their own realities. King Boniface asks a strange question when recalling his past loves, one of whom is a certain Zelda: 'Oh, Zelda Putziniu, did you finally go to Palestine?' Ferdy explains, as an aside: 'A small country in emerging Africa. Many zealots. Lots of folklore.'[13]

The reference to Zelda who went to Palestine is more than merely satirical for in the broadest cultural sense *The American Princess* expresses the central proccupation of early Israeli writing: the 'dichotomy' (a word occuring frequently in Hayyim Shoham's critical vocabulary) between a land envisioned by a generation which had matured at a distance from it and the land experienced by the generation which had inhabited it from childhood and would determine its future. Inasmuch as this is featured symbolically in *The American Princess*, the play is both a generational and an ideological statement exemplifying Aloni's premise of a crucial cultural war between fathers and sons in Israel. The Oedipal conflict also implies the sons' disappointment in their fathers' impenetrable principles, the resistance to modernism of a generation nurtured on an ethical ideology. Gershon Shaked confirms the play's 'relevance' by taking it as an expression of 'the emotional death of the Zionist dream'.[14]

Another reference in *The American Princess* to Israeli social dialectics is in the different natures of the ex-king and his son. The prince, Ferdy, denizen of a democratic post-royal world, a materialist and would-be wheeler-dealer, and the old father dreaming of a better past, lamenting the loss of values, resemble the Sobollian duo of Gershon and Boaz. If the play does contain a measure of allegory it suggests Aloni's comment on those members of his own generation who recreate the past in romantic, pastoral terms, a generation of kings reduced to greyness. Ferdy is crude, brash, ambitious and mercenary. Like Boaz and Dina in Sobol's *Going Home*, he mocks the king's clinging to the past and the hope for the restoration of his monarchy. The film allows him, in fantasy at least, to kill his father and inherit the crown. This is both an echo of the Oedipal story and an ideological allegory, similar to Boaz's schemes to deprive his father-in-law of his property. Some years earlier than Sobol, therefore, Aloni first raised the problem: Israel relegates an ideology and its values and substitutes a commercial, synthetic culture of commodity and self-aggrandisement. The 1982 version of *The American*

Princess was given greater piquancy and greater potential tension by the two central roles being played by a father and son, Yisrael and Moshe Becker.

However, to rest the play solely on Israeli socio-cultural foundations would be oversimplifying a complex multilateral work. The conflict between old values and technological materialism is not exclusively an Israeli concern. As Shoham has argued, the play's deep structure entails a metaphorical distant land devoid of recognisable topographical and cultural details. It also incorporates the universal concern with the unblemished past and the tarnished present, the old world which in memory alone is perfect, and modernity; idealism confronting pragmatism and losing its power in the modern world.

Despite his ventures into South America, Hell, New York and various mythical lands, including a Jaffa as unlike Jaffa as Brecht's Sechuan is unlike anywhere in China, Aloni is nevertheless an identified Hebrew playwright in his reading of his own cultural environment through the screen of 'universal' myths. With *Eddie King* (1975),[15] he reached an almost preordained culmination of his creative process. After having hinted at the story in many previous works, he finally transposed *Oedipus Rex* in its entirety to a contemporary setting, New York's Mafia underworld, with the Godfather as king. It was a critical failure. Audiences were mystified, and critics disputed the playwright's manipulation of the classical drama together with his reification of the Mafia. This was some time before *The Godfather* became a cult film.

Brought as a baby from Sicily to New York, Eddie King, the play's hero, 'established himself in the new world but never freed himself of the burden he had brought with him from "there"'.[16] Whether or not this is true of Aloni's generation, the one most burdened with quasi-psychological generalisations, Eddie remains the confused inhabitant of the old world while his rival, Creon, represents the future: a world of business, accountancy and the stock exchange. In the guise of Creon, the Boaz-Lifschitz figure again takes the stage.

Eddie King involves a second metaphor, that of immigrants who arrive in the new world laden not only with ancient moral baggage but with memories of a better place. While remaining on the margins of their new society they struggle to forge an identity within their self-created group. Eventually they challenge the old land with the new, old Sicily with America, past with present, a rural society with an urban one. The old world symbolises the newly-rejected values of the past, having shaped the new land's id. With Eddie's murder of his father, the gangster Don Laius, once again modernity supplants tradition. Perhaps Aloni's fascination with corrupt kings also has to do with the secularity of early Zionist culture, the breakdown of the relationship between the Jews and God.

In a whimsical one-act play, *Hakalah Vetzayad Haparparim* (The Bride and the Butterfly Hunter), (1967, revived 1980)[17] Aloni refers metaphorically to a different form of Oedipal relationship, that of the young pioneers with the land, always feminine, against the wishes of the fathers and also of God whose possession it remains. He alludes to the response of the pioneers to their encounter with the land, the suggestion of disappointment after the 'wedding night', the much explored disunion between expectation and fulfilment. Aloni utilises the *halutz* (pioneer) image to indicate the dangers of realising one's aspirations:

GETZ Generally they get into situations impossible even to imagine would happen – that is to say, before the wedding it would be impossible to imagine that they would happen after the wedding... like the pioneers that came to marry the country... I mean to say, to build the country ... they thought about it all the time, didn't they? ... and when they arrived.[18]

Disillusionment and nostalgia, the results of promise and desire, afflict each generation anew.

Aloni's contribution to Hebrew drama is therefore in his establishment of a unique metaphorical structure with which to examine a dominant element of the Jewish/Israeli unconscious. He has broken all the rules for the creation of what the experts believe to be national drama, conforming only with one play based on a biblical story. Otherwise, he recreates drama from its human sources, reviving a classical myth and allowing the distinctive consciousness of his own society to shape it. If there is a consistent narrative thread throughout, it is about a group (or nation) whose fate is a lonely journey towards self-recognition, at odds with its own history after having rejected the palliatives of tradition.

Despite his ventures into 'foreign' systems, Aloni is therefore among the most nationally identified of all Hebrew playwrights in his application of 'universal' myths to his own cultural text. All great drama is based upon a metaphor which interprets a specific national spirit and identity. Early Hebrew drama was defined by its adherence to its national myths and its exploitation of them. Aloni has transcended these myths to create a dramatic figuration of his own. Nevertheless, the sense of loss underlying his drama, the son's frantic attempt to usurp the father's throne, and the stubborn will of the individual confronting the group place his aesthetic sensibility within the Israeli literary tradition.

Consciously or not, Aloni has given the Zionist dialectic a philosophical dimension which it lacked even in Sobol's discursive analysis. If we are to apply Aloni's fixation with Oedipal rejection and usurpation to the ideological argument, we see that it is little more than an expression of rebellion. Sons reject their fathers and their fathers' gods. A revised ideology rejects and then displaces the old through its changed perspectives despite its inheritance of certain ancestral features, just as a rebellious son still resembles his father.[19] Interpretations of Zionist ideology demonstrate that the political tradition of successive Israeli generations has been built on disdain for the past.

Through this conflict of displacement and usurpation, Aloni is able to reconstitute the prerequisites for tragedy in Judaic terms. While his metaphysical battle (set within the framework of classical mythology) is primarily political in its confrontation between Zionism and Israel, the fatefulness of the confrontation moves it into the realm of tragedy. Not only does tragedy imply an element of choice, it also describes these choices as challenging metaphysical determinism. Killing the king inevitably leads to chaos, isolation and blindness; ultimately the land is laid waste.

CHAPTER 10

The vision of Hanokh Levin

Satirists often appear to be politically unaligned, or even conservative. According to Yitzhak Laor, '[Hanokh] Levin has a basic conservatism, generally characteristic of the writers of comedy'.[1] It is true that, unlike Sobol, Hanokh Levin's plays (apart from the satirical cabarets) rarely comment directly on Israeli or Zionist politics. However, his conclusions about modern Israel reiterate the doctrine expressed in the drama from early social realism to the present day: that 'normalisation' from the start has been equivocal, often an inversion of Zionism's great design. Levin's dour urban vision deviates entirely from the the founders' agrarian aspirations. His domestic black comedies illustrate – as well as the satires ever did – the bleak fall from ideological grace, the dark underside of *mamlakhtiyut*. His visual brutality is a fitting vision for the violence of modern existence in general and for twentieth-century Jewish fate in in particular. The physical and emotional dismemberment which underlies all his plays is indicative of his sense of ruin: ideological order become anarchy.[2] Dismemberment of the body denotes that of the body politic, a nation turning on itself. This constitutes the core of Levin's political conception throughout his drama.

Levin's genre of theatrical radicalism that had become almost commonplace abroad was a novelty in Israel, a reversal of the comparatively consensual drama of the preceding generation. Like Aloni's, his surrealistic world derives from the depth of the Israeli unconscious. He was born in Tel Aviv in 1943, the son of Polish immigrants. A precocious talent both as a playwright and a fiction writer, Levin achieved not only success but also notoriety with his early satirical cabarets which lampooned Israeli political and social complacency after the war in 1967. They entirely disrupted the gentle world of Ephraim Kishon's 'constructive satire'; nothing as outspoken, harsh and trenchant had ever been seen on the Israeli stage. Little that Levin has written subsequently has been free of controversy. His supporters have dubbed him an institution – ironic for one whose task from the start has been to subvert and rebel – and commend him for his daring. The older critics find him crude, superficial, repetitive, glib, decadent and pornographic. Either way, his undoubted talent has made him one of the most original playwrights and directors in Israel today, albeit endowed with a macabre imagination. There have been many instances in modern theatrical history of playwrights initially alienating audiences, only to become accepted and even venerated as the audiences develop the necessary receptive strategies. This is the case with Pinter and Beckett; even the outrageous Joe Orton has become something of a modern classic. In Israel Hanokh Levin has been the recipient of two establishment prizes, the Leah Porat Prize in 1983 and the Meskin Prize in 1984.

Levin's work falls into four categories: first, a group of satirical cabarets following the Six-Day War, of which *The Queen of the Bathtub* was one. These plays aroused critical and public controversies due in part to their novel style, but primarily because of their radical political content which ridiculed the Israeli public as much as its leaders. Levin followed these in the 1970s with his second wave of plays, comedy-dramas in the form either of farce or the Absurd in which the family, or a grotesque version of it, was central. The third category contained the 'metaphysical' plays of which *Hotza'ah Lahoreg* (Execution), (1979), *Yisurei Iyov* (The Torments of Job), (1981) and *Hazonah Hagedolah Mibavel* (The Great Whore of Babylon), (1982), were the most celebrated. In his fourth wave Levin returned to the style of the localised plays of the 1970s, and in 1993 he received universal accolades for *Hayeled Holem* (The Child Dreams) which was a departure in both style and language.

Levin's post-satirical 'domestic' plays were set in bourgeois neighbourhoods where the characters drift towards hopelessness and despair, ultimately succumbing to illness, death or subjugation. They are able to achieve self-definition only in apposition to others while a single character, usually a woman, provides the defining principle around which the other characters and the plot revolve. Levin stresses the dull parochialism of these people's lives, bound by the narrow moral conventions and aspirations of their milieu at the time, the standards of the public-at-large. He does not localise his plays by referring to recognisably Israeli or Jewish elements, but many reviewers are convinced that the target of his derision is a neighbourhood of Tel Aviv which closely resembles that of Levin's childhood:

You know the view from the balcony, the bus station, the café and the pharmacy, the local cinema and the smell of the sea; a stroll from here to the beach is almost as good as a journey abroad ... Even when he exiles his company to Babylon, Troy or ancient Canaan they exude the odour of onions in a Polish recipe and their roots are deeply fixed in the place where many of Levin's contemporaries grew up in the 50s.[3]

While his *dramatis personae* have attributive names with Yiddish overtones, little else in the plays is identifiable with Israel.

The 'domestic' plays reiterate a catalogue of characterisations functioning within deformed familial relationships, which may allegorise structures of social and political relationships. The paradigmatic *Hefetz* (1972)[4] examines a middle-class family and their lodger, Hefetz, viciously dissecting the inter-relationship of mother, father, daughter, son-in-law-to-be and lodger. Its themes were to become Levinic staples: the absolute lack of communication between individuals, mockery of the idealised Israeli youth, the sacrifice of the weak and helpless by the domineering (usually women), and the alienation of people from their fellows, all of which was repeated in almost every subsequent play. Levin's heroes exist within an hierarchical social framework, not the customary ranking of status, wealth or honour, but some imaginary law of human existence which fixes people in the hierarchy of oppressed and oppressor, with even the lowly exerting their power to oppress. They do not function mimetically or psychologically but as stereotypical creatures within his world.

The central motif of *Hefetz* is the sacrifice of a powerless man, Hefetz, selected to be the scapegoat of the bullying priestess-daughter, Fogra. His death, the play's *leitmotif*, binds the other characters by being the single significant event in their lives. The play follows in many details the precepts of the Absurd of the 1950s, restating its ideology that all mankind is lost, without identity, communication, affection or hope – a message Levin places in modern Israel and the modern Israeli family. Israeli audiences had never before been the target of this kind of rancour.

The people of *Hefetz* are ridiculous, loveless, ugly and dysfunctional. Their names are either allegorical (*hefetz*: 'object', 'thing') or meaningless (Clamansea: six letters of the Hebrew alphabet in sequential order). Levin's dramatic dialogue echoes the emphatic, truncated speech of childhood. His characters' conversations stand in complete contrast to their age, status and external appearance, to the point that a grotesque contradiction is created between them. Conflict between their search for personal fulfilment and the internal hierarchy of happiness and misery results in their debasement, which is predestined within the play's singular society. The means towards this perverse fulfilment are in themselves mean and perverted.

In Levin's plays human quality in every way undergoes a consistent process of reduction: the funeral is close to the wedding, the woman is flesh, erotic relationships are relationships of power and degradation between lumps of flesh without identity, the relationships of fathers and sons are relationships of mutual surrender, and so on. The characters undergo a continuous process of dehumanisation.[5]

Levin has discovered an image for this somewhat warped perception of social and psychological relationships. *Hefetz's* central metaphor is its most powerful element, dominating character, structure and language: a ritual sacrifice not only of the designated scapegoat but, one way or another, of every other character in the play. While each is Fogra's victim, Hefetz's specific tragedy sweetens the others' fate because he occupies the lowest rung on the human ladder. The intention is not cruelty or *schadenfreude* but the attribution of meaning to one life by the annihilation of another. As the archetypal victim, Hefetz is a central figure in the hierarchy of misery which constitutes the philosophical structure of all Levin's plays.

Fogra is the first of Levin's dominatrices who matures to become increasingly monstrous throughout the remainder of his drama. She struts through *Hefetz*, repeating her own definition here and throughout the other plays, ultimately becoming a brutal archetype. Fogra is twenty-four, the exact age of the State of Israel when the play was first performed. She is frigid, narcissistic and suffused with a twisted *joie de vivre* – the feminine mutation of the *sabra* myth and by extension, Zionist philosophy developed *ad absurdum*, a 'monstrous ideological travesty'.[6]

Who am I? Who actually is this Fogra that everyone talks about so much? They agree with me that this is a young, beautiful woman, note, young and beautiful, only 24, working with great accomplishment on her doctorate in physics, yes, physics, engaged to a rich, successful young man. She flows with life, loves to enjoy herself and draws pleasure from every single moment of her life. This is Fogra, my friends![7]

Originally appearing in the guise of Hulda in *The Queen of the Bathtub*, Fogra is a parody of the post-1948 idealisation of Israel's perfect youth; she is also the embodiment of Levin's view in his drama of all women as controlling matriarchs, destroyers of their men and their children. Levin exemplifies this in the character of Clamansea, the mother, and he also slyly inserts a note of more direct political satire by making her reminiscent of Golda Meir in *The Queen of the Bathtub*.

Levin's greatest gift is his ability to ritualise banal, commonplace events. His characters' petty, interpersonal loves, hates and jealousies, control and submission, which in themselves provide little dramatic interest, are intensified by their contextualisation within rituals of sacrifice, execution, feasts, games, weddings and funerals comically or grotesquely transformed. He incorporates elements from opera, the Passion, circus, oratorio, cabaret, Senecan and Greek drama. An important ritual in *Hefetz* is that of children's games and childish ceremonies which infantalise the adult characters.

Shitz (1975) defines the ideological – and to a large extent dramatic – framework in which the plays are set. Through the conflict between father- and son-in-law Levin censures his society for its preoccupation with materialism and consumerism at the expense of other values. The play implies that death in war is only marginally worse than the spiritual death of the Israeli bourgeoisie. For the the first time Israeli society was accused from the stage of gorging itself on possessions. *Shitz* also contained one of the most explicit indictments of the state's life-and-death power over the individual. Its bizarre plot involves Charches, another living-dead character in Israeli drama who, after having been killed in the war, returns to haunt his father-in-law Shitz, to prey on him for profit while Shitz in turn profits from Charches's death. In this play Levin's symbolism is associated almost exclusively with bowels and digestion, a metaphor he was to repeat often in both contradictory senses of waste and retention. The characters' names resemble sounds of disgust: Fefechtz Shitz is the father, Tzeshah, the mother, Sprachtzi, the daughter, and Charches, her flatulent husband.

Throughout his drama Levin exhibits his Swift-like loathing of those who control society, presenting them as grotesque, disfigured people, blown up by the failure of their own digestive processes. Their manipulation of their own waste is his metaphor for ideology become fetid, excremental. *Soharei Hagumi* (The Rubber Merchants), (1978), is structured on the central device of contraceptives and in this play, according to Michael Handelsaltz, Levin crossed every boundary of good taste. The hero, Shmuel Saprol has inherited a stock of ten thousand packs of contraceptives (signifying sterility) which he seeks to sell. This device, together with some social criticism, is subsumed by Levin's undeviating preoccupation with the existential deficiency of small, weak people.

These and many other black comedies with vivid, witty texts and music were among the greatest box office successes of the 1970s at the Cameri Theatre where Levin was the resident playwright until the mid-1980s. They ridiculed Israeli society, laid bare its defects and scoffed at its values through a virtuoso combination of scatology and the grotesque. Despite Levin's pessimism and mockery of certain Zionist values, he became the most popular playwright of the time. He had set out *épater les bourgeois* but was adored by them in a kind of communal self-abasement entirely consistent with his own dramatic masochism. Admirers praised his assault on Israel's self-satisfied materialism so soon after the war. He became a theatrical icon whom fashionable critics hesitated to attack, while the conservative and religious establishments mounted continual campaigns against him.

Levin's partiality to ritualisation reached its peak in his so-called 'metaphysical' or 'mythical' plays. These attempted to examine the sources of human suffering and evil, the 'large' issues. In keeping with the custom of Hebrew writers throughout the modern period, most of Levin's metaphysical plays relate to a text which he either cites or distorts. The first of these plays, *Execution*, (1979), is an inversion of the medieval morality plays, with female demons in place of angels. *The Torments of Job* and *The Great Whore of Babylon* are variations on the Passion. The title *The Great Whore of Babylon* is an allusion to St John's vision of Satan as a murderous and richly adorned prostitute, 'Babylon the Great' in Revelation 17.

With these plays Levin attempted to broaden his dramatic base by utilising the fundamental elements of theatre itself: archetypal stories of doomed heroes, myths or classical tales through which he extends his familiar preoccupations. It is not so much that Hefetz and others were 'prefigurations' of characters in these 'mythic' plays[8] but that Levin repeats his small lexicon of themes in these later *tours de force*. His allusive and intertextual technique gives these preoccupations a putative objectivity and perhaps some cosmic import. Levin's followers proposed that with these plays he crossed the border between the regional and the universal to provide the very essence of his dramatic statement. At the same time he reiterated and expanded his vision of dominance and degradation, of fatally powerful women and sacrifice, now in a primitive world of brutality and merciless environments.

Execution, a parody of the *Everyman* story, takes place in the celestial court, with female oppresssors and murderers replacing the heavenly process of prosecution and defence. These are evil angels, with ironically allegorical names such as 'Autumn Smiles', 'Nature's Tranquillity' and 'The Heavens Laughed', who invert emblems of sanctity into a satanic ceremony. Further departing from the Christian morality plays, *Execution* decrees the fate of the body rather than the soul.

The stage is constructed as a circus ring with the male victims wallowing in the sawdust while their tormentors, all women, sit in the circus audience's seats. This leaves no one with whom the real audience may identify, the victims or the play's vicious spectators. One of the men, Yellow Stains, is deemed worthy of a degree of mercy. He is allowed to propose three gifts to his tormenting angel, Autumn Smiles: he offers her love, servitude and compassion. Needless to say, the gifts are unacceptable so in addition to the castration he has already endured, he must suffer the amputation of all his limbs. When given the choice of suffering these mutilations or dying immediately he chooses the amputations. He remains onstage in a box without any limbs, only a head, having elected to remain alive at any price.

Execution was a celebration of violence as yet unparalleled on the Israeli stage, presenting in graphic detail, humour and *grand guignol* verve, excretion, blood, slaughter, dismemberment, castration, murder, rape, ritual killing and defilement of corpses. Superficially, the play emphasises the pitiless isolation people are forced to suffer in a world that demands their endurance despite being emasculated, assaulted and degraded. It has a political dimension as well: Autumn Smiles, an evolution of Fogra, has absolute control, exceeding even that of the official 'murderers'. She decides who lives and dies. With this symbol of the atrocious development of the *sabra*, Levin makes his point about power, violence and the state. On a deeper level the catalogue of horror makes the play a relevant vision for the post-Holocaust collective memory. In addition, *Execution* possesses a bitter inner logic which transcends the brutality of its scenes, and an insight into certain truths of human behaviour that are rarely faced.

Based on the biblical tale, *Yisurei Iyov* (The Torments of Job) brims with textual allusions, but the crucial difference is the shift of the biblical Job's theocentric world to Levin's anthropocentrism. In his play there is no contest between God and Satan and no reply from the whirlwind. In fact, God's absence is the play's theological point. Living in Roman times as a contemporary of Jesus, Job is a wealthy man, seen first at a great feast where, in accordance with his moral precepts, he dispenses largesse to beggars – but this is no more than the paltry remains of a meal. Then disasters befall him rapidly: the loss of his possessions, the loss of his children and his own unbearable physical ailment. He is derided and cast out and loses his faith in God. Subsequently he is visited by three friends whose cumulative advice restores his faith. Eliphaz represents the conventional belief in punishment as a consequence of sin; Bildad advises unquestioning submission to God, and Zophar proposes the merciful God whose love is that of a father for a helpless child. The biblical framework is abandoned at this point. A newly enthroned Emperor demands that Job renounce God. At first Job refuses to comply even though his hypocritical friends capitulate almost immediately. He is impaled through his rectum on a huge stake. Jesus passes by, dragging his cross. A circus arrives and its owner gathers a crowd to watch Job's passion and death. Shortly before his demise Job renounces his faith. His process of belief has therefore moved from his trust in the good order of the world, to denouncing God, to a restoration of belief in a merciful God, then to his final loss of faith when his agony becomes unbearable. The play ends as it began, with a chorus of beggars.

While it imitates tragic form, even to the presence of a chorus, *The Torments of Job* is not a tragedy. On the contrary, it flies in the face of tragic convention and is, rather, an anti-tragedy, even a parody. Levin mimics and at the same time subverts tragic form in various ways: his patronising and supercilious hero is afflicted but he dies without reconciliation; the presence of the deity is debated but not affirmed; the language throughout the play is portentous verse but it is laced with biblical cadences. While there is *anagnorisis* of a kind, it is reversed and ultimately there is no spiritual growth, purification or reconciliation, and therefore no catharsis. Levin's purpose is not redemption but irony.

Job dies in vain, without dignity. A character known as Cynical

Clown admonishes the circus audience: 'Don't ask for an explanation of ruin, a lesson or significance. Just watch the play: a man disintegrates and soon he'll die'.[9] Even Job's antagonist, a Roman officer, reproaches him after his opportunistic renunciation of God. 'A pity. For the same price you could have died as a man of principle'.[10] While literary tragedy implies a reaffirmation of life or a rebirth, Levin's Job does not affirm cosmic order or life, but the opposite, chaos, loss and death. If there is a form of rebirth in the play it is dispassionate and ironic, and thoroughly in keeping with Levin's philosophy: at the start of the play Job declares that each time his bowels are emptied and his digestion completed, he is born anew.[11] Levin sets out to tantalise his audience which is led by the content and style of the play to believe that there will be tragedy and meaning. At the last moment, however, this is wrested away.

Levin's parody of the Passion of Christ – from the Last Supper to the crucifixion – makes similarly subversive points. His theatrical iconography is deliberately Christian but his Job is Jesus's absolute converse. Jesus is a mystical hero and a man blessed with goodness and purity of heart, overcoming all obstacles in order to save mankind, while Job is an unredeemed failure, his suffering in vain. While Jesus on the cross became a holy myth, Job on the stake remains part of a jeering circus act, a mockery of salvation. Parallels with the gospel story extend throughout the play. Job refers obliquely to the miracle of the loaves and the fishes when he says sarcastically: 'What have we seen? A miracle? Or nature? A chicken bone feeds a dozen.'[12] Bildad speaks of the 'poor in spirit'; to strengthen the mockery the sardonic speech by the character called Pathetic Clown is a parody of *Ecce Homo*. Instead of Jesus' words 'My God, my God, why have you forsaken me?' Job cries: 'Don't leave me alone with God'.[13] Only here is the possibility of tragedy admitted: by his plea, Job is acknowledging the real mystery of God, dissociated from his friends' superficial blandishments and his own calculation.

Yet Levin's exercise is based on a story in the *Jewish* canon, a moral tale in which God's goodness is ultimately affirmed, together with his moral order. The philosophical problem in the biblical story is not that of atheism, but the more complex question of theodicy. Levin's Job can be seen in two ways. He is either a man whose faith will not be shaken by tribulation; only at the moment of his greatest agony does he deny God's existence. This is comparable, as some critics have pointed out, to Jesus's last cry on the cross. On the other hand, Job is weak-willed and confused with no opinion of his own, first eagerly agreeing with Zophar and then, far too late, surrendering to the Emperor.

From the quasi-tragedy of the first act with its almost conventional chastening of the hero the play moves firmly into the genre of the Absurd where everything becomes an ugly joke, including the hero himself. He denies God in terms that rob him of dignity, leaving him ridiculous. Action in the second half of the play involves a form of voluptuous sadism which some reviewers have likened to a Fellini film: to amplify the dissolute atmosphere of Job's Passion as a circus act, a prostitute uses his stake as a means of sexual gratification. Her cries of ecstasy below him mingle with those of his death throes.

Critics and scholars have vied with each other in discovering profound meaning in the play, some see it as mocking the bourgeoisie;[14] others, as an essay on the relationship between father and son.[15] Social criticism drives the first section which presents Job as an arrogant member of a wealthy élite throwing crumbs to the beggars. This is consistent with Levin's view of Israeli society greedily gorging itself without thought for the deprived. In his conflation of Job's great feast, his ultimate downfall and Jesus's crucifixion, Levin brings to mind Jesus's aphorism about a rich man's inability to achieve the kingdom of heaven. Scholars postulate a Levinian theology which is as significant as it is intellectually challenging. Dan Miron refers to Levin's 'debate' about the presence or absence of faith and the existence of God, a 'systematic dramatic investigation into disaster, degradation, suffering and pain that are the essence of human existence'.[16] However, God is not the subject of the play. If his existence is indeed being debated, it is in the most demeaning terms possible, predicated on mankind's – and society's – utter degradation.

In reading the play either as a tragedy or as a theological proposition Levin's ironic points are lost: God's care for the most wretched manifests itself by making them suffer adversity which they bear with resigned cheerfulness. To Job, God is something of a convenience. When life is good, he has faith; he loses it when he suffers, regains it with the hope of reward and renounces it for the sake of survival. His cry to the Romans reveals his moral flexibility even *in extremis*: 'There's no God. Take me off the stake. There's no God.'[17] On the other hand, Levin could be examining not God and theology but religion, postulating it as a circus inflamed by the

Figure 10   Design by Ruth Dar for Hanokh Levin, *Execution*, 1979.

powerful eroticism of martyrdom. According to Shimon Levi, Levin's theology is no more than a theatrical game or play: the word *mishak* means both.[18]

The Torments of Job does not, therefore, deviate from the central topic of Levin's other plays: mankind's hypocrisy, small-mindedness, self-interest, lack of nobility and above all, its imprisonment within reality without any means of escape, reality which art can attempt but will always fail to alter. Through his anti-tragedy Levin mocks humanity's desperate belief derived from religion and literature that suffering precedes redemption and therefore possesses significance, or that it engenders nobility. With one dramatic swoop he denies the validity of redemption with its implications for Jewish history and the foundation of Israel. He places ideology squarely within the boundaries of human choice. His irony in this play is fundamentally political.

For Levin, moreover, suffering has an ordinary, material meaning; people do not grow spiritually out of affliction but are diminished by it. Morality and principle are vanquished by adversity. Art and

Figure 11   Hanokh Levin, *The Torments of Job*, 1981.

ideology, therefore, lie. The functionary who has come to divest Job of all his belongings says to him: 'We're not in the theatre and you're not the main character in a play. Don't make monsters of us. We're all only human beings. We all go home to a wife, slippers and a bowl of hot soup.'[19] In his pessimism Levin succeeds in penetrating areas which art generally avoids, and strips away all possibility of art's transfigurativeness, its optimistic, positive and healing value.

Job's story proves the transcendence of body over spirit and the illusory nature of a life of the spirit. The earthy philosophy of the prostitute (a perverted portrait of Mary Magdalen at the foot of the cross), Levin's customary emphasis on the bowels, the feasting that opens the play and the blood and vomit that close it reinforce the primacy of the corporeal. Levin has created a mocking protest against illusion, positive teleologies which raise humankind from despair, and the myths that sustain all art and religion. Ophrat-Friedlander defines Levin's philosophy in the play as an 'inverted ritual': 'All birth means death, tragedy is a circus and all pleasure is suffering ... It is pseudo-dialectical, essentially static and circular, without any solution or positive synthesis, for there is no positive deity governing by means of affirmative law.'[20] Even paternal love is proved to be illusory.[21] Art is reduced to titillation: Job on the stake becomes a spectacle to be viewed and enjoyed by the crowd, one more example of the pornography of violence and martyrdom with which Levin mocks his audience.

CYNICAL CLOWN Hypnotized, you stand and watch someone's downfall.
    On your faces is a mixture of desire and fear
    Awaiting the predetermined and unrepeatable moment
    When a body is kicked into the earth.[22]

Without faith and without 'the relief occasioned by art', there is nothing left but a void, in Levin's characterisation, a 'black hole'. If he is seriously making a theological point in the play, it is within the general framework not of atheism or theodicy but of misogyny. The 'black hole' is a woman's vagina, 'woman's fatal openness'.[23] The prostitite sings a crude song about the black hole between her legs which can accommodate a penis of 'African' proportions and then the circus manager shouts to Job on the stake: 'Hey, you man there, what do you think now? Is there a God? Do you see something there? Is there? Or only a black hole that fits the size of Africa? Eh?'[24] God is, then, a terrifying nothingness and all that is left is the dark and mysterious secrecy of a woman. Levin's substitution of God with this black hole is permeated with disgust: God has somehow become a woman's power, the incomprehensible power that Levin's plays consistently detest and fear, expressed viscerally by Shakespeare's King Lear:

    Behold yond simpering dame,
    Whose face between her forks presages snow,
    That minces virtue, and does shake the head
    To hear of pleasure's name –
    The fitchew nor the soiled horse goes to 't
    With a more riotous appetite.
    Down from the waist they are Centaurs
    Though women all above:
    But to the girdle do the gods inherit.
    Beneath is all the fiends';
    There's hell, there's darkness, there's the sulphurous pit,
    Burning, scalding, stench, consumption; – fie fie fie! pah, pah!
                           (Act IV, scene 6)

For Levin the gods and the fiends alike rule the parts beneath the girdle.

Although the Holocaust should not be imposed on every literary text, its presence is almost unavoidable in Levin's violent scenarios. In many of his plays there are oblique, perhaps unconscious references to it even if only in their emphasis on dehumanisation before destruction (as in *The Torments of Job*, *Hefetz* and *Execution*). There is no other event in human history which so resists transformation into art, in which there is no possibility of the catharsis of tragedy, which did not ennoble the sufferer and which demonstrated the degradation of both victim and oppressor. In the play the sudden loss of Job's home, his family and his health is inexplicable, and his suffering is surreal and pointless. He is victimised for no reason by the Romans who, like storm troopers, invade his house to seize his possessions. They also remove his gold teeth.

The pace of *The Torments of Job* was slow and the music repetitive and monotonous, so that the final impression was one of 'terrible coldness'. Many critics commented on Levin's ability as a director as opposed to his talent as a playwright. Elyakim Yaron criticises him for underestimating the intelligence of his public, for example preventing them from making their own connection between the crucifixion and Job's elevation on the stake, by having Jesus appear onstage dragging his cross.[25] Giora Manor notes that Levin imposes upon the audience so much of suffering and torment that they become indifferent to Job and more concerned about the actor who is perched for a long while atop a stake with his arms outstretched.[26]

Levin's 'metaphysical' theatre has something in it of Antonin Artaud's creed: 'I believe our present social system is iniquitous and should be destroyed ... There are too many signs that everything that used to sustain our lives no longer does so, that we are all mad, desperate and sick.' For Artaud, the theorist of the Theatre of Cruelty, theatre's function is to liberate forces in the audience's unconscious by giving direct expression to dreams and obsessions. He envisioned a theatre of 'timeless debauchery' in which cruelty reflects a vision of the world, both ethical and metaphysical. This theatre deals with the metaphysical concerns of ancient rites, 'an exorcism to make our demons flow'. It must reflect 'atrocious crimes ... superhuman devotions, as the ancient myths do'. The notion of cruelty stems from the mystical forces of 'a theatre in which violent physical images crush and hypnotize the sensibility of the spectator seized by the theatre as by a whirlwind of higher forces'. Artaud conceives of theatre as total spectacle: it must have the 'ceremonial quality of a religious rite' made up of violent and concentrated action 'pushed beyond all limits'.[27]

Artaud had an overarching agenda: violence and brutality are evoked not for their own sake but as part of a process of purification, a means of ridding society of its institutionalised violence. He believes that after experiencing the staged cruelty his spectator will never again want to go to war or to commit violent acts.[28] Whereas Artaud expresses a purpose for his Theatre of Cruelty, Levin avoids the sense of catharsis. His plays appear to lack any overarching *redemptive* purpose for which he substitutes a boundless and impotent rage against a society which offers the individual nothing but filth and corruption. His least 'cruel' and most poetic drama, *The Child Dreams*, concludes that there is no salvation either in this world or the next.

After the period of 'mythic' plays it seemed that Levin had reached the end of his creativity, but with *Orzei Hamizvadot* (The Suitcase Packers), (1983)[29] he entered a new and more mature phase. This, Levin's eighteenth play, revisits the modern social arena. Unlike his earlier work, it focuses on the collective rather than individual life in the familiar urban neighbourhood to which he now returns. *The Suitcase Packers* recapitulates many of the topics and personalities portrayed in previous work. If there is anything new it is in the method with which the earlier motifs are treated.

The Suitcase Packers, subtitled 'A play with eight funerals', presents certain episodes in the lives of five neighbouring families, each of which contains some element of physical or emotional illness. It has been interpreted as a portrait of mankind's journey through life, 'showing how life goes on and doesn't add up to much'.[30] It is a parable of meaninglessness, frustration and mean aspiration, deriving its power solely from the playwright's misanthropic anger. It concerns a number of departures which lead nowhere, and a series of deaths and funerals. Illness and death are the only events of substance, punctuated by the characters setting out with their suitcases, wandering around and either dying or feebly returning to their point of departure. Needless to say, in this Levinian world, only one of them reaches her destination: Nina, a young woman who escapes physically and emotionally by marrying and moving to Vienna. The funerals degenerate into surrealistic parodies as the drama continues and death becomes commonplace.

The action takes place on the street in front of the characters' houses, reminiscent in its overall concept of Elmer Rice's *Street Scene* (1929). Rice's play, which portrayed life in a New York City working-class tenement, blended a representative group into a truthful but somewhat bleak portrayal of a milieu in a certain period and place. Whereas this group included various nationalities, individual histories, cultures and occupations, Levin presents a homogeneous group trapped within the stifling conformity of its own history, culture, religion and nationality.

The first funeral is that of Shabbetai Shuster who dies of constipation, the inability to move or let go. Amaziah, the son of another of the families, and the purpose of his parents' lives, dies of a brain tumour after setting out for America. Avner, a hunchback who is rejected by his family, commits suicide; others die of unspecified causes. A previously deceased husband returns as a youthful ghost to entice his aged, disintegrating widow. Dreams are the only escape for the living. Even the local prostitute packs her bag and leaves for Switzerland (Levin's recurring and ironic utopia). Lola Globchik, one of Levin's heartless female caricatures, persuades her weak-willed husband to place his aged mother in an institution from which she escapes, doggedly dragging her suitcase with her until she is reduced to crawling on all fours. The hunchback, Avner, is similarly evicted from his brother's house by his shrewish sister-in-law, a textbook *yachne* (complaining, slatternly woman). Bella, Nina's ugly sister, forbids Avner even to dream about her, thereby exercising her own cruel power.

The play is a stylised mixture of realism and fantasy containing caricatures sunken in their 'kitschy pathos', in Avraham Oz's phrase. They are representative of the social class the playwright seems to detest. One (unnamed) reviewer writes that because the play is compounded of small Israeli and Jewish details of reality, one must be Israeli or at least Jewish to understand it.[31] Others have pointed out that Levin's language contains echoes of cadences specific to the Polish immigrants in Israel. His setting is familiar to his viewers who are able to recognise Tel Aviv although its name is not mentioned. 'Even though no time or place is specified it is clear by all the signs that he means a veteran Ashkenazi neighbourhood in the vicinity of the central station.'[32] Each character is drawn from among the petit bourgeoisie in contemporary Israeli society. Most of these, according to the play, are unpleasant female stereotypes: the *yakhne* and the *yente* (fussy woman), the hard and unsympathetic daughter-in-law, the hateful sister-in-law, the nagging wife. A more positive character is the old woman who refuses to be put away, a portrait of forsaken but resilient old age.

Everyone in the play has vague dreams of 'elsewhere', anywhere outside their own locality. 'No one is waiting for us in London but there despair is easier to bear.'[33] This unhappiness may have something to do with both the wandering nature of the Jew and the search for greener pastures. The state has failed to prevent people from wanting to leave it, due to the 'age-old notion of the Jews that they can live anywhere with their invisible, portable God'.[34] Levin contradicts the search for the 'something better' that, according to his characters, exists only beyond Israel's shores, for they do not escape – or dream of escape – only to other places: they escape by dying, by illness or madness. The obsession with escape relates to an existential rather than an Israeli or Jewish phenomenon, not only that of the wandering Jew or of *yerida* (settling abroad), although these occur in the play. It is the dream of escape from the social strictures that dominate the individuals' lives.

In Levin's society the family is all-important. Generally he implicates Foucault's imagination of power in his metaphor of the oppressive social institution of the family. This powerful institution both subjugates the individuals within it and collaborates with them for the perpetuation of its rules and conventions. Levin's families in *The Suitcase Packers* tacitly accept their subjugation within a system which is never questioned. Despite themselves, his people function according to the received norms of family behaviour, with the peculiarities of *Jewish* family behaviour adding their own shackles. Characters fall in love, marry, have children (Tzipporah, the unkind sister-in-law is constantly pregnant), the old are rejected, parents manipulate their children, siblings quarrel, widows compete for a man's affection, Nina manages to marry a doctor. However banal, this is far more the stuff of life than most readers or members of the audience would care to admit. Levin has captured the sense of a stifling community, imprisoned by familial mores which are upheld generation after generation despite every attempt to surmount them. Each generation is indistinguishable from the other. The younger people fail to develop a world view of their own and remain unvarying components of their parents' texts.

This renders the characters' endless and untiring striving for fulfilment highly ironic. They are searching for escape or accomplishment *within* their social framework and its standards. For example, Levin's female characters exemplify the social conventions and sustain them: mothers plan for their children, young women seek marriage and wives rule their husbands' lives. The definitive objective of the female characters is the wedding and the purchase of an apartment. There is no adultery in the play, no incest, murder or corruption and only a hint of homosexuality. The play's universe is, in fact, moral, its prescriptive horizons and moral norms the most likely reason for the characters' gloom.

Levin's people are therefore unable to avoid their petit bourgeois world even in imagination. For example, Nina's marriage to a doctor ironically highlights an aspiration enshrined in Jewish popular culture. Yet 'marrying a doctor' binds her even more inexorably to the environment which has set the parameters of her achievement. Levin is less concerned with his characters' lives and fortunes than with the *community* they constitute. They are bounded by a logical consistency based on their kind of milieu, in a portrayal that has resonances for any homogeneous Jewish community not only in Israel but in the diaspora as well.

The action of the *The Suitcase Packers* took place on a bare stage, its unlit centre like a dark crater from which the characters emerged. Extended over it were visible lighting grids which lit the stage from above and also presented an ominous series of shapes to the audience, becoming part of the claustrophobic design. The play was directed by the London-based director, Michael Alfreds (the founder of the group *Shared Experience*), a departure for Levin who until then had always directed his own plays. Alfreds brought warmth and sympathy to Levin's characters, and added depth to the text: 'In this respect the greatness of the play – which is among the cleanest and most discursive of Levin's plays, concentrating on the delineation of the characters and the situations and astonishing again and again with its secular poetry compounded of day-to-day language – becomes the greatness of the production.'[35] Handelsaltz cites one scene in which two characters dance: Alfreds's direction left it sad and moving whereas Levin's would have alienated it and rendered it cold, hard and mocking.

There are many parallels between Levin's work and that of Joe Orton (1933–67), the English playwright whose farces reflected the growing political dissent in Britain of the 1960s. Like Levin, Orton expressed his savage, irreverent vision through sexual games in addition to violence and dehumanisation and, like Levin, Orton is preoccupied with scatology, much of it rendered wittily. While working in the tradition of British farce he subverted it by overstepping its boundaries, and this structural iconoclasm corresponds to his overall aim which was to be boundlessly outrageous.

The substantial difference between the two playwrights is that of orientation: Orton, a homosexual, battered his society as an outsider, a pariah. Levin, on the other hand, speaks with a critical voice from within the social consensus. Despite their differences, the two playwrights' agendas were ideologically similar: Orton turned farce into a weapon of sexual and class warfare while Levin used it as an instrument for battering social complacency and constraint.

Like Levin, Orton progressed in violence from play to play. The primary function of Orton's licence was to arouse 'the most violent reactions possible within the average (by definition bourgeois) audience'.[36] Orton himself noted, 'Sex is the only way to infuriate them. Much more fucking and they'll be screaming hysterics in next to no time.'[37] Initially his plays were remarkably successful in provoking extreme responses. Public rejection forced the first production of *Loot* to close before it reached London although, very much in the Levinian fashion, it won high critical acclaim. *What the Butler Saw* was greeted with booing and hissing in 1969. According to one of the actors, 'members of the audience really wanted to jump onto the stage and kill us all.' This is all familiar in relation to Levin's theatre. For example, the casts of both of his satires, *The Queen of the Bathtub* and *The Patriot*, received death threats.

The key to Orton's approach, as it is to Levin's, is the manner of treating conventionally unpleasant or sad situations as a source of comedy. One of Orton's central images is a funeral, in fact the original title of *Loot* was *Funeral Games*. According to Innes, this technique trivialises public standards of seriousness.[38] It also allows the audience's laughter to soften the impact of distasteful truths. Like Levin, Orton believed in the absolute realism of presentation. According to his own 'principle of contradiction', while the play is not written naturalistically it must be directed and acted with absolute realism. 'No "stylisation", no "camp", no attempt to match the author's extravagance of dialogue with extravagance of direction.'[39] Levin, as director, sustained the contradiction in his 'domestic' plays, resulting in a very specific grotesquerie.

There was nothing of Orton or Artaud in Levin's *Hayeled Holem*

(The Child Dreams), (1993),[40] a much praised, *apparent* departure for Levin. From an external perspective, this play demonstrates the difference between contemporary theatre in western Europe and the Israeli dramatic tradition derived in the main from Russian stylisation and the Expressionist theatre. The play is largely declamatory, rhetorical both in language and in visual effect, closer in spirit and style to Strindberg than to Brecht with whose work it has been frequently compared. While the audience was unable to identify with any character, the entire play constituted an emotional experience, resembling a profound ritual. Audiences, so accustomed to Levin's nihilism, were astonished that a play of his could offer them a vestige of tragic beauty.

To suit his preoccupation, if not obsession, with European allegorical forms, *The Child Dreams* is constructed in the style of a medieval religious allegory, including human typology and the notion of a journey or quest. Despite his emotional nihilism Levin is very much in control of his form and encloses chaos in an organised and controlled structure. His play is in four acts (rather than the classical five-act structure), each corresponding to one of the stations of suffering, similar in intent to *The Pilgrim's Progress*. Each stop implies a challenge or a test for the play's characters. They are not named but designated, all existing within a dreamlike continuum which moves from symbol to symbol, beginning with a slow procession of displaced people seeking shelter and ending with a group of dead children. The images on the stage are European rather than Israeli although the locale is unspecific. Lack of specificity renders the play an allegory of people's lives in which death and degradation await them at every turn.

Levin's protagonist is a child suddenly forced to confront the most terrifying experiences of life without the consoling illusions of loving parents, family security or a home. The first act takes place in his home: a father and mother are leaning affectionately over the bed of their sleeping son but their idyllic world, for which there is no precedent in any previous play of Levin's, is suddenly breached by a dying man streaming with blood, followed by jackbooted soldiers armed with machine guns, and a woman dressed in red. They kill the father and banish the rest of the populace, including the mother and the frightened child. No reason for the killing or the appearance of the cruel woman is given, but she is familiar as the Levinian stereotype of a beautiful, sadistic female. In the second act the mother attempts to board a refugee ship with her child in order to escape the unidentified oppressors. The ship's captain permits her on board on condition that she has intercourse with him. She hesitates but the child's screams persuade her to make the sacrifice. Act Three takes place in the port of an island at which the ship, now offstage, has arrived. A uniformed official at the island, also in the company of a beautiful woman, refuses the refugees permission to disembark, but he is prepared to take the child, due to the presence of a group of journalists who will report his benevolence. Remembering the mother's promise never to allow the two to be parted, the child refuses to leave her. In the final act the mother crosses a railway track and lays down the body of her dead child who is then transferred to heaven where other dead children await the coming of the Messiah, an allusion to Beckett's Godot. The Messiah arrives, a furtive man dressed in a raincoat, carrying a suitcase of watches but unable to influence time or restore life. Eventually the soldiers follow and threaten him; he chooses not to save himself but to perish with the children. Levin has turned the Messiah into a caricature and his death into an ironic joke, robbing the children and the grieving mother of any hope for the future.

In *The Child Dreams* Levin has not moved far from the philosophical preoccupations of his earlier plays, despite the innocence of his victims who represent a pure rather than a tainted sacrifice. They are victims of circumstance, units of suffering in a world that seeks their destruction in the private, intimate, and in the public domains. It is the first of his plays in which the majority of the characters are not monsters in human form, but people confronting the political realities of twentieth-century life. Not only that, but they are forced to grapple with moral dilemmas for which they are poorly equipped. At the same time, certain Levinian staples are presented in altered form, one being the theme of bereavement, especially the loss of children. The final scene represents a protest at the death of young people, reminiscent of the satires in which soldiers protest against their own death.[41] Other preoccupations are the oppressing army, the helpless victim, bureaucracy and corrupt power, sadistic women, people whose indifference allows them to stand by while others suffer.

Everyone is denounced in this play: God, the Messiah and humankind. Levin characteristically preaches the negation of all humankind's sustaining dreams and illusions. For example, he cites the resilience which permits life to continue in the face even of the loss of a child. This is not a positive response, however, but an example of humankind's emotional shallowness. The world of the play becomes political when evil is located in recognisable characters: murdering soldiers, a captain who threatens rape, the bureaucrat who is prepared to show mercy for the sake of propaganda. Even art, represented by a poet, is impotent. Again institutionalised power stalks the individual, denying all hope of deliverance.

While overall *The Child Dreams* is an allegory of a child's proleptic nightmare of modern political life, the topic of the Holocaust is unavoidable. The play begins with the child's singing in order to soften the murderers' hearts. The song is about the end of summer and the ominous advent of night, a song reminiscent of one sung in Lanzmann's *Shoah*, also by a child. The sudden onslaught of jackbooted soldiers, their senseless killing, the refugee ship, the island people who turn it away, the railway tracks in the final scene, all provide examples of Holocaust iconography. On the other hand, the episodes in the play resonate with twentieth-century history for which war, refugees, displacement and loss constitute the primary images.

The relationship between mother and son establishes the core of the play's metaphorical system of human interaction. Made on the basis of adult experience, the mother's decisions appear to the child as treachery. Levin explores the difficulty of each to trust the other, and their inability either to reject or to live without the other. He raises the question of separation, the mother's dilemmas of choice always made in her child's favour. A time comes when the mother, having sacrificed so much for him, wants to be free of him. After rejecting him with a wounding verbal onslaught, she cries: 'Take him away from me! For God's sake, tear this child away from me!' With all the political symbolism and the 'large' issues of war and oppression, this is the play's only expression of the pain of close human relationships.

Levin has made this play empty of human compassion and the saving grace of irony. He offers no solutions and rejects any religious answer. He disdains the conclusions of Camus and Artaud, both of whom divined some purpose in the misery of daily life. His own conclusions are reminiscent of a celebrated poem by the veteran Israeli poet, Hayyim Guri, based on the biblical tale of the *Akedah*, in which the angel appears and stays Abraham's hand.

Isaac, as the story goes, was not sacrificed,
He lived for many years,
Saw all that was good until his eyes grew dim.

But he bequeathed that hour to his heirs.
They are born
With a knife in their hearts.[42]

Levin's audience and critics appear to luxuriate in his brand of pain, the more desperately pessimistic, the more brutal, the more they celebrated it. Ziva Shamir concludes that the play offers an inverted optimism although the fundamental values – including a mother's love for her son, the hope for meaning out of suffering – are repudiated, for even the most miserable life is better than the one Levin portrays in his play. It is, therefore, almost a cathartic response.[43] However, lacking grace and spiritual growth, the play is not a tragedy. In fact, so relentless is Levin's onslaught that it is easy to agree with Avraham Oz that 'Levin's cry against the world ... borders on kitsch'.[44] Levin's earlier plays possessed layers of humour, even *Execution's* black cabaret celebrated its irony and wit. *The Child Dreams* is a conglomeration of wretched images, both visual and verbal. Society, perhaps mistakenly, looks to the artist for enlightenment. While Levin is offering from the stage realistic images of contemporary suffering, he is achieving no more than the television screen or newspaper photographs. His discourse offers no consolation, no solution, no hope, merely a report upon disaster. In an age when viewers are almost inured to images of violence and pain, he does not offer a method of defamiliarisation or recruit the audience's compassion to the desire for change.

Despite the differences in the style and language of his plays, Levin is accused by his critics of constantly repeating himself. His plays are variations on a theme according to Hayyim Shoham and Dan Miron; Nissim Kalderon is less charitable: 'Levin has discovered a transition the size of a pinhead from the politics of truth and he nags at it endlessly.'[45] 'The plays are joined to each other with an internal thematic or poetic bond by means of a Levinic code, either verbal or non-verbal in the form of a theme and variations.'[46] On the other hand, Michael Handelsaltz, one of Levin's champions, argues that his plays should be viewed as a single developing saga. In his view, every play bears something of its predecessor and develops it until its message becomes fully-fledged.[47] 'Both reduction and repetition (of themes) are indespensable constituents of his dramatic strategy: both function not only with the structural organisation of his work but are also crucial constituents of his ideological critique of Israeli society and its communal dreams.'[48]

For all this, Levin's theatre obeys the injunction of 'relevance'. His early satires captured a piece of the national mood and at the very least provided a comedy of parody, something which few other serious Israeli playwrights have done. He is perhaps the most consistently political of them all, taking many social issues into his forum rather than a single phenomenon such as Zionism or the Israeli-Palestinian conflict. His hierarchy of oppressions arises from the internal dissension of his own society. It is also a revolt against political reality.

Levin places, so to speak, a mirror to the society in which he lives. The society chooses – and reality proves this, for it is not for nothing that Levin is the most controversial playwright in Israel – to shatter the mirror which reflects its ugly face. At the time of *Hefetz* Professor Eddy Zemah said that Levin sketched a society in the process of becoming fascist [*fashizatziah*] ... Today I know that Zemah's view was profound and that Levin was blessed with an almost prophetic talent. Israeli society did indeed undergo a process of becoming fascist and gradually came to resemble Levin's characters ... Hanokh Levin tries again and again to make a crack in the wall of his audience's indifference to human suffering...[49]

Levin no doubt wants his viewers to derive a portrait of his society from his distorted pictures of gluttony, corruption, cruelty, moral relativity and denial and the constant pain of loss, albeit often relieved by his comic prowess. More significantly, the violence in his drama reflects the stored images of humanity's darkest era, together with warfare and bereavement. His taunting scatology is his answer to the questionable 'purity' of ideology.

Levin has undoubtedly touched some nerves and so allowed his society the possibility of confrontation with itself, a means of self-mockery, objectivising pain, even laughing at it, reaching problems which may never otherwise surface. This, rather than political alignment or non-alignment, may be the reason for his popularity on the one hand, and the loathing of his work, on the other.

Levin's is a universe divested of traditional absolutes. His is an intensely *personal* vision despite his fondness for both Judaic and European mythology. Judaism offers no hope of salvation. 'God is not there for anyone in the world of Hanokh Levin.'[50] His emphasis on sacrifice has little to do with the romantic idea of divine creation after destruction. Friedrich Schlegel, for example, idealised human sacrifice, annihilation and death as the basis and necessary condition of the eternity for which all people hope. Levin's view rejects this corrupt romantic idealism. His is not a noble sacrifice, a tragic sacrifice, only a pessimistic metaphor of the inevitable progression of human life. If there is no God, no redemption at all, there can be no redemption in Zionism, which Levin's theatre has brutally confirmed. Nevertheless his work represents a significant achievement within the context of Israeli drama. His plays are among the few since Aloni's to have transcended the here and now to provide a 'universal' message which is derived from, and ultimately directed at, Israel of the past thirty years but which is no less applicable in any modern society.

Figure 12   Tehiya Danon as Um Naji in, *Gorodish* (Hillel Mittelpunkt), 1993.

Afterword

The progressive political role of art becomes that of exposing and interrogating ideology ... the most powerful weapon of social control.[1]

More than any other art, theatre asks for relevance.[2]

Throughout this book the point has been made that plays with recognisably political content – including those that 'target ideology' – do not constitute the entire body of original drama produced in Israel. A variety of topics and an abundance of forms have graced the Israeli stage since the earliest times in the drama's development. So-called 'political' playwrights themselves consistently produce material of less confined interest. Hillel Mittelpunkt, for example, has written delicately poetic allegories of human relationships. Yet of those outside the political canon, only Yosef Bar Yosef's works have crossed Israel's borders to achieve recognition abroad.

International success is not of course the sole criterion for a play's value, although Bar Yosef's exceptional drama richly deserves it. One fears that in other cases such success is often more a matter of sensation than quality. Few plays seen outside Israel have combined both, one being Sobol's *Ghetto*. Nevertheless there is no doubt that the most discussed plays in Israel and abroad and the playwrights best known, are those dedicated to some form of political discourse. Political playwrights usually wish to confront foreign audiences with local problems under the banner of dissidence, although in Israel 'dissidence' cuts a different shape. In the face of an historically accrued, but fallacious, belief in Jewish ideological unity, they confirm to foreign audiences the existence of a liberal consensus in Israel which opposes certain instances of government policy, particularly those concerning the Palestinians.

Whatever the genre, documentary, realism, satire, historical allegory or symbolism, the drama's social and political themes dissolve into the single overriding preoccupation: Israel's 'secular religion', Zionism. To the drama, 'Zionism' is a multipartite phenomenon, with conquest at its core and issues of identity, diaspora and religion its buttresses. Each play on the topic clarifies some prismatic feature, each displays a different face while converging on the same problem. Ultimately the debate is not political but ethical, regarding the new society's moral vision, so effectively summarised in Sobol's *The Night of the Twentieth*. Underlying the settlers' anxiety is the principle of their enterprise, their intuition that it may be worthless without a predetermined ethical design. Moshe, one of the pioneers, resisting his transformation into a 'manifesto', says, 'Once in a lifetime we have an opportunity like this to start everything from the beginning. Must we therefore do it like automatons? Because of pressure? Rotten myths?'[3] He is implying that he and his companions should venture beyond the 'amoral vagaries of myth' (another of Avraham Oz's luminous phrases)[4] despite all the potential hazards of being out of step with the hegemonic ideology.

Because the debate encompasses morality rather than *realpolitik* it transcends party politics. It examines sense and purpose rather than practicality, soul rather than body. Body and soul – Herzl and Freud – designate the ostensibly antagonistic elements, Israel and Zionism respectively. The corruption of one inevitably corrupts the other, but repair will follow repair. Like others interested in the country's moral welfare, political playwrights, prophetically immersed in the nation's soul, transcend their function of diarist to become its counsellors. The fact that the drama's interests relate to matters of cultural proportion rather than temporal process proves that Israel has not lost its awareness of the moral precepts which have qualified Jewish culture from the start.

In addition to its almost obsessive preoccupation with Zionist and post-Zionist moral ideals, the drama is also seeking something which can be regarded as a representative hero or 'self',[5] having rejected the *sabra* icon. Whichever self ultimately evolves, it will be unlikely to resemble its forebear. The *sabra*-hero is dead. The visual and verbal iconography he inspired have changed. The image that originally energised the drama's various styles, developments and influences has vanished. From Levin to the latest plays by young playwrights, many of them by women, the *sabra* has become a grotesque distortion of himself, violent, militaristic, empty and manipulative.

In one play he organises rape, in another he is a crude, vodka-swilling, machine-gun-toting thug. These portrayals often say less about the nation-building *palmahnik* than about the materialistic, Americanised, television-dominated writers who vilify him.

So far, in its search for a replacement Israeli identity, the drama has only offered a *negative* judgment through examples of what the Israeli should not be. Danny Horowitz is one of few who attempts to define some kind of uniqueness for his generation, something removed from a collectively sanctioned image. 'When you begin to serve a concept you become addicted to it, and you lose touch with reality . . . It is not by chance that plays were written about Weininger and Kastner and Yair [codename of Avraham Stern, the leader of the Stern Gang]. All three were individualists and we, in turn, sense the need to disengage from a stereotypical view of reality.'[6] Horowitz's protest against the primacy of the collective is ironically embodied in a group of men acculturated to the diaspora whose destinies did little to recommend individuality.

Even so, manipulated by the playwright, they say something about Israel and the Israeli. Gorodish, Stern, Eli Geva in Danny Horowitz's, *A Lesson for the Homeland* (1983), Kastner, Weininger, Herzl and Freud in Yosef Mundi's, *It Goes Around* (1970), Bitanya's pioneers and others speak as the playwrights' surrogates, stepping out of their time and place to join the debate on modern Israel. The playwrights make them relevant spokesmen for our time, and Israeli audiences and critics alike seek relevance, a word interpreted in Israeli dramatic criticism entirely in political terms. Perhaps its kind of relevance justifies the existence of drama in a culture that still regards theatre with suspicion; but it is also a dramatic principle.

A well-known German scholar claimed that if all the history books in the world disappeared and only plays remained, there would be no lack of knowledge about the development of human society.[7] This is true of Israel because of the immediacy of its history and the relationship between society and stage. Israeli theatre has preserved its traditional polemical function, to comment and commentate almost to the extent of participation in social processes. In fact, it is frequently on the brink of *becoming* a social process. More than an artistic medium for interpreting reality, Israeli drama affects reality by accentuating issues which might otherwise have remained less graphically illuminated for the public, such as Israeli-Palestinian and religious-secular relations. Israeli political drama, therefore, is not observed only as theatre, art or an artistic experience, but as a stimulus to discussion, often relating to something known by the audience but not shown on the stage. The artist exploits the stage as a forum.

> The Israeli theatre repertoire ... has a documentary value equal to that of other types of surveys and may even reveal what other sources do not, for the very reason that it expresses faithfully the subjective outlook of a particular group ... [Theatre texts] fulfil a central role in the ongoing change in our collective self-image.[8]

The violence of the public arguments, stimulated by Hebrew plays or skilfully manipulative adaptations of foreign works, witnesses the drama's centrality and authority in the country's intellectual life.

Its very character as an essential component of political discourse places the drama in danger. First, while the viewers wish to see reality reflected on the stage, they disapprove when the portrait differs from their experience. 'It doesn't happen like that in real life', is a repeated critical maxim. Critics, censors and audiences take a play as a slice of life rather than an invention, and for this reason permit the artist little licence. Second, representations of reality in political plays often offend more than the reality itself. The director Oded Feldman commented after the furious response to Sobol's *Jerusalem Syndrome* that the public takes the events in the Occupied Territories as a matter of course but loses all restraint when they see them portrayed on the stage. A source of complaint against censorship was the notion of banning the representation instead of the real.

In Israel there is a similarity between the material in an original political play and on the pages of a serious cultural journal. For better or worse, this has given the political drama an extraordinary character. Its very discursiveness is the balm which allows a sometimes flawed voice to be eloquently heard. This is its invaluable contribution to its country, its literature and its culture as a whole.

Notes

INTRODUCTION

1 Anita Shapira, 'Introduction', Yehuda Reinharz and Anita Shapira (eds.), *Essential Papers on Zionism* (London, Cassell, 1996), p. 12.
2 See Amos Elon, *The Israelis: Founders and Sons* (London, Sphere Books, 1971), p. 11.
3 Yaakov Hasdai, *Truth in the Shadow of War* (Zmora, Bitan, 1979), p. 80.
4 Gershon Shaked, *The Shadows Within* (Philadelphia, Jewish Publication Society), p. 150.
5 Adir Cohen, 'From the struggles of the original play' [Hebrew], *Moznayim*, vol. 12, no. 5–6, April–May 1961, p. 435.
6 Emanuel Sivan, *Myth, Portrait and Memory* [Hebrew] (Tel Aviv, Ma'arakhot), p. 122.
7 Shosh Weitz (ed.), *Summary of the Activities of Public Institutions for Culture and Art in Israel* [Hebrew] (Centre for Information and Research, July, 1994), pp. 31–46.
8 Dan Urian, 'Introduction' in *Contemporary Theatre Review*, vol. 3, no. 2, 1995, p. 7.
9 Moshe Shamir quoted by Avraham Oz, 'Chasing the subject: the tragic as trope and genre and the politics of Israeli drama' [Hebrew], *Contemporary Theatre Review*, vol. 3, no. 2, 1995, p. 141.
10 Dan Urian, 'The stereotype of the religious Jew in Israeli theatre', *Assaph C*, no. 10, 1994, p. 134.
11 Dan Urian, 'Introduction' in *Contemporary Theatre Review*, vol. 3, no. 2, 1995, p. 7.
12 Ben-Ami Feingold, 'Israeli theatre now' [Hebrew], *Moznayim*, vol. 57, no. 2, December 1992, pp. 34–6.
13 Susan Bennett, *Theatre Audiences: A Theory of Production and Reception* (London, Routledge, 1990) p. 94.
14 Urian, 'Stereotype of the religious', p. 134.
15 Marvin Carlson, *Theatre Semiotics (Signs of Life)* (Bloomington and Indianapolis, Indiana University Press, 1990), p. 12.
16 Urian, 'The stereotype of the religious', p. 132.

1 THE 'ENTERPRISE' AND ITS REINFORCEMENT IN THE DRAMA
OF THE 1950S

1 Max Brod (ed.), *The Diaries of Franz Kafka 1910–1923* (Harmondsworth, Penguin Books, 1978), p. 148.

2 Michael Keren, *The Pen and the Sword. Israeli Intellectuals and the Making of the Nation State* (San Francisco and London, Westview Press, 1989), p. 27.

3 Hayyim Hazaz, 'Creation, the act of victory over chaos' [Hebrew], *Moznayim*, vol. 23, no. 2, July 1966, p. 133.

4 Itamar Even-Zohar, 'Hebrew literature in Israel: an historical model' [Hebrew], *Hasifrut*, vol. 4, no. 3, July 1973, p. 432.

5 Keren, *Pen and the Sword*, p. 35.

6 *Ma'aleh* 2 January 1957, quoted in Gid'on Ophrat, *Israeli Drama* [Hebrew] (Jerusalem, Tcherikover Publishers, 1975), p. 86.

7 Leah Porat, quoted in Ophrat, *Israeli Drama*, p. 85. This is a somewhat Zhdanovist viewpoint. Andrei Zhdanov was Stalin's chief cultural commissar who, in 1934, set out the official doctrine of Socialist Realism: artists and architects were to follow the creed of 'revolutionary romanticism' and depict the officially sanctioned vision of the new society.

8 See Dan Miron, *Facing the Silent Brother* [Hebrew] (Jerusalem, Keter, 1992), p. 200.

9 Yoram Matmor, *Mahazeh Ragil* (An Ordinary Play), (1956), in *Proza*, no. 19–20 January–February 1978, pp. 36–47.

10 Moshe Shamir quoted by Avraham Oz in 'Chasing the subject', p. 141.

11 Elite corps of the pre-Israel Defence Force army, the Haganah. The *Palmah* was disbanded with the creation of the I. D. F. in 1948.

12 See Emmanuel Sivan, *Myth, Portrait and Memory* [Hebrew] (Tel Aviv, Ma'arakhot, 1991), p. 193.

13 Israel Goor, 'The comrades' Jimmy and Habimah's Jimmy', *Batzipiah Lateatron, Bamah*, no. 87–88, Summer 1981, pp. 92ff.

14 Performed at the Cameri Theatre.

15 Waves of immigration from 1881 to 1933.

16 Mossinzon, *In the Wastes of the Negev*, Or Am, 1989, p. 82.

17 Ibid., p. 102.

18 Danny Horowitz, 'Eli Geva, the teacher of the homeland' [Hebrew], *Yedi'ot Aharonot*, October 1993.

19 Cohen, 'From the struggles', p. 434.

20 Yisrael Goor, 'Chapters of the original play in the State of Israel' [Hebrew], *Bamah*, no. 38–39, Summer 1968, p. 8.

21 Cohen, 'From the struggles', p. 434.

22 Quoted in Ophrat, *Israeli Drama*, p. 36. See also Goor, 'Chapters of the original play', pp. 12, 14.

23 Performed at the Cameri Theatre.

24 After an incident in his first version of his play had been censored, Shaham described the horror with which a 'higher authority' viewed a

scene in which the soldiers send an Arab prisoner to fetch wood, hoping he will explode a mine and save an Israeli life. This 'authority' was apparently offended by the military realism of the play. Quoted in Ophrat, *Israeli Drama*, p. 37.

25 Natan Shaham, 'They Will Arrive Tomorrow', in *Bamah*, no. 66, Summer-Autumn 1975, p. 17.

26 Hayyim Shoham, *Challenge and Reality in Israeli Drama* [Hebrew] (Bar Ilan University Press), 1975, p. 75.

27 Yisrael Goor, 'Baring the soul at the time of attack' [Hebrew]. *Bamah*, no. 40, Winter 1969, p. 129.

28 In 1958 Yizhar was refused one of the most prestigious of Israel's literary prizes, the Bialik Prize, not because of any qualitative judgment of his writing, but because of his iconoclastic ideological stance.

29 David Canaani, quoted in Yitzhak Laor, 'We are the twelve in the pits' dust' [Hebrew], *Ha'aretz*, 29 April 1990; also in Laor, *We Are Writing You, Homeland* [Hebrew] (Hakibbutz Hameuchad, 1995), p. 52.

30 Ibid.

31 Cohen, 'From the struggles', p. 435.

32 See Nurit Gertz, *Hirbat Hiz`ah and the Next Morning* [Hebrew] (Tel Aviv, Tel Aviv University Press, 1983), p. 70.

33 See Lucien Goldmann, *The Hidden God* (London, Routledge and Kegan Paul, 1956).

34 Dina Porat, 'Attitudes of the young State of Israel towards the Holocaust and its survivors', Laurence J. Silberstein (ed.), *New Perspectives on Israeli History* (New York and London, University of New York Press, 1991), p. 166. See also Sivan, *Myth, Portrait and Memory*, pp. 76–7, 98.

35 See Sivan, *Myth, Portrait and Memory*, p. 76.

36 Yigal Mossinzon, *In the Wastes of the Negev*, p. 38.

37 Ibid., p. 35.

38 Myron J. Aronoff, 'Myths, symbols and rituals of the emerging state' in Silberstein, *New Perspectives*, p. 181.

39 Laor, *We Are Writing You, Homeland*, p. 52.

40 Goor, 'Jimmy', p. 94.

41 See Sivan, *Myth, Portrait and Memory*, pp. 35–39.

42 Laor, 'We are the twelve', p. 58.

43 Performed at the Cameri Theatre.

44 Nahman Ben-Ami, 'The heroes are tired' [Hebrew], *Al Hamishmar*, 13 November 1956.

45 'With slow steps ...' [Hebrew] (author not named), *Proza*, no. 19–20, January-February 1978, p. 36.

46 Ibid., p. 37.

47 Ibid., p. 38.

48 Matmor, *An Ordinary Play*, p. 44.

49 Ehud Ben Ezer, 'Breaking through and besieged' [Hebrew], in *Keshet*, no. 3, Summer 1968, p. 124.

50 Matmor, *An Ordinary Play*, p. 39.
51 See Mitchell Cohen, *Zion and State* (New York, Columbia University Press, 1992), pp. 201–60.
52 Matmor, *An Ordinary Play*, p. 40.
53 Matmor's satirical comments about the drama of his day imply the nature of many of the dramatic norms, not least of all, the *Palmah* hero. His 'author' says of Yitzhak, the moral arbiter in the play: 'Yitzhak isn't the hero. He's not active or positive enough'.
54 'With slow steps . . .', p. 38.
55 Leah Porat quoted in 'With slow steps . . .', p. 38.
56 'With slow steps . . .', *Proza*, p. 38.
57 See Shimon Levi, *The Altar and the Stage* [Hebrew] (Or Am, 1992), p. 185.
58 Matmor, *An Ordinary Play*, p. 44.
59 Hayyim Gamzu, '*An Ordinary Play* at the Cameri' [Hebrew], *Ha'aretz*, 13 November 1956.
60 Matmor, *An Ordinary Play*, p. 42.
61 In a story by Aharon Meged, 'An unusual deed', in D. Rabikovitz (ed.), *New Israeli Writers* (New York, 1969), a similar stereotypical wife is named Ziona.
62 Matmor, *An Ordinary Play*, p. 46.
63 For example, in Yehudit Hendel's *The Street of Steps* [Hebrew] and Yosef Bar Yosef's *Tura*.
64 See, for example: Natan Shaham, *Call Me Siomka* (1950); Aharon Meged, *Hedva and I* (1954); Moshe Shamir, *A House in Good Order* (1961); Ehud Ben Ezer, *The Quarry* (1964) [all Hebrew].

2 ZIONISM ON THE STAGE: YEARS OF PROTEST

1 See Susan Bennett, *Theatre Audiences: A Theory of Production and Reception* (London, Routledge, 1990), p. 112.
2 Shmuel Schneitzer, *Ma`ariv*, 5 November 1982.
3 '*Protocol*: Oh what a lovely cultural war' [Hebrew], *Nekudah*, 2 May 1984, p. 70. Author's name not listed.
4 Ibid.
5 Amos Oz, *In the Land of Israel* (London, Flamingo, 1983), pp. 151–2.
6 At a meeting at the Israel Museum where a 'heroic' experiment to bring together artists from the Right and the Left under the auspices of the journals *Akhshav* and *Nekudah*, 'the Right did not appear with [its] writers', only representatives of the religious groups. (*Ha'aretz*, 7 December 1990).
7 'Oh what a lovely cultural war', *Nekudah*, 3 June 1988, p. 70.
8 Dan Urian, *The Judaic Nature of Israeli Theatre: a Search for Indentity* (trans. Naomi Paz), unpublished manuscript, p. 93.
9 Avraham Oz, 'A note on the tragic Israeli situation as a challenge to the theatre' [Hebrew], *Siman Keriah*, no. 12–13, 1981. See also 'Chasing the

subject: the tragic as trope and genre and the politics of Israeli drama'
in *Contemporary Theatre Review*, vol. 3, no. 2, pp. 137ff.

10 Performed at the Haifa Municipal Theatre.

11 Eric Bentley, *The Theatre of War*. (London, Eyre Methuen, 1972),
p. 358.

12 David Alexander, *The Court Jester and the Ruler. Political Satire in Israel
1948–1984* [Hebrew] (Tel Aviv, Sifriat Poalim, 1986), p. 145.

13 Ibid.

14 Performed at the Cameri Theatre.

15 See Yigal Boorstein, 'The people of "Everything's Okay"' [Hebrew],
Ha'aretz, 15 May 1970.

16 Hanokh Levin, *The Queen of the Bathtub* [Hebrew] in *Mah Eikhpat
Latzippor* (Hakibbutz Hameuchad, 1987), p. 66.

17 Mossinzon, *In the Wastes of the Negev*, p. 20.

18 The word *sabra* is a corruption of the Hebrew word *tzabar* which means
both a native-born Israeli and a prickly pear.

19 Levin, *Queen of the Bathtub*, p. 66.

20 Mossinzon, *In the Wastes of the Negev*, p. 50.

21 Levin, *Queen of the Bathtub*, p. 66.

22 Mossinzon, *In the Wastes of the Negev*, p. 14.

23 Ibid.

24 Levin, *Queen of the Bathtub*, p. 89.

25 Ibid., p. 91.

26 Ibid.

27 Ibid., p. 89.

28 Boorstein, 'Everything's okay', pp. 61–2.

29 Ibid.

30 See Moshe Zimmerman, *The End of the Myth: Hebrew Drama Following the
Six-Day War* [Hebrew], (unpublished Ph.D thesis, Tel Aviv University,
1991), p. 65.

31 Ibid.

32 Performed at the Tzavta Theatre.

33 Alexander, *The Court Jester*, p. 142.

34 Amos Kenan, *Comrades Tell Stories About Jesus* [Hebrew] in *Mahazot* (Tel
Aviv, Proza Books, 1978), p. 15.

35 Ibid., p. 14.

36 Ibid., p. 15.

37 This refers to Moshe Shamir's *Hu Halakh Basadot* (He Walked in the
Fields), credited as the first Israeli play. It was produced in 1948 on the
back of army lorries in the battlefield. It achieved great popular success
and both disseminated and reflected many of the popular doctrines of
the day.

38 Shosh Avigal, 'When and why are plays banned in their entirety?'
[Hebrew], *Hadashot*, 28 July 1989.

39 Oz, 'A note on the tragic situation', pp. 284ff.

40 Ibid.
41 A Jew of Spanish origin, now predominantly from the Middle East and Africa.
42 Peformed at the Haifa Municipal Theatre.
43 N. Ben Ami, 'Two plays at the Haifa Theatre' [Hebrew], *Ma'ariv,* 8 July 1975.
44 Performed at the Carmeri Theatre.
45 See Zimmerman, *The End of the Myth,* p. 112.
46 Prostitute of Jericho who saved the spies sent by Joshua by hiding them in her house (Joshua 2:1–21; 6:17, 22–25).
47 Josef Mundi, *Moshel Yeriho* (The Ruler of Jericho), (Tel Aviv, Akshav, 1975), p. 56.
48 Ibid., p. 35.
49 For example, S. Yizhar, *Hashavui* (The Prisoner) 1948; Amos Kenan, *Haderekh el Ein Harod* (The Road to Ein Harod) 1984, 1985; David Grossman, *Hazeman Hatzahov* (The Yellow Wind) 1987.
50 Mundi, *The Ruler of Jericho,* p. 25.
51 Israel Goor, 'A distorted reflection' [Hebrew], *Batzipiyah Lateatron, Bamah* no. 87–88, Summer 1981, p. 68.
52 Goor, 'A distorted reflection', p. 68.
53 N. Oren, *Yedi'ot Aharonot,* 5th September 1980.
54 Bennett, *Theatre Audiences,* p. 112.
55 '*The Palestinian Girl* in the mirror of psychohistory', [Hebrew] *Ma'ariv* 1st November 1985.
56 E. D. Hirsch's term, quoted in Robert Boyers, *Atrocity and Amnesia* (Oxford and New York, Oxford University Press, 1985), p. 6.
57 T. Rubinstein, 'A group – get up and go' [Hebrew], *Iton 77,* no. 40–41, April–May, 1983, p. 39.
58 'A. B. Yehoshua, 'A summary of the festival of "alternative theatre" in Acre', [Hebrew] *Iton 77,* no. 24, 1980, p. 8.
59 Giora Manor, 'A return to realism?' [Hebrew], *Bamah,* 94, Winter, 1983, p. 5.
60 Michael Handelsaltz, 'Even the good are bad' [Hebrew], *Ha'aretz,* 20 October 1983.
61 See Graham Holderness, *The Politics of Theatre and Drama* (Basingstoke and London, Macmillan, 1992), p. 12.
62 Playwright Motti Lerner in a lecture at the Oxford Centre for Hebrew and Jewish Studies, 1989.
63 Michael H. Heim and Simon Karlinsky (ed.), *Letters of Anton Checkhov* (London, The Bodley Head, 1973) p. 200.

3 THE ISRAELI-PALESTINIAN WAR

1 See Dan Urian, 'Theatre and the Intifada' in *Contemporary Theatre Review,* vol. 3, no. 2, 1995, pp. 207–20; also 'The emergence of the Arab image

in Israeli theatre 1948–1982' in *Israel Affairs*, vol. 1, no. 4, Summer 1995, pp. 101–27.

2 Shosh Avigal, 'Everyone wants to live', *Modern Hebrew Literature*, no. 11, Autumn-Winter 1993, p. 19.

3 Aviva Sha'avi, 'Sobol syndrome' [Hebrew], *Yedi'ot Aharonot* 15th January 1988.

4 Performed at the Tzavta and Cameri theatres, revived at the Beer Sheva Theatre.

5 Performed at the Tzavta Theatre.

6 Miriam Kainy *Kmo Kadur Barosh* (Like a Bullet in the Head), photocopy, p. 27.

7 Ibid., p. 34.

8 Performed at the Neve Tzedek Theatre.

9 Performed at the Haifa Municipal Theatre.

10 A militant right-wing organisation headed by Rabbi Meir Kahane advocating the expulsion of the Arabs from Israel.

11 Yehoshua Sobol, *Hapalestina'it* (The Palestinian Girl) (Or Am, 1985), pp. 44–5.

12 Ibid., p. 72.

13 Yitzhak Laor, *Ephraim Returns to the Army*, photocopy, p. 26.

14 Ibid., p. 38.

15 Ibid., p. 13.

16 Avraham Oz takes a less positive view of the play, deeming it 'a convenient instrument of self-exoneration in the tradition of liberal Zionist apologetics, its political idiom infected by condescension and voyeurism'. In an interview, according to Oz, Hazor revealed that one of the earlier versions of the play located the action in pre-1948 Palestine, the characters being members of an anti-British underground group, the Stern Gang. Oz, 'Chasing the subject', *Contemporary Theatre Review*, vol. 3, part 2, 1995, p. 151.

17 Ran Gilboa, 'After all there's something new in Acre' [Hebrew] *Ha'ir*, 10 October 1990.

18 Performed at the Cameri Theatre.

19 A. P. Foulkes, *Literature and Propaganda* (London and New York, Methuen, 1983), p. 79.

20 Motti Lerner, *Hevlei Mashiah* (The Pangs of the Messiah), (Or Am, 1988), p. 83.

21 Ibid., p. 27.

22 Giora Manor, *Al Hamishmar* 21 June 1987.

23 Michael Handelsaltz, *Ha'aretz*, 23 June 1987.

24 'You can't argue', *Jerusalem Post* 23 October 1987.

25 Gidi Avivi, 'The pangs of Ofra' [Hebrew], *Kol Ha'ir* 27 March 1987.

26 Ibid.

27 Boyers, *Atrocity and Amnesia*, p. 19.

28 For an exposition of urban space as a political forum see Mitchell

Berman, *All That is Solid Melts Into Air* (London and New York, Verso, 1983).

29 Lerner, *Pangs of the Messiah*, p. 47.

30 Leviticus 26, 27ff in *The Palestinian Girl*, p. 49.

31 A. B. Yehoshua's *Na'im*. Na'im, an Arab boy, quotes from one of the Hebrew poet H. N. Bialik's poems. Amos Kenan's Mahmoud in *The Road to Ein Harod* quotes part of a nationalistic poem by the Hebrew poet Saul Tchernichowsky.

4 ZIONISM ON THE STAGE: SOBOL'S CASE

1 Herbert Lindenberger, *Historical Drama* (Chicago, University of Chicago Press, 1975), p. 12.

2 Ibid., p. 6.

3 Eric Bentley, *The Theatre of War* (London, Eyre, Methuen, 1972), p. 358.

4 Yosef Mundi, 'My theatre' [Hebrew], *Iton 77*, no. 84–85, January–February 1987, p. 103.

5 Bennett, *Theatre Audiences*, p. 161.

6 The 1927 act permitting theatre censorship in Israel was repealed in 1991.

7 Shoshana Weitz, 'The socio-political role of Israeli theatre' *Ariel* n.d.

8 Yehoshua Sobol, 'An artist in his land' [Hebrew], *Bamahaneh*, no. 10–11, September 1983, p. 15.

9 Sobol in Clive Sinclair, 'Joshua Sobol: Interview', *Index on Censorship*, vol. 14, no. 1, February 1985, p. 25.

10 Sobol in Yehudit Livna, 'What's bothering Yoash Shapiro?' [Hebrew], *Davar*, 14 March 1974.

11 Amos Oz, 'The way of the wind' in *Where the Jackals Howl* (London (trans. Maurie Goldberg-Bartura), Fontana Books, 1983).

12 Yehoshua Sobol, *Sylvester '72* (photocopy, 1974), p. 14.

13 Sobol in Livna, 'Yoash Shapiro'.

14 Sobol, *Sylvester '72*, p. 11.

15 Ibid., p. 4.

16 Yisrael Goor, 'Another well-parked evening at the Stage 2 of the Haifa Municipal Theatre' [Hebrew], *Batzippiyah Lateatron* [In the hope of a theatre]. *Bamah*, no. 87–88, Summer 1988, p. 62.

17 Sobol, *Sylvester '72*, p. 23.

18 Boaz Evron, 'An allegory of father and sons' [Hebrew], *Yedi'ot Aharonot*, 10 April 1974.

19 Ibid.

20 Sobol, *Sylvester '72*, p. 29.

21 Ibid., pp. 32–3.

22 J. L. Styan, *Modern Drama in Theory and Practice 3* (New York and Cambridge, Cambridge University Press, 1991) pp. 182–3.

23 Lecture, Oxford, 18 May 1995.

24 Performed at the Habimah Theatre.

25 David Horowitz, *My Yesterday* [Hebrew]. (Tel Aviv and Jerusalem, Schocken Books, 1970), p. 105.

26 *Kehiliyatenu* (a collection published by kibbutz Hashomer Hatza'ir on the Haifa-Jadeh road) [Hebrew], 1922, p. 55.

27 Yehuda Yaari, *When the Candle Was Burning* (1932; London, Gollancz, 1947).

28 Elkanah Margalit, *The Shomer Hatza'ir: From a Youth Group to Revolutionary Marxism 1913–1936* [Hebrew] (Hakibbutz Hameuchad, 1971), pp. 97–99.

29 Amos Elon, *The Israelis – Founders and Sons* (London, Sphere Books, 1971), p. 148.

30 David Horowitz, *My Yesterday*, p. 106.

31 Yehoshua Sobol, *The Night of the Twentieth* [Hebrew] in *Proza*, no. 3, p. 18.

32 Ibid., p. 9.

33 Yaari, *When the Candle Was Burning*, p. 146.

34 *Kehiliyatenu*, p. 55.

35 The name given to a group of disillusioned anti-bourgeois young intellectuals of the 1920s in Germany and Austria who strove for pure and simple values to contrast with the formality and authoritarianism of their societies.

36 Some of Gershon's aphorisms in *Sylvester '72* were derived from Bitanya: for example, 'I used to say, "You'll understand that individual salvation and the collective enterprise depend on erotic completion" and "There is no salvation for the Hebrew individual in isolation. The collective enterprise is based on the erotic!"'

37 'Searching for roots' [Hebrew], *Ha'aretz* 9 September 1977.

38 Sobol, *Night of the Twentieth*, p. 18.

39 Ibid.

40 Ibid.

41 Ibid., p. 9.

42 Performed at the Habima Theatre.

43 Yehoshua Sobol, 'Good day to you, Boazite Israel' [Hebrew], *Hotam*, 8 February 1974.

44 Emanuel Bar Kadma, 'Thirty years, three plays, one story' [Hebrew], *Yediot Aharonot*, 1 December 1978.

45 'It is well known ... that the artistic director of Habimah initiated, *inter alia*, a production of an Israeli *Oresteia* and gave the responsibility to Yehoshua Sobol. The latter of course rose to the challenge: he sat and wrote. When some of our critics came to evaluate the two parts of the trilogy that had already been staged by Habimah ... they began a kind of 'comparative study' which of course flattered Aeschylus more than it did Sobol.' Goor, *In the Hope of a Theatre*, p. 82.

46 Bar Kadma, 'Thirty years, three plays', p. 30.

47 Ibid.

48 Yehoshua Sobol, *Going Home* (photocopied manuscript)

49 Performed at the Habimah Theatre.
50 Peter Loewenberg, *Decoding the Past* (Berkeley and Los Angeles, London, University of California Press, 1985), p. 115. Herzl was inspired by the opera's pageantry and colour. The second Zionist Congress (1898) opened festively to the sounds of *Tannhäuser*.
51 Loewenberg, *Decoding the Past*, p. 119.
52 Yehoshua Sobol, *Nefesh Yehudi – Halaylah Ha'aharon Shel Otto Weininger* (A Jewish Soul: The Last Night of Otto Weininger), (Or Am, 1982), p. 39.
53 Ibid., p. 107.
54 Ibid., p. 50.
55 Michael Taub (ed.), *Modern Israeli Drama*. (Portsmouth, Heinemann, 1993), p. xv.
56 Sobol, *A Jewish Soul*, p. 109.
57 Sarit Fuchs, 'To make love and to die' [Hebrew], *Ma'ariv,* 1 October 1982.
58 Sobol in Sinclair, 'Interview', p. 54.
59 Sarit Fuchs, 'To make love and to die'.
60 Dan Urian, 'The controversy over *A Jewish Soul*' [Hebrew], *Bamah* no. 100, 1985, p. 82.
61 Ibid.
62 Amos Oz, *Israeli Literature: A Case of Reality Reflecting Fiction The Colorado College Studies* no. 21, 1985, p. 18.
63 In sympathy with German Jews who protested at the staging of *The Palestinian Girl* in Dusseldorf, the Israeli ambassador to Bonn, Yitzhak Ben-Ari, expressed the fear that 'the extreme Left in Israel is feeding the extreme German Right'. David Witztum, 'Let the Jews act for us' [Hebrew], *Koteret Rashit*, 18 November 1987.
64 Hannah Rosenthal, 'A playwright's soul' [Hebrew], *Al Hamishmar* 28 June 1985.
65 Sarit Fuchs, 'A rebellious Jewish soul' [Hebrew], *Ma'ariv,* 28 September 1983.
66 Hannah Rosenthal, 'Clamped in Haifa' [Hebrew], *Al Hamishmar,* 25 March 1988.
67 Sobol was awarded the Meskin Prize in 1983 for *A Jewish Soul*.
68 See Amos Oz, *Menuhah Nekhonah* (A Perfect Peace) (1982); A. B. Yehoshua:, *Gerushim Me'uharim* (Late Divorce), (1982).
69 Peter Finkelgrün, quoted in Witztum, 'Let the Jews act for us'.
70 Rosenthal, 'A playwright's soul'.
71 Hannah Rosenthal, 'Clamped in Haifa'.

5 HERO'S END

1 Performed at the Beersheba Theatre.
2 Performed at the Cameri Theatre.
3 See Tami Louvitz, 'Top secret' [Hebrew], *Ma'ariv,* 1 October 1993.
4 Thought to be based on the Israeli sculptor Yigal Tumarkin.

5 A great Jewish warrior who led a revolt against the Syrians in the second century BCE.
6 Hillel Mittelpunkt, *Gorodish* (Or Am, 1992), p. 6
7 Louvitz, 'Top secret'.
8 Hillel Mittelpunkt, *Gorodish*, (Or Am, 1992), p. 38.
9 'Operation Dovecote' is, according to Mittelpunkt's Gorodish, an action in the event of the Egyptians attacking Sinai.
10 Mittelpunkt, *Gorodish*, p. 65–66.
11 Amnon Levi, 'A terrifying thesis' [Hebrew], *Hadashot* 22 November 1993.
12 Lahat in Michael Handelsaltz, 'Returning to the tribal campfire' [Hebrew], *Ha'aretz* 29 November 1993.
13 Adam Baruch, 'Mittelpunkt kills Gorodish in the name of the youth of '73' [Hebrew], *Ha`olam Hazeh*, 24 November 1993.
14 Helen Kaye, 'True blue – and white', *The Jerusalem Post*, 26 November 1993.
15 See Handelsaltz, 'Returning to the tribal campfire'.
16 Mitterpunkt, *Gorodish*, p. 80.
17 Daniela Fisher, n.d.
18 Calev Ben David, 'The General cried at dawn', *The Jerusalem Report*, 13 January 1994, p. 44.
19 The plural form of *Palmahnik*, a member of the *Palmah*.
20 Adam Baruch, note to the programme of *Gorodish*.
21 Carmit Miron in *Zu Haderekh* 15 December 1993.
22 Adam Baruch, 'Mittelpunkt kills Gorodish in the name of the youth of '73'.
23 Handelsaltz, 'Returning to the tribal campfire'.
24 Shabtai Tevet, 'A few comments about *Gorodish*' [Hebrew], *Ha'aretz* 10 December 1993.
25 Ben Ami Feingold, 'Gorodish', *Hatzofeh*, 30 November 1993.
26 Styan, *Modern Drama*, p. 183.
27 Mitterpunkt, *Gorodish*, p. 42.
28 Feingold, 'Gorodish'.
29 *Hatzofeh*, 24 December 1993.

6 THE ISSUE OF RELIGION

1 Shaul Meizlish, 'Haredi culture at the Cameri' [Hebrew], *Davar*, 22 October 1993.
2 See Shapira and Reinharz (eds), *Essential Papers on Zionism*, pp. 12–3.
3 William Frankel, *Israel Observed* (London, Thames and Hudson, 1980), p. 198.
4 Dan Urian, 'The stereotype of the religious Jew in Israeli theatre', *Assaph C*, no. 10, 1994, pp. 134, 151.
5 Members of ultra-Orthodox sects.
6 The Israeli media invariably refer to the antagonists as 'religious' and

'secular' (*dati* and *hiloni*), terms which are political labels rather than indicative adjectives. 'Secular' indicates non-observance of the minutiae of Orthodox doctrine. It is used in this sense in this book.

7 Amos Oz, *In the Land of Israel* (London, Fontana, 1982), p. 115.

8 See, for example, Joseph Perl, *The Revealer of Secrets* (trans. Dov Taylor) (Colorado, Westview Press, 1996).

9 Performed at the Haifa Municipal Theatre.

10 Performed at the Haifa Municipal Theatre.

11 Performed at the Haifa Municipal Theatre.

12 Performed at the Tzavta Theatre.

13 Joshua 1:3; see also Deuteronomy 12:24.

14 Performed at the Cameri Theatre.

15 Mishna is the collection of Oral Law which forms the basis of the Talmud, the body of commentaries on the Oral Law; Midrash is the homiletical interpretation of the Bible; Aggadah (literally 'legend') the homiletical passages in rabbinic literature.

16 Performed at the Acre Festival and revived at the Khan Theatre.

17 Aharon Meged, 'The sober madness' [Hebrew], *Davar*, 12 December 1982.

18 David Grossman, 'Con lui è morto l'Ebreo Nuovo' [The New Jew has Died with Him] (undated photocopy): 'With his death the era of the *sabra* came to an end'.

19 Performed at the Khan Theatre.

20 Performed at the Beer Sheba Theatre.

21 Giora Manor, 'One fears for you, Israel' [Hebrew], *Al Hamishmar* 15 May 1986.

22 Hayyim Nagid, 'The banning proves what is written in *The Last Secular Jew*' [Hebrew], *Ma'ariv*, 2 December 1986.

23 Yoav, 'Between the aroma and the rottenness' [Hebrew], *Davar* 19 December 1986.

24 Performed at the Cameri Theatre.

25 Naomi Golan, 'The Cameri war with the Hebrew Halakhah' [Hebrew], *Hatzofeh*, 4 June 1993.

26 '*Fleischer*, unclean' [Hebrew], *Hatzofeh*, 4 June 1993.

27 Ibid.

28 Ilan Shahar, 'The storm around Fuchs and Hund' [Hebrew], *Ha'aretz* 30 May 1993.

29 Amir Oryan, 'The rite of religion and the ritual of tea', [Hebrew], *Ha'ir* [Tel Aviv], 4 June 1993.

30 Even-Or in Naomi Golan, '*Fleischer*', *Hatsofeh*, 4 June 1993.

31 'Jerusalem of Black', *The Jerusalem Report*, 29 December, 1994, p. 56.

32 *Ma'ariv*, 21 May 1993.

33 One-time Minister of Education in Rabin's administration.

34 Rivka Kanarik and A. Kadmi, 'In the days when the reapers are reaped', *Yom Hashishi*, Jerusalem, 21 May 1993.

35 Helen Kaye, 'The play's the thing to catch consciences', *Jerusalem Post*, 2 July 1993.

36 'A paranoid melodrama for the bourgeoisie' [Hebrew], *Ma'ariv*, 4 June 1993.

37 Sarit Fuchs, 'Emotional manipulation' [Hebrew], *Ha'aretz*, 1 June 1993.

38 Amir Oryan, *Ha'ir*, 4 June 1993.

39 Ibid.

40 Ibid.

41 Ibid.

42 See Urian, 'Stereotype of the religious', p. 151.

43 Performed at the Cameri Theatre.

44 *The Ultra-Orthodox* [Hebrew] (Jerusalem, Keter, 1989).

45 Daniela Fisher, 'A rebel despite herself' [Hebrew], *Al Hamishmar*, 3 September 1993.

46 *The Theatre Essays of Arthur Miller*, Robert A. Martin (ed.), (London, Methuen Drama, 1994), p. 259.

47 Daniela Fisher, 'A rebel despite herself'.

48 Hayyim Nagid, 'Making war in his courts' [Hebrew], *Davar*, 19 September 1993.

49 See Bennett, *Theatre Audiences*; Carlsson, *Semiotics*. Also, Janelle G. Reinelt and Joseph R. Roach (eds), *Critical Theory and Performance* (Ann Arbor, University of Michigan Press, 1992).

50 Rob Nixon, 'Appropriations of *The Tempest*', *Critical Inquiry*, Spring 1987, p. 558.

51 Samuel Schnitzer, 'Racism is celebrated on our stages' [Hebrew], *Ma'ariv*, 20 May 1994.

52 Ibid.

53 Ibid.

54 Shelomo Zand, 'Shylock goes to Sheinken', [Hebrew], *Ma'ariv*, 6 May 1994. The reference is to Baruch Goldstein, a religious settler who murdered 39 Palestinians at prayer in a mosque. Sheinken is a fashionable street in Tel Aviv.

55 Ibid.

56 Ibid.

57 Nitzan in N. Zeevi, 'Shylock made in Israel' [Hebrew], *Yated*, 13 May 1994.

58 Ibid.

59 Nitzan in Ilan Sofer, 'Shylock. From an enlightened man to a religious fanatic' [Hebrew], *Globes*, 29 April 1994.

7 THE POLITICAL USES OF THE HOLOCAUST

1 Michael Handelsaltz, 'The entire world is against us' [Hebrew], *Ha'aretz*, 16 November 1989.

2 Geoffrey H. Hartman, 'The cinema animal', in Yosefa Loshitzsky (ed.), *Spielberg's Holocaust. Critical Perspectives on Schindler's List* (Indiana University Press, 1997), p. 68.

3 Claude Lanzmann, 'Why Spielberg has distorted the truth', *The Manchester Guardian*, 3 April 1994.

4 David Patterson, *The Shriek of Silence* (Kentucky, University Press of Kentucky, 1992), pp. 7–8.

5 Sara R. Horowitz, 'But is it good for the Jews? Schindler and the aesthetics of atrocity', Loshitzsky, *Spielberg's Holocaust*, p. 3.

6 Ibid.

7 Primo Levi, *If This Is a Man* (Harmondsworth, Penguin Books, 1979).

8 David Jacobson, 'Aharon Appelfeld and the Holocaust' in *AJS Review*, vol. 13, nos. 1 and 2, Spring and Fall 1988, p. 131.

9 Tom Segev, *The Seventh Million* [Hebrew] (Jerusalem, Keter & Domino, 1991), pp. 383–84.

10 'Israeli theater and the Holocaust', *Israeli Holocaust Drama*, Michael Taub (ed.), (New York, Syracuse University Press, 1996), p. 12.

11 Avishai Margalit, 'The uses of the Holocaust', *The New York Review of Books*, 17 February 1994, p. 8.

12 James E. Young, *The Texture of Memory* (New Haven, Yale University Press, 1993), p. 211.

13 David Jacobson, 'Aharon Appelfeld', p. 132.

14 Ben Ami Feingold, *The Holocaust in Israeli Drama* [Hebrew] (Tel Aviv, Hakibbutz Hameuchad, 1989), p. 27.

15 See Alan Mintz, *Hurban – Responses to Catastrophe in Hebrew Literature* (Columbia University Press, 1984), p. 162.

16 Jacobson, 'Aharon Appelfeld', p. 130.

17 Ibid., p. 132. See also Yael Zerubavel, *Recovered Roots. Collective Memory and the Making of Israeli National Tradition* (Chicago: Chicago University Press, 1995), p. 72.

18 Zerubavel, *Recovered Roots*, p. 75.

19 Hayyim Hazaz, 'The sermon' [Hebrew], in *Sippurim Nivharim* (Tel Aviv, Dvir La'am, 1952), p. 189.

20 Mintz, *Hurban*, p. 161.

21 Yehoshua Sobol, *The Night of the Twentieth* in *Proza* 19–20, January-February 1978, p. 9.

22 Amos Elon, 'The politics of memory' in *The New York Review of Books*, 7 October 1993, p. 3.

23 Mossinzon, *In the Wastes of the Negev*, p. 42.

24 Bruno Bettelheim reinforced this image of the passive Jewish victim. In his opinion, 'A certain type of ghetto thinking has as its purpose the avoidance of taking action. It is a type of deadening of the senses and emotions, so that one can bow down to the mujik who pulls one's beard, laugh with the baron at his anti-Semitic stories, degrade oneself so that one will be permitted to survive.' (*Freud's Vienna and Other Essays*

(New York, Knopf, 1990), p. 260). Hebrew writers also deplored this facility, seeing it not as a psychological defence but as a cultural failure.

25 Segev, *Seventh Million*, p. 164.

26 Ibid.

27 Segev, *Seventh Million* [Hebrew], p. 97.

28 Oz, 'Chasing the subject', p. 140.

29 See Dina Porat, 'Attitudes of the young State of Israel toward the Holocaust and its survivors: a debate over identity and values' in *New Perspectives on Israeli History* (New York and London, New York University Press, 1991) pp. 163 ff.

30 Porat, 'Attitudes of the young State', p. 164.

31 See Yehuda Bauer, *The Jewish Emergence from Powerlessness* (Toronto, University of Toronto Press, 1979); Leon Cohen, *From Greece to Birkenau, The Crematoria Workers' Uprising* (Tel Aviv, Salonika Jewry Research Centre, 1996).

32 See Moshe Zimmerman, *The End of the Myth. Hebrew Drama after the Six-Day War*, p. 97.

33 *Tcherli Katcherli* is a meaningless name indicative of the type of nickname given to the young *sabras*.

34 Performed at the Khan Theatre.

35 Danny Horowitz, *Tcherli Katcherli* (Or Am, 1992), p. 43.

36 Ibid., p. 50.

37 Ziva Ben–Porat, 'A *sabra* whose name is Tcherli' [Hebrew], Introduction to *Tcherli Katcherli* (Or Am, 1992), p. 17.

38 Horowitz, *Tcherli Katcherli*, p. 68.

39 Zimmerman, *The End of the Myth*, p. 99.

40 Performed at the Cameri Theatre.

41 Jewish council.

42 Mapai, the Israeli Labour Party, was in power.

43 The underground defence and resistance organisation founded in 1931 by the Revisionist Zionists, hostile to the Haganah.

44 Right-wing Revisionist party, founded in 1948.

45 The Court found that Halevi had based his conclusions on a lack of recognition of the conditions that the Jews in general, and those serving on the Relief Committee in particular, had suffered during the occupation of Hungary.

46 Yehiam Weitz, 'Political dimensions of Holocaust memory in Israel during the 1950s', *Israel Affairs*, Robert Wistrich and David Ohana (eds), vol. 1, no. 3, Spring 1995, p. 130.

47 Segev, *Seventh Million*, p. 251.

48 See Chapter 8.

49 'From public sources, particularly newspapers, it is difficult to determine to what extent at that time [the ultra-Orthodox world] viewed the Holocaust as its main weapon to be used against secular Zionists.' Weitz, quoting Dina Porat, in 'Political dimensions', p. 131.

50 *Davar*, 12 July 1985.
51 Motti Lerner, *Kastner* (Or Am, 1988), p. 149.
52 Styan, *Modern Drama*, pp. 182–3.
53 Lerner, *Kastner*, p. 137. This passage is adapted from the transcript of the 'Kastner Trial'.
54 Brand travelled to Istanbul to negotiate with the Americans but was imprisoned by the British in Aleppo as an enemy agent.
55 Lerner, *Kostner*, p. 37.
56 Weitz, 'Political dimensions', p. 130.
57 Taub, *Israeli Holocaust Drama*, p. 15.
58 *Davar*, 12 July 1985.
59 Jim Allen, *Perdition* (London and Atlantic Highlands, Ithaca Press, 1987), p. 67.
60 Cesarani in Victoria Radin, 'Playing dirty', *The New Statesman* 6 February 1987.
61 See David Rose, 'Rewriting the Holocaust', *Guardian* 14 January 1987.

8 THE HOLOCAUST AS POLITICAL ANALOGY

1   Hedda Boshes, 'The prostitution and corruption of language', n.d.
2   Dan Almagor, *Yediot Aharonot*, 16 December 1988.
3   Segev, *Seventh Million*, pp. 382ff.
4   Performed at the Haifa Municipal Theatre.
5   Sobol in 'Joshua Sobol – Interview', pp. 24–5.
6   Programme notes for the National Theatre production in London, 1989.
7   Sobol in 'Joshua Sobol – Interview', p. 25.
8   Ibid.
9   John Gross, *Sunday Telegraph*, 30 April 1989.
10 Charles Spencer, *Daily Telegraph* 29 April 1989.
11 Christopher Edwards, *The Spectator*, 6 May 1989.
12 David Witztum, 'Let the Jews act for us', *Koteret Rashit*, 18 November 1987.
13 For a discussion of 'cultural resistance' see Lawrence Langer, 'Cultural resistance to genocide', *Admitting the Holocaust* (New York, Oxford University Press, 1995), pp. 51–63.
14 Programme note for *Ghetto*, 1989.
15 See George Steiner, (In a post-culture', *In Bluebeard's Castle* (London, Faber and Faber, 1971), p. 61ff.
16 Paul A. Taylor, *The Independent*, 29 April 1989.
17 Yehoshua Sobol, *Ghetto*, (Or Am, 1984), p. 41.
18 Ibid., p. 79. In the London production he faces the audience and says: 'For the sake of your clean conscience I plunged into filth. I couldn't

afford a clean conscience. Could I?' Yehoshua Sobol, *Ghetto* (London, Nick Helm Books, 1989), p. 48.

19 Sobol, *Ghetto*, p. 55.

20 Ibid., p. 36.

21 Sobol in 'Joshua Sobol – Interview', p. 24.

22 Feingold, *Drama of the Holocaust*, p. 129, n. 11. See also Dafna Clifford, *Unifying Elements in European-Jewish Fiction 1890–1945* (Unpublished D.Phil. thesis, Oxford, 1994): '[I]t is now recognised that the German-Jewish symbiosis was never the *folie à deux* imagined by German Jews, in that Germany never wanted its Jews as much as its Jews wanted Germany.' (p. 11).

23 Sinclair, 'Joshua Sobol – Interview', p. 25.

24 Quoted by Feingold, *Drama of the Holocaust*, p. 109.

25 Sobol, *Ghetto*, p. 65.

26 Ibid.

27 Ibid., p. 83.

28 Ibid., p. 84.

29 Ibid.

30 Keith Gore, 'In extremis', *The Oxford Magazine*, Fourth Week, Trinity Term 1989, p. 15.

31 Michael Ratcliffe, *The Observer*, 30 April 1989.

32 Irving Wardle, *The Times*, 29 April 1989.

33 Shlomo Shapir, '*Ghetto* in Berlin – success and amazement' [Hebrew], n.d.

34 Michael Handelsaltz, 'Why did *Ghetto* fail?' [Hebrew] Ha'aretz, 16 June 1989.

35 Gore, 'In extremis'.

36 Charles Spencer, *Daily Telegraph*, 29 April 1989.

37 Clive Hirshhorn, *Sunday Express*, 30 April 1989.

38 Michael Handelsaltz, 'Viewers and collaborators', [Hebrew] *Ha'aretz*, 4 October 1991.

39 Ibid.

40 See Elyakim Yaron, 'A Jewish soul' [Hebrew], *Ma'ariv*, 4 October 1991.

41 *Davar*, 13 April 1993.

42 Yigael Abiran, *Davar* 14 April 1992.

43 Shosh Avigal, *Hadashot*, 17 April 1992.

44 Performed at the Habimah Theatre.

45 Yosef Mundi, *Leylot Frankfurt Ha'alizim* (Happy Nights in Frankfurt), (Jerusalem, Schocken Books, 1988), p. 117.

46 Ibid., p. 121.

47 Ibid., p. 122.

48 Yoram Kaniuk, 'Native Israeli literature and the specter of Jewish history' [interview with Esther Fuchs], *Modern Hebrew Literature*, Fall/Winter 1983, p. 64.

9 METAPHOR AND MYTHOLOGY

1 See Michael Gurewitz, Hayyim Shoham, Sh. Shapera, Gershon Shaked, 'A discussion about Nissim Aloni' [Hebrew], *Bamah*, Spring-Summer 1983, p. 72.

2 Gurewitz et al., 'Discussion', p. 75. See also the article by Aloni (1951) quoted in *Proza* 19–20, January/February, 1978, p. 78: 'It is our duty to go to war for the country's Hebrewness [*ivriyyutah*] for every moment wasted allows the diaspora [*galut*] to hammer another nail into this land called Israel and soon, in our time – if we are not there yet – we'll find ourselves in a Jewish ghetto, oppressed, humiliated, bearing the yellow star.'

3 Performed at the Habimah Theatre.

4 See G. Abramson, *The Distant Self* (Oxford, Oxford Centre for Post-graduate Hebrew Studies, 1982).

5 Nissim Aloni, 'The young men who went to war', *Proza* 19–20, January–February 1978, p. 44.

6 Malcolm Bradbury and James MacFarlane (eds), *Modernism* (Harmondsworth, Penguin Books, 1976), p. 277.

7 See Alan Mintz, *Banished from Their Father's Table. Loss of Faith and Hebrew Autobiography* (Bloomington and Indianapolis, Indiana University Press, 1989), pp. 82–4.

8 M. Z. Feierberg, *Whither* [Hebrew], (7th ed.), (Tel Aviv, Dvir, 1964), p. 135.

9 Aloni, quoted by Michael Ohad, 'Analysis of a myth' [Hebrew], *Ha'aretz* 31 January 1975.

10 Theo Hermans (ed.), *The Manipulation of Literature* (London and Sydney, Croom Helm, 1985), p. 164.

11 Performed at the Habimah Theatre.

12 Hayyim Shoham, 'Nissim Aloni's *The American Princess*' [Hebrew], *Iton 77*, January, 1983.

13 Nissim Aloni, *Hanesikhah Ha'amerika'it* (The American Princess), (Amikam, 1963), p. 12.

14 Gurewitz et al., 'Discussion', p. 87.

15 Performed at the Habimah Theatre, and then revived by the Haifa Municipal Theatre in conjunction with the Israel Festival in 1990.

16 Moshe Natan, 'The king is dead – long live the poor man' [Hebrew], *Ma'ariv*, 6 May 1975.

17 Performed at the Bimot Theatre.

18 Nissim Aloni, *Hakalah Vetzayad Haparparim: Haniftar Mitparea* (The Bride and the Butterfly Hunter; The Deceased on the Rampage), (Hakibbutz Hameuchad, 1990), p. 29.

19 Foucault recognised the ambiguity in this wilful separation in *The Archeology of Knowledge and the Discourse on Language* (Pantheon, New York, 1972), as did the Hebrew literary scholar Barukh Kurzweil in his

question regarding the continuity of modern Hebrew literature: '*Hemshekh o mahapekhah*' (Continuation or revolution)?

10 THE VISION OF HANOKH LEVIN

1 Yitzhak Laor, *We Are Writing You, Homeland* [Hebrew] (Hakibbutz Hameuchad, 1995), p. 172.

2 Avraham Oz, 'Dried dreams and bloody subjects. Body politics in the theatre of Hanokh Levin' in *JTD (Haifa University Studies in Theatre and Drama)*, no. 1, Autumn 1995, p. 133.

3 Shosh Avigal, 'Levin's family wants to live' [Hebrew], *Davar*, 3 May 1985.

4 Performed at the Haifa Municipal Theatre.

5 Ben Ami Feingold, 'Answers without questions' n.d.

6 Oz, 'Dried dreams, p. 128.

7 Hanokh Levin, *Hefetz* (Tel Aviv, Siman Keriah, 1972), p. 17.

8 Shimon Levi, *The Altar and the Stage (Mekatrim Babamot)*, (Or Am, 1992), p. 196.

9 Hanokh Levin, *Yisurei Iyov Ve'aherim* (The Torments of Job, and Other Plays), (Hakibbutz Hameuchad, 1988), p. 101.

10 Ibid., p. 99.

11 See Gidon Ophrat-Friedlander, 'Death and the possibility of rebirth' [Hebrew], *Ha'aretz* 11 December 1981.

12 Levin, *The Torments of Job*, p. 60.

13 Ibid., p. 94.

14 Daniel Ben-Levin, 'The Torments of Job and the torments of Sisyphus' [Hebrew], *Al Hamishmar*, 11 September 1981.

15 Michael Handelsaltz, 'There is no God and that's final' [Hebrew], *Ha'aretz*, 17 April 1981.

16 Dan Miron, 'The degradation, the humiliation and the pain' [Hebrew], *Hadoar*, vol. 24, 1 May 1981, p. 389. Also in *Ma`ariv*, 27 March 1981.

17 Levin, *The Torments of Job*, p. 99.

18 Levi, *The Altar and the Stage*, p. 200.

19 Levin, *The Torments of Job*, p. 69.

20 Ophrat-Friedlander, *Ha'aretz*, 1981.

21 See Boaz Evron, 'The torments of the body are stronger than faith' [Hebrew], *Yedi'ot Aharonot*, 23 April 1981.

22 Levin, *The Torments of Job*, p. 101.

23 Oz, 'Dried dreams', p. 119.

24 Levin, *The Torments of Job*, p. 97.

25 Elyakim Yaron, 'The execution of Job' [Hebrew], *Ma'ariv*, 23 April 1981.

26 Giora Manor, 'The torments of Hanokh' [Hebrew], *Al Hamishmar*, 6 June 1981.

27 See Antonin Artaud, *The Theatre and its Double*, (trans. Mary C.

Richards), (New York, Grove Press, 1958). Elyakim Yaron admonishes Levin for potentially losing control of his text within his theatrical fireworks, the 'glorious sea of aesthetics'. Similarly, Giora Manor accuses the director of having vanquished the playwright and he criticises the play's 'colourful extravaganza' (*The Torments of Hanokh*).

28 Ibid.
29 Performed at the Cameri Theatre.
30 Harold Atkins, *The Daily Telegraph* (London), 16 April 1985.
31 'Not nice, not bad' [Hebrew], *Ha'aretz*, 5 September 1985.
32 Michael Wulff, 'Depressed' [Hebrew], *Al Hamishmar*, 19 August 1983.
33 Hanokh Levin, *Orzei Hamizvadot* (The Suitcase Packers), (Hakibbutz Hameuchad, 1983), p. 56.
34 Giora Manor, 'Levin's beauty' (or 'Lovely Levin') [Hebrew], n.d.
35 Michael Handelsaltz, 'A comedy of funerals' [Hebrew], *Ha'aretz*, 14 March 1983.
36 Christopher Innes, *Modern British Drama 1890–1990* (Cambridge, Cambridge University Press, 1992), p. 269.
37 Joe Orton, *The Orton Diaries* (London, Methuen, 1986), p. 125.
38 Innes, *Modern British Theatre*, p. 270.
39 Ibid.
40 Performed at the Haifa Municipal Theatre, the Habima Theatre, and the Israel Festival.
41 Shosh Weitz, 'What beautiful pain' [Hebrew], *Yedi'ot Aharonot*, 24 May 1993.
42 Hayyim Guri, 'Heritage' in *Shoshanat Ruhot* (Hakibbutz Hameuchad, 1960), p. 83.
43 Ziva Shamir, 'Man's instinct is bad and terrible from the time of his youth' [Hebrew], *Ta'amim*, December 1993.
44 Oz, 'Dried dreams', p. 141.
45 Quoted by Hayyim Shoham, *Theatre and Drama in Search of an Audience* [Hebrew], (Or Am, 1989), p. 62.
46 Feingold, 'Answers without questions'.
47 'The encouragement of the play and the suppression of the playwright' [Hebrew], n.d.
48 Oz, 'Dried dreams', p. 122.
49 Michael Handelsaltz, 'A crack in the wall of indifference' [Hebrew], *Ha'aretz*, 27 February 1983.
50 Oz, 'Dried dreams', p. 131.

AFTERWORD

1 Holderness, *Politics of Theatre*, p. 9.
2 Arthur Miller, *The Theatre Essays of Arthur Miller*, (London, Methuen, 1994), p. 258.
3 Yehoshua Sobol, *The Night of the Twentieth* in *Proza*, no. 3, p. 19.

4 Oz, 'Chasing the subject', p. 137.

5 A European search for 'self' took place during the first half of the twentieth century, resulting in the many opposed 'selfs' of Pirandello, Anouilh, Genet, Claudel, Sartre, Beckett and Osborne, among others.

6 Shosh Avigal, 'New directions. Hebrew theatre in the 1990s', *Modern Hebrew Literature*, no. 11, Autumn/Winter 1993, p. 20.

7 See Elyakim Yaron, *Ma'ariv*, 26 November 1993.

8 Urian, 'The stereotype of the religious', p. 132.

Select bibliography

1. ENGLISH BOOKS

Abramson, Glenda, *Modern Hebrew Drama*, London, Weidenfeld and Nicolson, 1979.

J. Barnes (ed.), *The Writer in Australia*, Melbourne, Oxford, Oxford University Press, 1969. Toronto, University of Toronto Press, 1979.

Bennett, Susan, *Theatre Audiences: A Theory of Production and Reception*, London, Routledge, 1990.

Bentley, Eric, *The Theatre of War*, London, Eyre, Methuen, 1972.

The Theory of the Modern Stage, Harmondsworth, Penguin Books, 1984.

Berman, Mitchell, *All That is Solid Melts into Air*, London and New York, Verso, 1983.

Bettleheim, Bruno, *Freud's Vienna and Other Essays*, New York, Knopf, 1990.

Bhabha, Homi K. (ed.), *Nation and Narration*, London, Routledge, 1990.

Boyers, Robert, *Atrocity and Amnesia*, New York and Oxford, Oxford University Press, 1985.

Brenton, Howard, *Hot Irons*, London, Nick Hern Books, 1995.

Brod, Max (ed.), *The Diaries of Franz Kafka 1910–1923*, Harmondsworth, Penguin Books, 1978.

Calvocoressi, Peter, *Freedom to Publish*, Almqvist & Wiksell International, Stockholm, 1980.

Carlson, Marvin, *Theatre Semiotics (Signs of Life)*, Bloomington and Indianapolis, Indiana University Press, 1990.

Case, Sue Ellen and Reinelt, Janelle (eds.), *The Performance of Power*, Iowa City, University of Iowa Press, 1991.

Chaney, David, *Fictions of Collective Life: Public Drama in Late Modern Culture*. London and New York, Routledge, 1993.

Cohen, Mitchell, *Zion and State*, New York, Columbia University Press, 1992.

Elon, Amos, *The Israelis – Founders and Sons*, London, Sphere Books. 1971.

Herzl, London, Weidenfeld and Nicolson, 1975.

Elsom, John, *Cold War Theatre*, London and New York, Routledge, 1992.

Post-War British Theatre, London and Boston, Routledge and Kegan Paul, 1976.

Foulkes, A. P., *Literature and Propaganda*, London and New York, Methuen, 1983.

Frankel, William, *Israel Observed*, Thames and Hudson, 1980.

Fussell, Paul, *The Great War and Modern Memory*, London, Oxford and New York, Oxford University Press, 1975.

Girling, John, *Myths and Politics in Western Societies*, Transaction Publishers, 1993.

Goldmann, Lucien, *The Hidden God*, London, Routledge and Kegan Paul, 1956.

Gonen, Jay Y., *The Psychohistory of Zion*, New York, Mason/Charter, 1975.

Hasdai, Yaakov, *Truth in the Shadow of War*, Zmora, 1979.

Havel, Vaclav, *The Power of the Powerless: Citizens against the State in Central-Eastern Europe*, Armonk, Sharpe, 1985.

Hilton, Julian (ed.), *New Directions in Theatre*, Macmillan, 1993.

Holderness, Graham, *The Politics of Theatre and Drama*, Basingstoke and London, Macmillan, 1992.

Hubner, Zygmunt, *Theatre and Politics*, Illinois, Northwestern University Press, 1988.

Innes, Christopher, *Modern British Drama, 1890–1990*, Cambridge, Cambridge University Press, 1992.

Jacobs, Naomi, *The Character of Truth: Historical Figures in Contemporary Fiction*, Carbondale and Edwardsville, Southern Illinois University Press, 1990.

Keren, Michael, *The Pen and the Sword. Israeli Intellectuals and the Making of the Nation State*, Boulder, San Francisco, London, Westview Press, 1989.

Langer, Lawrence, *Admitting the Holocaust*, New York, Oxford University Press, 1995.

Lindenberger, Herbert, *Historical Drama*, University of Chicago Press, 1975.

Loewenberg, Peter, *Decoding the Past*, Berkeley, Los Angeles, London, University of California Press, 1985.

Merrett, Christopher, *A Culture of Censorship (Secrecy and Intellectual Repression in South Africa)*, Cape Town, Mercer University Press, 1994.

Oz, Amos, *Where the Jackals Howl*, Fontana Books, 1983.

In the Land of Israel, London, Minneapolis, Flamingo, 1983.

Reinelt, Janelle G. and Roach, Joseph R. (eds), *Critical Theory and Performance*, Ann Arbor, University of Michigan Press, 1992.

Reinharz, Yehuda and Shapira, Anita (eds), *Essential Papers on Zionism*, London, Cassell, 1996.

Rolef, Susan Hattis, *Political Dictionary of the State of Israel*, New York, Macmillan, 1987.

Rutherford, Andrew, *The Literature of War*, London, Macmillan Press, 1989.

Shaked, Gershon, *The Shadows Within*, Philadelphia, J.P.S., 1987.

Silberstein, Laurence J. (ed.), *New Perspectives on Israeli History*, New York and London, New York University Press, 1991.

Skloot, Robert, *The Darkness We Carry*, Wisconsin, University of Wisconsin Press, 1988.

The Theatre of the Holocaust, Wisconsin, University of Wisconsin Press, 1982.

Styan, J. L., *Modern Drama in Theory and Practice 3*, New York and Cambridge, Cambridge University Press, 1991.

Szondi, Peter, *Theory of the Modern Drama* (trans. Michael Hays), Minneapolis, University of Minnesota, 1987.

Taub, Michael, trans. and ed., *Modern Israeli Drama*, Heinemann, London, 1993.

Israeli Holocaust Drama, New York, Syracuse University Press, 1996.

Urian, Dan (ed.) *Contemporary Theatre Review*, vol. 3, no. 2, 1995.

Yaari, Yehuda, *When the Candle Was Burning*, London, Gollancz, 1947.

Young, James E., *The Texture of Memory*, New Haven, Yale University Press, 1993

Zerubavel, Yael, *Recovered Roots (Collective Memory and the Making of Israeli National Tradition)*, Chicago and London, University of Chicago Press, 1995.

ENGLISH JOURNALS

Israel Studies (Israel), *Israel Affairs* (London), *Jewish Theatre and Drama* (later *The Journal of Theatre and Drama*), *Prooftexts, A. J. S. Review, Contemporary Theatre Review, Ariel, Assaph, Critical Inquiry, Index on Censorship, The Jerusalem Report*.

HEBREW BOOKS

Alexander, David, *Leitzan Hehatzer Vehashalit: Satirah Politit Beyisra'el 1948–1984* [The court jester and the ruler: political satire in Israel 1948–1984], Sifriat Poalim, 1986.

Feingold, Ben Ami, *Hashoah Badrama Ha'ivrit* [The Holocaust in Hebrew Drama], Hakibbutz Hameuchad, 1989.

Goor, Israel, *Batzipiah Lateatron*, a special issue of *Bamah*, no. 87–88 (Summer 1981).

Horowitz, Dan, *Tkhelet Ve'avak* [The Heavens and the Earth. A Self-portrait of the 1948 Generation], Keter, 1993.

Horowitz, David, *Ha'etmol Sheli* [My Yesterday], Schocken Books, 1970.

Kehiliyatenu: Kovetz Hotza'at Kibbutz 'Hashomer Hatza'ir' Bakvish Haifa-jadeh [Kehiliyatenu: A Collection Published by Kibbutz Hashomer Hatzair on the Haifa-Jadeh Road], 1922.

Laor, Yitzhak, *Anu Kotvim Otakh Moledet* [We Are Writing You, Homeland], Hakibbutz Hameuchad, 1995.

Levi, Shimon, *Mekatrim Babamot* [The Altar and the Stage], Or Am, 1992.

Margalit, Elkanah, *Hashomer Hatza'ir: Me'adat Ne'urim Lemarxism Mehapkhani 1913–1936* [The *Shomer Hatza'ir*: From a Youth Group to Revolutionary Marxism 1913–1936], Hakibbutz Hameuchad, 1971.

Ophrat, Gid'on, *Hadrama Hayisra'elit* [Israeli drama], Tcherikover Publishers, 1975.

Segev, Tom, *Hamilyon Hashevi'i*, Keter & Domino, 1991.

Shoham, Hayyim, *Etgar Umetzi'ut Badrama Hayisra'elit* [Challenge and Reality in Israeli drama], Bar Ilan University Press, 1975; Or Am, 1989.

    Teatron Udrama Mehapsim Kahal [Theatre and Drama in Search of an Audience] Or Am, 1989.

Sivan, Emmanuel, *Mitos, Diyukan Vezikkaron* [Myth, Portrait and Memory], Tel Aviv: Ma'arakhot, 1991.

Urian, Dan, *Demut Ha'aravi Bateatron Hayisra'eli* [The Figure of the Arab in Israeli Theatre], Or Am, 1996.

Zimmerman, Moshe, *Ketz Hamitos: Hadrama Ha'ivrit Mimilhemet Sheshet Hayamim* [The End of the Myth: Hebrew Drama after the Six-Day War], unpublished Ph.D thesis, Tel Aviv University, 1991.

HEBREW JOURNALS

Bamah, Proza, Iton 77, Siman Keri'ah, Hasifrut, Moznayim, Keshet.

HEBREW PLAYS

(Photocopied plays are available from the Israel Goor Theatre Museum and Archive at the Hebrew University of Jerusalem.)

Aloni, Nissim

    Bigdei Hamelekh (photocopy).

    Eddie King, Siman Keriah, 1975.

    Hakalah Vetzayad Haparparim Siman Keriah/ Hakibbutz Hameuchad, 1980.

    Hanesikhah Ha'amerikait, Sifrei Amikam, 1963.

Danon, Rami (see Levi, Amnon).

Even-Or, Yigal, *Fleischer* (photocopy).

Hasfari, Shmuel

    Gisato shel Goldin (photocopy).

    Hahiloni Ha'aharon (photocopy).

    Tashmad, 1982 (photocopy).

Hazor, Ilan, *Re'ulim*, Or Am, 1991.

Horowitz, Danny, *Tcherli Katcherli*, Or Am, 1992.

Kainy, Miriam

    Kmo Kadur Barosh (photocopy).

    Hashiv'ah (photocopy).

Keinan, Amos, *Haverim Mesapprim 'al Yeshu*, Sifriat Proza, 1978.

Laor, Yitzhak, *Ephraim Hozer Latzava*, 1989 (photocopy).

Lerner, Motti,.

    Hevlei Mashiah, Or Am 1988.

    Kastner, Or Am, 1988.

Levi, Amnon and Danon, Rami, *Sheindele* (photocopy).
Levin, Hanokh
  Hayeled Holem (photocopy).
  Hefetz, Siman Keriah, 1972.
  Hotza'ah Lahoreg in *Yisurei Iyov Ve'aherim*, Siman Keriah, 1988.
  Malkat Ha'ambatya in *Mah Eikhpat Latzippor*, Siman Keriah, 1987.
  Orzei Mizvadot, Or Am, 1983.
  Yisurei Iyov in *Yisurei Iyov Ve'aherim*, Siman Keriah, 1988.
Matmor, Yoram, *Mahazeh Ragil* 1956, *Proza*, 19–20, January–February 1978.
Mittelpunkt, Hillel
  Ahim Laneshek, Kinneret, 1992.
  Gorodish, Or Am, 1993.
Mossinzon, Yigal, *Be'arvot Hanegev,* Or Am, 1989.
Mundi, Joseph,
  Leilot Frankfurt Ha'alizim, Schocken, 1988.
  Moshel Yeriho, Akhshav, 1975.
Shaham, Natan, *Hem Yagi'u Mahar*, Sifriat Poalim, 1949; World Zionist
  Organisation, 1957.
Sobol, Yehoshua,
  Ghetto, Or Am, 1984.
  Habayta, Habayta (photocopy).
  Hapalestina'it Or Am, 1985.
  Leyl Ha'esrim, *Proza*, 1977.
  Nefesh Yehudi, Or Am, 1982.
  Sylvester '72, (photocopy).
Yehoshua, A. B., *Laylah Bemai*, Schocken, 1974.

SELECTION OF HEBREW PLAYS PUBLISHED IN ENGLISH TRANSLATION

Aloni, Nissim, *The American Princess*, Institute for the Translation of Hebrew
  Literature, Israel (henceforth, Institute); Michael Taub (trans. and ed.),
  Modern Israeli Drama, Heinemann, 1993 (henceforth, Taub 1993).
Bar Yosef, Yosef, *Difficult People*, Institute.
Goldberg, Leah, *The Lady of the Castle*, Institute; Michael Taub (ed.), *Israeli
  Holocaust Drama*, New York, University of Syracuse, 1995, (henceforth
  Taub 1995).
Horowitz, Danny, *Breakdown and Bereavement*, Institute.
Lerner, Motti, *Kastner*, Taub 1995.
Levin, Hanokh, *Yaakobi and Leidenthal*, Institute.
  The Sorrows of Job, Taub 1993.
Meged, Aharon, *Hanna Senesh*, Taub 1995.
Mittelpunkt, Hillel, *Buba*, *Modern International Drama*, vol. 2, no. 1 Fall 1987;
  also in Taub, 1995.
Sobol, Yehoshua, *Ghetto*, London, Nick Hern Books, 1989.

A Jewish Soul – The Last Night of Otto Weininger, Modern International Drama,
  vol. 22, no. 2, Spring 1989; Taub 1995.
The Night of the Twentieth, Institute.
Adam, Taub 1995.
Tomer, Ben Zion, *The Children of the Shadow*, Institute; Taub 1995.
Yehoshua, A. B., *A Night in May*, Institute.
Possessions, Taub, 1993.

Index